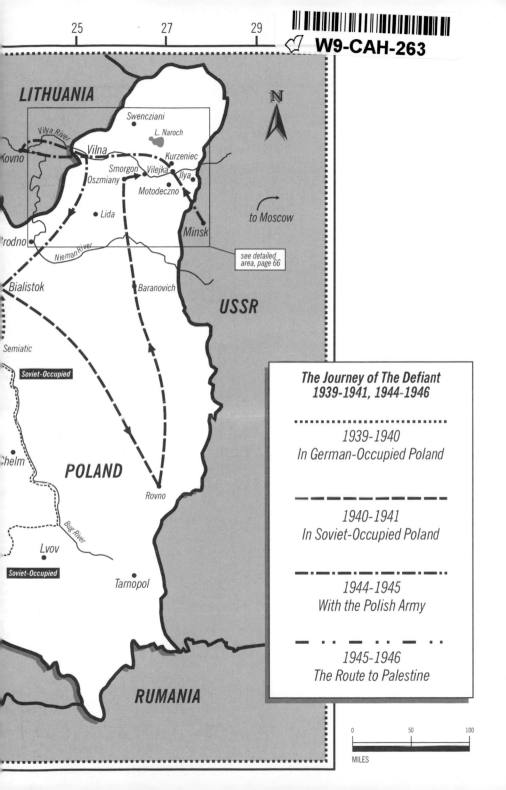

The Journey of The Defiant
1939-1941, 1944-1946

············ 1939-1940
In German-Occupied Poland

— — — — 1940-1941
In Soviet-Occupied Poland

—··—··— 1944-1945
With the Polish Army

— ·· — ·· — 1945-1946
The Route to Palestine

THE DEFIANT

THE DEFIANT

A True Story

SHALOM YORAN

Translated by Varda Yoran

ST. MARTIN'S PRESS ⚹ NEW YORK

Book design by Scott Levine

Library of Congress Cataloging-in-Publication Data

Yoran, Shalom.
    The defiant : a true story / Shalom Yoran ; translated by
Varda Yoran.
        p.   cm.
    ISBN 0-312-14585-3
    1. Yoran, Shalom. 2. Jews—Poland—Biography.
3. Holocaust, Jewish (1939–1945)—Poland—Personal nar-
ratives.   4. World War, 1939–1945—Jewish resistance—
Poland.   I. Title.
DS135.P63Y67   1996
940.53'18'09438—dc20   96-22409
                                                            CIP

First Edition: September 1996

10   9   8   7   6   5   4   3   2   1

This book is dedicated to the memory of my mother, a warm, intelligent and vivacious woman—the greatest influence in my life. And to my father—quiet and gentle, a truly good man. Their lives were abruptly ended. Not even a gravestone marks their passage through life. But to me and my family, and to the friends who knew and loved them, their spirit lives on.

CONTENTS

ACKNOWLEDGMENTS

My appreciation and thanks to the people who were most instrumental in helping turn my memoirs into a book.

To my wife Varda for translating into English my experiences and emotions. Her consistent support and encouragement helped me to re-enter and to relive the most difficult years of my life.

To Edwin Wintle for his critique and invaluable input in shaping my book. And for all the hats that he wore—literary adviser, legal representative, agent, coordinator and friend.

To Alan Adelson, Executive Director of the Jewish Heritage Project, for the dedication, advice, and personal effort he put into strengthening and publishing this book.

To my beloved daughters, Yaelle and Dafna, for adding such an important dimension to my life, and for sharing and taking to heart all my stories throughout their entire lives.

AUTHOR'S PREFACE

These are the recollections of the most devastating years of my life, during a period in history that was horrendous and terrifying beyond words—World War II. These memoirs were written in 1946 in Israel, while the events were still fresh in my mind. I recounted the facts of my experiences—raw, unembellished, unexaggerated. I could not bring myself to read my memoirs until recently; I was afraid to relive the suffering. Even now, almost half a century later, as my wife Varda translated my experiences from Polish into English, discussing the atrocities was physically painful to me.

I was a teenager then, and grew into manhood as a Jewish resistance fighter in the forests of eastern Europe. I coped with situations as they arose—hunger, thirst, cold, terror, pain, danger, terrible loss, hatred and bigotry, physical and emotional fatigue, and despair, not grasping the magnitude of the historical events of which I was a part. I encountered the worst and the best in people, from the ultimate in human baseness to friendship, bravery, consideration, and loyalty beyond belief.

What can be done in the face of murder and genocide, whether directed at Jews or anyone else? Looking back, I came to understand that if more Jews had defied extermination by resisting, many might have survived. If there is a lesson to be gleaned, it is that no person should succumb to brutality without putting up a resistance. Individually it can save one's life; en masse it can change the course of history.

1

THE GERMAN-POLISH WAR

My mind was slowly floating back into awareness. My body was aching. Lying on my back on a thick blanket of fresh snow, I carefully turned my head slightly to one side. Out of the corner of my eye I saw a broken stick on the ground beside me. I remembered that the last thing that happened before I passed out was the crack of the stick landing on my head. What had prevented it from crushing my skull was my fur cap, which was no longer on my head. Through half-closed lids I could clearly see five figures silhouetted against the powdery whiteness. One of them was sitting astride me, with his back to me. A second man had just yanked off my damp boots, which had stuck stubbornly to my feet. The other three men were a little further away, arguing in subdued voices. While I was unconscious, all my clothing had been removed and I was left with only my underpants on.

The young man straddling me turned around to face me and with his left hand groped my bare chest for my heart; his right one, gripping a knife, was raised and about to stab. He turned to the others and asked them, "Shall I kill him?"

My mind leapt into focus. Am I going to die now, so young, without even a chance to take revenge against the Nazis? A shout escaped my throat.

"I want to live!"

German army invaded Poland and turned my life upside down, it felt like a lifetime. It seems impossible that the word "home" can describe both this crude underground dwelling and the pleasant house in which I had lived with my family just three years before. But home it was, and though it was not all that far from the small town where I grew up, that home now seemed worlds away.

My family's home was in Raciaz, a typical small Polish town about fifty miles from Warsaw and thirty-seven miles from the German border. A few thousand people lived there, almost half of whom were Jewish. In the center of town was a large empty square surrounded by shops, the town hall and the elementary school. There was no local high school. The synagogue, a Hebrew school, and the Catholic church were nearby. Compared to most of the buildings, which were made of wood, the brick town hall was imposing, with wide steps leading up to the entrance. Twice a week farmers from the surrounding villages brought their produce on their horse-drawn carts and turned the square into an outdoor market. There was no public transportation. People either walked or rode in horsecarts or on horseback. When it rained or snowed, the roads leading to the town, and even the streets, turned to deep mud or slush.

Though some of the shops were owned by Jews, on the whole the Jewish community was quite poor. Most of them were craftsmen—tailors, shoemakers, blacksmiths, bakers or peddlers. There were, however, a few Jewish doctors, a pharmacist, and several teachers.

We lived at the edge of town, about half a mile from its center, across the street from the railroad station. Many of the more remote towns and villages did not even have trains to connect them to the rest of the country.

My father, Shmuel Sznycer, owned and managed a lumberyard. Our house was located on a large lot of land, surrounded by a fence. On the property were the factory, the piles of logs, cut lumber, machines and equipment. Beyond that were fields. Tracks from the station extended into our property, and the lumber was deposited straight into our yard. The chief mechanic Plato, a German who had worked for our family for twenty years, the accountant Kozak, the watchman Yan and his family, as well as our housekeeper Michasia and several other employees lived in small houses on the grounds of the lumberyard, right near our house.

My mother's youngest brother, my uncle Shlomo, was a junior partner in my father's business and lived in our house. My mother had thirteen siblings; some lived with their families in Palestine, and the rest lived in or near Warsaw. My father was one of six. His family lived in Plonsk, about nineteen miles from us. During summer vacations our house would fill up with relatives who would come to visit and stay for months at a time. There were ten rooms in our house, and enough space to accommodate them all. Although the outhouse was in the yard and there was no running water in the house, we were considered affluent by the standards of those times.

My mother Hannah was the dominating influence in the family. She was highly intelligent, warm, and an ardent Zionist. She was one of the representatives of the Jews at the town hall and was greatly respected. She was a well-read woman, had unconventional taste, and decided to call me by the name of a Turkish sultan, Selim, about whom she had read. She loved going to the theater in Warsaw, and back home would reenact the entire play for us, her enthralled audience.

My father was busy running the lumber mill and left our up bringing to my mother. He was a quiet man—religious, but not fanatically so. On weekends he would want my brother and me to accompany him to the synagogue, but we preferred to stay home, and have breakfast served in bed. Father would come into our room and reprimand us. "What would you do if I weren't here to provide you with such comfort? How would you survive?" And we would reply that if the necessity arose we would cope.

The year was 1939, and my only brother, Musio, had just graduated from high school in Warsaw. He was four years older than I, dark-haired, tall and thin, and more the scholarly type. I was fair and freckle-faced. I preferred sports and impressing girls, but I maintained fairly good grades at school. I was fourteen and about to enter high school in Warsaw in the fall.

Sometimes, through the closed door to my parents' bedroom, which was adjacent to ours, we would hear their recurring arguments regarding the future. Mother wanted to resettle in Palestine immediately. My father said we should wait until my brother and I finished our education.

There was tension in the air, a foreboding of war. My father tried to convince everybody that war would not break out, but my mother, Musio, and I, seeing the Polish army mobilizing, were convinced that it was inevitable.

On Thursday, August 30, 1939, the radio announced that the Germans had served the Polish government an ultimatum consisting of sixteen demands, which the Polish government rejected. Now war was definitely imminent. In preparation, we spent the entire day building an air-raid shelter in one of the rooms. We reinforced the walls, propped the ceiling with logs, and sealed off the doors and windows against the possibility of a gas attack, which was rumored as the Germans' most terrifying weapon. We pasted strips of paper on all the windows in the house.

On Friday morning, Plato came in and said that he could hear the ground rumbling from artillery fire, coming from the direction of the German border. Nobody wanted to believe him and preferred to think that he was just creating panic. From our house we could see the railway station, full of mobilized soldiers. The tension and concern kept growing. We continued to work on the shelter.

The accountant Kozak and I were in the yard collecting firewood when we saw the first airplanes overhead. We tried to convince ourselves that the Polish air force was supervising a smooth mobilization. At that moment we heard a tremendous explosion. The ground shook, windows rattled and smashed—a bomb had been dropped. I did not realize the significance of it all until I saw a black cloud rising from the ground. All the people at the train station began to run in panic. Only then I understood that we were being attacked by the Germans.

An airplane was flying toward us. People all around were trying to hide behind piles of wood in our lumberyard. Some fell to the ground and tried to cover their heads with their hands. Some ran around wildly. For no apparent reason, unable to think rationally, I ran into the nearby fields, fell to the ground, and tried to watch the airplanes which were circling around so low that I could see the pilots. I had the feeling that they were chasing me personally.

Another round of bombs. The ground shook. I was hurled up in the air and down again. A cloud of heavy smoke was floating toward us, and someone shouted that this was gas. Another wave of panic began. Someone else shouted that this was only smoke from the bombs. I covered my mouth with a handkerchief and ran for home. By then the airplanes had vanished. Everybody was in the shelter, safe. They all crowded around me, asking what had happened to me, and why I was dirty, and if I was hurt. Uncle Shlomo felt ill and said he wouldn't survive another such attack.

Two hours later, that September 1, the radio announced that Poland was at war, that the German army had crossed into Poland and had begun to bombard Polish towns. Until now war was something we learned about in school, or heard spoken of as a probability. This was real. And I was frightened.

The airplanes kept coming back in waves, and we kept hiding in the shelter, among the piles of wood in the yard, or in the fields. Miraculously, neither the house nor the lumberyard were hit.

Trains full of Polish soldiers were moving toward the German border. Everybody was asking the same question—"What will happen now? What will happen now?"

On Saturday the airplanes were still flying overhead but not bombing. From afar we could clearly hear artillery fire. The radio blared marches and serious classical music, but gave no information. By nightfall fires were visible on the horizon, and the bombardments moved closer. Nobody knew whether to stay or flee, whether it was safer indoors or outside. All through Sunday airplanes continued circling over our town and the artillery fire grew ever closer.

On September 3, the radio announced that England and France had declared war on Germany. That caused a degree of optimism and hope. But that afternoon panic struck again, caused by the sight of the Polish army retreating through Raciaz. The soldiers were fleeing on foot, on horseback, and by train. The rumor was that the Germans had broken through the Polish defense at the front. By night there was complete terror and we began to pack, with the intention of taking the train to Warsaw, the capital.

We went to the crowded railroad station. After we boarded the train, my brother Musio insisted that we get off, as the Germans would surely bomb all the trains. The train left with Uncle Shlomo and the accountant Kozak. My parents, my brother, and I stayed behind and tried to find another way to reach Warsaw.

By Monday everyone was fleeing. We chose to go through Drobin, Plonsk, across the Visla River, and from there to Warsaw.

My mother managed to catch a ride with some friends to Drobin and told us to meet her there. Carrying our valises, father, Musio and I set out on foot along the main road. Again we witnessed the once-proud Polish soldiers on the run, in disarray, fear and panic in their faces, glancing backward as though expecting to see the Germans chasing them. They shouted, "Hurry! Save yourselves! The Germans are right behind us!"

Just as we left the town we heard airplanes approaching and moments later Raciaz was bombed again. There was bedlam on the road out of town—people, horses, goats, cats, dogs, carts, cows, all rushing to escape. We were part of the exodus.

The five miles to Drobin were the first of many I would trudge during the next four years. Already my feet were blistered and chafed.

We met my mother at a prearranged place in Drobin and together continued on our way toward Plonsk. Plonsk was situated on both sides of the Visla River, and everyone hoped that the Germans would be stopped at the river. All along the way everyone and everything was in flight, using any possible means of transportation. We left the main road and took short cuts along side roads. On the way a Polish landowner, a friend of my father's, picked us up in his horse-drawn cart and we traveled that way until nightfall, hearing explosions throughout the entire journey.

Just as we stopped to rest and unhitched the horses, a man came running toward us, shouting hysterically that the Germans were only four miles away, on the main road. He too was yelling, "Save yourselves!" We immediately hitched up the horses and for the rest of the night galloped as fast as they could take us toward Plonsk. The landowner turned to us, knowing that we were Jews, and said, "Let us now each pray to our own God to save us." Like the Polish soldiers I had seen all day, I found myself peering fearfully into the darkness behind me, to see if the Germans were already at our heels.

Before dawn we reached Plonsk, and the Visla River. Shoving through the mobs of soldiers, cannons and other refugees, it took us four hours to get across the river. The sight of Polish soldiers, cannons, machine guns and artillery on the other side gave us a false sense of safety. We were convinced that the Germans would be stopped here. Having parted from our Polish friend, we continued on foot to Gombin, another small town somewhat like Raciaz. There we hoped to find some means of reaching Warsaw.

Somewhere along the way I lost one shoe but continued my march with one stockinged foot. I must have been quite a sight. We were all tired and hungry, and after six miles my father began to feel unwell. We stopped at a roadside inn where the only food we could get was some stale biscuits. After a short rest we continued on our way and reached Gombin by the afternoon.

The town was full of refugees fleeing from other areas. The last bus to Warsaw had just left. We later learned that the Germans, coming from another direction, had cut off the road between Gombin and Warsaw, and our plan to reach the capital could not be realized. We were stranded in Gombin, not sure what to do next. We located a friend of my mother's by the name of Wolfovitch, a local resident. She received us warmly into her home. The war hadn't affected Gombin yet; apart from the chaotic movement of the Polish army units to and from the front, and the distant sound of bombardment, Gombin seemed safe—a haven for us refugees. There was no shortage of food or other supplies. We settled in with the Wolfovitch family, and began preparations for Rosh Hashanah, the Jewish New Year. I helped my mother with the shopping and other chores.

For a week we went about our lives in relative calm, though the front was getting nearer by the day, and the artillery sounds were louder and clearer. It was rumored that the Germans had been stopped, as we had hoped, on the banks of the Visla River, but there was no official information to confirm or deny these rumors. We were constantly trying to find a way to go east to Warsaw, but no transportation was available. The Polish soldiers were milling around and nobody seemed to know where the Germans really were.

On the day of Rosh Hashanah, we attended morning services at the local synagogue. In the middle of our prayers we heard an explosion, and people began fleeing frantically in all directions. This was the first artillery attack on the town of Gombin. Evidently the

Germans were closer than we had all believed.

That afternoon we heard sirens. I was alone in the Wolfovitch home. I rushed outside searching for my family. I was in an open field when I was caught in a full-fledged air attack. I threw myself on the muddy ground behind a stable, irrationally feeling at that moment that any structure, however flimsy, was a source of protection against the flying bombs. There were three airplanes circling above me, and they were all bombing.

Each time they flew directly overhead, I buried my face in the mud. The cold was penetrating. I counted—one, two, three, four, five. . . They had passed me. At that instant, a bomb fell very close to me, and I was hit by pieces of wood and brick. Then the pilot began strafing the area with machine guns. This was even worse. My heart was pounding against the ground beneath me. Each time I heard a series of shots I was sure I had been hit. Hesitantly, I lifted my head out of the mud and could see the airplanes directly above me. Bullets whistled. Flying debris from the stable felt like a vicious animal attacking me. This is the end, I thought. I lay there, believing that in an instant I would be dead.

When the planes finally receded into the distance, I realized that not only was I alive, I wasn't even hurt. It was incredible! Just a few inches above my head, the stable was riddled with bullet holes. The raid must have lasted some twenty minutes, leaving me drained and exhausted. I staggered back to the Wolfovitch home and to my relief found my entire family safe. They had all been hiding in the cellar throughout the raid, worrying about me. When I walked in, all muddy and pale, Mother hugged me, tears of relief in her eyes.

Throughout the next day, artillery and aircraft attacks continued. At first we hid in the cellar, but we later realized that in the event of a direct hit, the house would cave in and we would all be buried alive. We would be safer above ground.

We sat huddled together on the bed, our hands interlocked, trying to give each other moral support. We were emotionally drained from this constant state of tension, and my greatest wish was that the bombing would stop long enough for me to fall peacefully asleep. But instead the planes kept coming. As each one approached, we recognized first the roar of the engine, then the whistle of the dive, and then we anticipated the dreaded sound of the explosion.

Each time we buried our faces in our hands, and I could hear my father softly praying. We expected each bomb to hit the Wolfovitch house. In fact, bombs fell all around us, but missed us.

People from the surrounding buildings, half-crazed with fear and pain, rushed into the house. Toward evening we heard a whistle so shrill and piercing directly overhead that to me it seemed that a direct hit was inevitable. During the split-second of silence that followed, in my heart I said my goodbyes to the world. And then came the explosion, so powerful that it threw us all to the ground. The house seemed to be lifted into the air. Doors and windows were torn off their hinges and disappeared.

My mother rose, urging, "Get out before the house collapses!"

I shouted back that we should stay indoors because the planes were waiting to shoot at each person who came out. At that moment we heard the machine guns again, and the people who had run outside were falling. That was the German system; first they bombed the houses, and then with machine guns they shot the people as they tried to escape.

Miraculously, the Wolfovitch house survived relatively intact, even with the ten-yard-deep pit that had been burnt into the ground just outside the front door.

With the following daybreak, the bombing resumed. The entire city of Gombin was aflame. Again we sat huddled on the bed. If we were meant to die, at least we would all die together. With occasional intervals, the bombing lasted throughout the day. Though we hadn't eaten all day, I felt no hunger—just utter weariness and a desire to fall asleep.

People kept coming in and out, seeking emotional support from each other. At one point an elderly Jew burst into the house, wild-eyed with terror, and begged us to help him dig his wife and children out from under the debris of his collapsed house. But as long as the bombing continued no one moved to help him.

Later, during one of the lapses in the bombing, Menahem, a schoolmate of mine from Raciaz who had also arrived in Gombin, came in to see how I was holding up. When the bombardment resumed, he ran to the next house to join his family. I later found him outside, lying unconscious, with both legs blown off. I remembered how I had enjoyed meeting his familiar face in this strange place just a few days ago. He was the first casualty of war that I encountered, and it left me shaken for a long time.

By evening, the planes left and did not return all night. The town was a burning shambles, with hardly a building intact. Though the Wolfovitch house survived again, we resolved to flee Gombin in the morning—we knew we wouldn't survive a repetition of that day. We spent the night hiding in the fields.

At daybreak we returned to the house to collect our things. We were to leave Gombin with ten other people. While my parents were getting ready, I was standing by the window on the second floor. I heard a long whistle and the powerful explosion of an artillery shell. I was thrown sideways. Accompanied by artillery bombardment, we left the city and managed to reach safety at a small village with only a few houses. We found refuge in one of the nearby farmhouses. By mid-morning we heard the airplanes bombing Gombin again, but here it was quiet, and again we were sure we had found safety.

Suddenly small artillery and heavy machine-gun shells were being shot over the farmhouse. Airplanes followed and began to bomb the forest around us.

We had moved from one danger to another. German paratroopers were being dropped from the sky and two of them landed in the yard of the farmhouse. They immediately started firing their machine guns in the direction of the woods. My father prayed all the time that they would not turn and start shooting on the farmhouse. Utter weariness overcame me—I could hardly keep my eyes open.

We later found out that the Germans were trying to surround and capture several units of the Polish army hiding in the woods. From afar we could see four Polish artillery guns with their crews, dragged by horses, trying to flee. Some ten minutes later they were running back, obviously aware that they were surrounded. Their artillery guns got stuck in the mud and the soldiers tried desperately to get their horses to pull them out. Finally they left the guns and fled by foot into the forest. We heard airplanes, but this time no bombs. A local peasant brought us leaflets dropped by plane. They were meant to convince the Polish soldiers to surrender, by saying that the Jews and Beck (a Polish leader at that time) had betrayed them.

The fighting in the nearby woods was intense but brief. By four o'clock it was quiet. Someone came to tell us that the Germans were already in Gombin. This was it then. The German occupation had caught up with us! With the news came a momentary feeling of relief—no more bombardments. But would I ever overcome the terror I felt each time I heard an approaching airplane? Then a new fear overwhelmed me. What would happen now? Musio and I went into the yard and on a distant road saw German motorcycles, helmets, and long gray overcoats, an image until then familiar only in the newsreels. I said to my brother, "That's them! That's how we saw them in the pictures showing the occupation of Prague!"

We all returned through fields to the devastated town of Gombin, and saw our first Germans at close range. There was a young officer and several soldiers looking at the ruined town. The officer had a green coat, a cap, and a hard young face. I was afraid to make eye contact with them. They were laughing. "See what our Luftwaffe (air force) has done!" Since Yiddish, the language most widely used by the Jews of Europe, resembles German, it was easy for us to get the general gist of what was said.

That came day we heard that Russia had declared war on Poland and had started occupying its eastern part. We had nowhere to go now and felt it would be safer at home, even under the Germans. So we decided that we might as well return to our own home at Raciaz, and started on foot, walking alongside the road.

Along the main road we saw the German army—tanks, motorized columns, artillery, droves of well-dressed, happy soldiers in carts, trucks, and on horseback. They were all singing along to accordions played by other soldiers. One officer stuck in my mind—freckle-faced, helmet low over his brow, arrogantly ordering all civilians to keep to the right. A shabby man was directing them, probably one of their many spies. Yes, we were definitely under German occupation. But I hadn't fully grasped the meaning of that yet.

Many people were heading the same way, mainly Jews, and we formed quite a crowd. The air was filled with conflicting rumors. Germans had met Jews and had done nothing to them, so they couldn't be all bad. After all, they couldn't distinguish between Jews and non-Jews, and there were Jews still living in Germany. Then someone said that a German had told him, with his hand gesturing a cut throat, "All Jews kaput!" That became the chief topic of concern for everyone. When the Poles began to point out the Jewish groups, the Germans started shouting to us: "We are waiting for you! All Jews kaput! Hitler will take care of you!"

With heads bowed, humiliated, we walked on. My parents and a few others tried to put some distance between themselves and the Germans by walking further away from the road, but the Germans started shouting at them. They quickly came back to the roadside.

The number of refugees on the road was increasing constantly. All the bridges across the Visla River were destroyed and the only way to cross was by boat. At each place where boats crossed, there were long lines of people already waiting. Rumors began circulating that as soon as any Jews crossed the Visla, they would be singled out and taken to forced labor. We walked on, parallel to the river.

We waited in a bombed-out house for three days. There was no food available. At first we tried to find something in the fields, and dug up some potatoes, which mother cooked. Then we began a "food-acquisition" campaign. We sneaked into farmyards to milk cows. We found some bowls and all ate from the same ones. My mother cooked whatever we could find. We began to become familiar with hunger.

On the fourth day at 6 A.M. we made our way to the riverside and finally a farmer agreed to take us across in his boat, after he had given us some peasant clothing. We paid him lavishly. We continued walking on to Raciaz, in shabby peasant clothes to avoid being recognized as Jews.

It was getting dark when we finally arrived at our hometown. From afar we could see the chimney of our house. It was still standing. We were met quite civilly by our gentile employees Yan the watchman and even the German chief mechanic Plato. Our home was intact, but the interior of our house had been ransacked. So we moved into the house where the accountant Kozak had previously lived.

2

THE FIRST GERMAN OCCUPATION

September 22–November 9, 1939

Within the first month of the war, the Germans had already taken over our lumberyard—there was a sign at the entrance saying "Beshlagmant" (requisitioned)—but we were allowed to stay on in Kozak's house. Almost all those who had fled from Raciaz trickled back and tried to adjust to life under the Germans. We were all awaiting news. When would England and France finally defeat Germany? We found out that the USSR had taken over the entire eastern section of Poland, up to the Bug River. We contemplated trying to cross over to Russian-held territory, but it was very far away. We were constantly debating whether we should attempt it. Musio and I were now as much a part of the discussions as my parents.

One evening the Shamash (the caretaker of the synagogue) rushed in and notified us that at eight o'clock the following morning all the Jewish men between the ages of seventeen and sixty were to come to the market square. Panic struck, but everyone intended to go, for fear of reprisal. I was too young, but my father and brother would go. It was the eve of Yom Kippur, the Day of Atonement, the holiest day in the Jewish year. That night we held our own Kol Nidre service at home, and went to bed fearing the next day.

On the morning of Yom Kippur Father and Musio went to the square. They were gone for several hours, and Mother and I didn't know what to think. Suddenly Father rushed in and grabbed several boxes of cigarettes. He had been given ten minutes to bring two hundred cigarettes for the Germans.

Exhausted from running the half-mile from town to our house, there was no way my father could be back at the square in time. So I took the cigarettes from him and hurried to the town square, toward the school building where everyone had been assembled. At the entrance to the schoolyard stood a German guard in black uniform, pale-faced and expressionless, a skull glistening on his collar—the emblem of the Gestapo.

The Gestapo was the name of the Nazi secret police, one of the most dreaded organizations created by Hitler. N-A-Z-I were the initials of the German political party headed by Hitler, which took over the German government in 1933, proclaiming Hitler as the Führer (leader) of the Third Reich. The fanatically loyal members of this party enforced all the autocracy over the Jews, the occupied countries, and all elements considered inferior by the Nazis.

A group of Poles was trying to look into the schoolyard to see what was happening to the Jews. The Gestapo man coldly said, "Dirty pigs, get away." The people didn't understand him. With calm and deliberate movements, he came up to one of the Poles and kicked him in the stomach several times. The people understood and dispersed.

I went up to the Gestapo guard and told him that I had brought the cigarettes. He asked me, "Jude?" I nodded. He grabbed me and shoved me into the yard. There were the Jewish men, assembled in groups of four, surrounded by armed Gestapo guards. Ten men were facing the wall with arms raised, and several Gestapo had rifles aimed at them. These were the hostages used to ensure that nobody "misbehaved." In the middle of the yard were long tables laden with vodka, wine, cigarettes, and other goodies that the Jews had been ordered to bring. The mayor of Raciaz was standing at one of the tables. A local doctor of German extraction who had recently been made mayor of the town by the Germans, he was a good friend of our family. I handed him the cigarettes. He asked me loudly, so the Gestapo would hear, how old I was. I said, "I'm fourteen." He yelled, "Get out!" In an instant I was gone. Back home I found Mother agitated and worried. I told her what I had seen and tried to calm her.

Meanwhile my father had returned to the schoolyard. Around 8 P.M. he and Musio returned home. They filled us in on what had happened.

When the men had assembled at the town square, they were grouped in fours and made to run around the square, and to shout, "The Jews want war!" "Jews are swine!" and slogans in that vein. In order to scare them, shots were occasionally fired into the air. Then, surrounded by armed Gestapo aiming rifles at them, they were led to the schoolyard. One of the officers made a speech that began by cursing Jews in general, and went on to curse the captive men in particular. He said that from that day forth the Germans were "Herrenvolk" (superior race) and the Jews were their slaves. Then the Jews were made to sweep the town square. They were told that every morning all Jewish males between the ages of seventeen and sixty were to appear for gymnastics and parading, and then they were to clean up the town. Musio said such humiliation was beyond tolerance. But this was just the debut performance of Gestapo tactics, and very mild compared to what happened later. Being Yom Kippur, we hadn't eaten all day and broke the fast with heavy hearts.

That Yom Kippur marked the beginning of a new life for us. We moved back into our own home, repaired the damage done to the house, and settled in. Yan did most of the shopping. Some of the villagers brought their produce to our door. Father was allowed to continue to run his business, even though it had been confiscated by the Germans. The money he made by selling wood for construction went to the city hall. He managed however to keep some of it, and that covered our expenses. Mother buried all our valuables in the garden. Plato, who was of German descent, continued to live in our compound with his family. He tried to protect us from Nazi vandalism and abuse.

German gendarmes (police) were brought in to keep order in the town and to keep an eye on the Jews. Luckily, there was no permanent Gestapo unit in Raciaz. They were stationed in Scierpz, the county capital, and came to Raciaz for "guest appearances." Whenever they came, we would hide in our lumberyard, so as not to catch their attention. One never knew when it would occur to them to drag someone off to some unknown destination.

The local German gendarmes changed every week, and life in

the town depended upon the personality and mood of whoever was on duty. Some took bribes and made life bearable. Some were violent and cruel. They beat people, dragged them to work, and abused them.

The Germans took over control of the railway station and, because we lived across the street and ours was a large house, the new German station commander took over our house too, but allowed us to stay in a small part of it. Since my mother spoke fluent German and could communicate with him, he became somewhat friendly toward her. He told us that he was not a Nazi but a social democrat. He was angry at the Nazis for taking his children away into the Hitler Youth organization and did not approve of the Nazi policies toward the Jews. He even predicted that the Germans would lose the war. But still, being a good German, he felt obligated to support Hitler because Hitler was fighting for his Fatherland, which was more important than one's personal political views.

Another railway employee however—a twenty-year-old engineer named Alfred—spoke of Hitler as one speaks of a god. With tears in his eyes, he told us that he had once stood near Hitler at a parade. As we became friendlier, he said he had no personal antagonism against us as Jews, in spite of the propaganda depicting us as devils. He found us to be as human as himself. But he still believed that Hitler's views should not be questioned and all orders fulfilled exactly. Proof of Alfred's blind adulation came one day, when we saw him whipping the Jews who were unloading the trains.

The Jews in Raciaz now worked everywhere without pay—slave labor. It was especially pleasing to the Germans to give the hardest physical work to people who had never done manual labor, and to see them collapse. My father, brother, and I were not taken to work in the town because we were under the jurisdiction of the railway gendarmes, and continued to work in the lumberyard. Mother was made to sew for the railway workers, including flags with the Nazi swastika for the station. Just by seeing the tension in her back, bent over the sewing machine, I could feel the revulsion and hatred she felt and the emotional effort it took to put on the detested insignias, though she never said a word to us so as not to add more pain to our lives.

All means of communication, even within Poland, were disrupted. There was no mail and no phone connections in homes. We didn't know what was happening to the rest of our numerous relatives, whether they were safe in their homes or wandering around trying to escape the Germans. We had such a large family but were all alone.

The Germans had begun demanding collective "contributions" of gold, jewelry, and money from the Jews. My mother was chosen by the Jewish community to be one of the representatives in this matter. Each time she went to a meeting with the German county chief she would return devastated.

Another Jewish family from Raciaz, our friends the Vigdoroviches, came to stay in our house. There seemed to be a greater sense of security in numbers. Their only daughter Estusia was a nice girl, about my own age. Living in such close proximity, our friendship deepened.

We kept bringing up the idea of getting away to Soviet-occupied territory, but had not yet formulated any concrete plans. Some Polish people whom my father knew offered to hide us in their village not far from Raciaz, and that was another option we were considering.

Our friend the mayor kept suggesting that we run away, as our future seemed very bleak to him. But where were we to go? And how? We discussed the situation with the Vigdoroviches and we put off making a decision.

Our German mechanic Plato gradually began to absorb the Nazi propaganda, and to believe himself to be of the superior race. Though he was still polite to us, he started to see us as his inferiors. He strutted around our property as though he owned it, and began to show disdain to our Polish customers.

Since I was still considered a "youngster" I was sent into town to do the family errands. On one such occasion, I saw a German gendarme beat a Jew over the head with a stick until blood oozed from his ears. I sneaked through the town in constant fear of being caught, beaten, and humiliated.

A new German commander came to town, and with him came new unrest. Luckily, however, the permanent German contingency at the railway station had gradually developed a more personal relationship with us and even helped us. They occasionally brought us food, and most important of all, protected us from being taken to work by the gendarmes.

The routine we settled into lasted until November 6, when we first saw a train fully loaded with civilians come into the station. There was a commotion. Nobody knew what it all meant. No one was allowed near the train. Mrs. Vigdorovich suddenly screamed that she recognized her father in one of the box cars. She called out to him, but he was too far away to hear her. His presence meant that these were Jews from Scierpz, a small town some about twelve miles from Raciaz. We stood mesmerized at the window. We saw two young men escape from the train. Guards chased after them but did not catch them.

We later found out that all the Jews from Scierpz had been deported by train without any belongings. No one knew where they were being sent. Any disobedience during the process was punished by death.

We tried to think clearly, without succumbing to panic. After weighing all the alternatives, we decided to run away before they tried to deport us, and began to pack. But before dark, the Shamash came shouting to everybody that the following morning all Jews, young and old, men, women, and children, were to assemble at the synagogue. Anyone found hiding would be shot. It was too late to start running away, because civilians were not allowed to travel along the roads at night, and the following day we expected that the Nazis would send patrols on the roads to stop the Jews from trying to escape. We decided not to go to the synagogue, and hoped nobody would notice our absence. Father and Musio hid among the lumber in our factory. Mother and I hid in the yard by the house in the dark. The Vigdoroviches hid somewhere too. In the morning mother and I returned to the house.

Around noon the next day a messenger from the mayor came to my mother and said that the German gebbitz-commissar (county chief) insisted on seeing her personally. He had noticed her absence because he had dealt with her on previous occasions as the only woman representative of the Jews of Raciaz. She had to go. Left alone, I ran to tell my father of the new turn of events, and stayed with him in hiding.

Night fell and Mother didn't return. We were all frantic, especially my father. Plato, who knew where we were hiding, came to tell us of the horrendous things he had seen in town. In a house-to-house hunt for Jews, those discovered were beaten and tortured. For some reason nobody came to search for us. All the Jews were then pushed into the synagogue. Plato could see no more.

When it was dark, we came out of hiding and lay down near the compound entrance, to be able to see who was coming. We were terribly frightened. Each squeak of the gate brought a new surge of emotions. Was it my mother, or the Gestapo?

At eleven o'clock at night she arrived, pale, not responding to our joy at seeing her. She went into her bedroom and burst into tears. I had never seen her cry before. For at least half an hour she was inconsolable. When she finally collected herself she described what she had witnessed.

She had walked through the deserted streets to the synagogue where the Jews had been assembled. She was shocked to find the courtyard strewn with dead bodies, including that of a friend who had been beaten to death. The men were gathered in one hall, and the women in another. All the women were ordered to undress and to parade naked before the Holy Ark, where the German commander stood on a podium with his entourage. Each woman brought her clothes and was thoroughly searched for jewels and valuables. To keep them scared, they were occasionally whipped. Then these petrified women were told to sing something happy. One woman, known for her beautiful voice, was brought forth, and began to sing "Kol Nidre," the opening prayer of the Yom Kippur services. The Germans meanwhile removed the Torah from its case and began to destroy it. One of them took a prayer shawl and placed a fragment of the Torah scroll on his head and began to dance. The commander, whip in hand, looked ferociously at the herd of naked women, his slaves. The German stopped dancing. Total silence except for the sound of "Kol Nidre." Every woman heard in that voice her own personal grief, helplessness, humiliation, and pain.

The commander lashed his whip and shouted, "I want something happy, something pleasing to my ear!" The woman immediately switched to a popular melody. Then each woman was made to go up to the podium to display her beauty. Anyone who tried to cover herself was beaten. Was my mother among these women? I don't know—she never told us. We didn't ask. She didn't know why she was called there, as she didn't even see the Gebietskommissar.

The commander occasionally went to the hall where the naked men were assembled. Their clothes were searched. If anything was found, they were beaten for concealing it. If nothing was found, they were beaten for having nothing. They were sent under guard to bring valuables from home. Finally the two halls were locked up for the night. The people were told that the following morning they would be sent home, under guard, to bring ten pounds of food per family to the train and they would then be deported. In the evening the mayor came and had my mother released. He told her, "Run away!" He explained that Raciaz and the surrounding areas near the German border had been annexed to Greater Germany, and that the Jews in that area were stripped of their possessions and would be deported to an unknown destination in the east. Central Poland, around Warsaw and Krakow, called "General Government," was Polish territory though under German rule, where Jews were still allowed to live. We should get away from the annexed territory.

The mayor's assistant brought Mother home. We packed two suitcases and decided to leave at dawn. We planned to go to Plonsk, where Father's family lived. That city was not annexed to Germany but was part of the General Government.

3

SEEKING REFUGE ONCE MORE

November 10–December 29, 1939

5 A.M. We hadn't slept all night. We were leaving our home once again—chased away. The Vigdorovich family would come with us. The Polish watchman Yan was going to take our horse and cart out of Raciaz to the road to Plonsk as he would not arouse suspicion, and we were to cross the fields on foot and meet up with him on the way. It was a risk worth taking. So at dawn on November 10 we went through a gap in the fence surrounding our compound, and sneaked away from our home. Michasia the housekeeper helped us and accompanied us to our meeting place with Yan. We arrived at the designated spot, and Mother and Mrs. Vigdorovich got on the cart with our few belongings. We tearfully said goodbye to our loyal Michasia and Yan, and the rest of us began to walk beside the wagon.

In drizzling rain and the gray morning light, we plodded along dressed in old coats. From afar I turned back to look at our home, our lumber factory, my entire youth, the happiness and security I had felt there, all left behind. Banished. Going where? I wanted to cry, but choked back my emotions and walked on.

We were scared to come face to face with the Germans. Each time we saw a German vehicle slowing down, we were sure they were going to stop us. But we must have looked like any ordinary farmer's family and didn't arouse suspicion.

Darkness fell as we were approaching Plonsk. On the outskirts of the city we heard a shout, "Halt! Everybody get off!" The women quickly jumped off the cart. A German patrol searched through our belongings and, not recognizing that we were Jewish, let us through.

We arrived at the home of father's sister Tola, where she lived with her husband and two children. The Vigdoroviches went to their relatives in Plonsk. When father's other siblings and their families heard of our arrival, they all gathered to meet us. The joy of being together was salted by the depressing stories we exchanged. We learned that Plonsk was relatively quiet. The German governor, when adequately bribed, behaved humanely.

We learned that Uncle Eisenberg had died of a heart attack on the first day of the occupation when a German had beaten him and threatened him with a gun. Uncle Zelig, father's oldest brother, who had studied at the Heder (religious school) with David Ben-Gurion, had his story to tell. Elderly and lame, formerly deputy mayor of Plonsk and director of a bank, he was one of the first ten hostages taken by the Germans to guarantee the cooperation of the population. He was taken by train to a remote station, and, despite his limp, was made to run back to Plonsk. The Germans, on bicycles, shot at the hostages to scare them, and beat whoever fell. Somewhere, running through a village, my uncle managed to escape and hide in a barn. The owner of the barn let him stay, and notified the local Jews. They brought him back safely to Plonsk. Weak and terrified, it took quite some time for him to regain the full use of his legs.

Our first few days in Plonsk went by uneventfully. I walked around town with Estusha, the Vigdoroviches' daughter. My friendship with her had by now developed into a crush. She was pretty, blonde and slim, and I was proud to be seen with her. She was shy and quiet, but intelligent, and I enjoyed her company. We kissed, but both of us were hesitant about going any further. We were sometimes joined by my cousin, Tola's son, who was our age. We spent a great deal of time at my Uncle Bogaty's flour mill, playing cards, talking, and speculating about the future. Then our parents decided we should all go to Warsaw, and try to sneak from there into Russian-held territory. There was no place for us under German occupation. We suspected that it wouldn't be too long before the Jews of Plonsk would suffer even more at the hands of the Germans.

Sure enough, within a few days the rounding up of Jews began in Plonsk, using the same tactics we had witnessed in Raciaz—beatings, exercise, humiliation. We managed to avoid being caught by being constantly alert to the goings-on, and by spending most of our time indoors. The Germans would grab people off the streets at random, either to drag them to work or to terrorize them.

With my fair hair and freckles, I did not look like the stereotypical Jew and was not usually recognized by the Germans as such. Once, when I was in the streets, a group of Jews was being grabbed for work. I didn't know what to do. Running would betray my identity. I decided to walk calmly along. It worked. I wasn't stopped and escaped with only a scare.

We learned to distinguish the various uniforms worn by the Germans. The immaculate green uniforms with the sparkling insignia of skull and daggers was worn by the SS, the military arm of the Nazis. The brown uniforms were worn by the SA, the party members who handled civilian affairs. The Gestapo wore black uniforms with skull and daggers, as well as swastikas on red armbands. From a window looking onto the marketplace I watched the daily hunt for Jews. When the Germans spotted one, they would stalk him. They would close in on him without appearing to look at him, and when they were near enough, they would pounce. One more Jew to clean their boots or their floors—a personal slave. They particularly enjoyed singling out attractive girls.

For easier identification, all the Jews were ordered to wear a yellow patch with the word "Jude" on it, sewn to the left side of their garments. I did not wear it. Jews were not allowed to walk on the sidewalks, and had to bow to every passing German. One elderly man I saw apparently failed to bow low enough to satisfy a German, and was pushed to the ground and made to crawl in the mud, and then to pass that German ten times, bowing to the ground each time.

Every day, when the Jews were forced to exercise on the square, a water cannon stood by, ready to hose down anyone who wasn't doing it right. When they were supposed to run, a German on a bicycle set the pace for everyone to follow. Failing to do fifty pushups was punishable by a German jumping up and down on the man's back until he lost consciousness.

We took turns at the window overlooking the square, on the lookout for Germans. Whenever the hunt was on, we ran away to hide in Uncle Zelig's attic.

During lunch one day an SS man unexpectedly came in. All we young men tried to escape into the attic through the rear door. He spotted us and began to chase after us. Luckily he listened to my mother's and Aunt Tola's pleas to let us alone. He had come for a special purpose, and nothing else really mattered to him. He wanted my uncle to sign a paper stating that he was selling his house to the German for 30,000 zloty—money which of course my uncle never saw. But Uncle Zelig quickly signed the paper.

That young German, named Helmut Breiele, spoke a little Polish. He spotted the blue Keren Kayemet collection box for Palestine and questioned my mother about it. He then delivered a speech about the Jews, who were out to destroy his Führer. "The Jews are devils and should all be exterminated. But because the Germans are a very cultured nation, they refrain from doing this and they allow the Jews to live, but only as slaves."

We spent only two weeks in Plonsk. Then, according to our plan, our horse and cart were to take us on the road again—to Warsaw. The Vigdorovich family had to go their separate way.

It was a blow to me, and destroyed my hopes of continuing my romance with Estusha. We parted sadly, hoping to meet again.

My aunt Bronka had come back to Plonsk from Lvov, a town in the east of Poland under Russian occupation, and described life there. It wasn't easy, but at least the Jews were allowed to live as humans. We dared to hope to reach the Russian-occupied part of Poland, and to be free of oppression.

We managed to get permits from the local authorities to go to Warsaw, and left Plonsk at the crack of dawn. Our trip was, for a change, quite uneventful. We were stopped by German patrols, searched, and let through. We saw ruin and devastation everywhere; entire towns had been destroyed.

We covered thirty miles and by evening we arrived in Warsaw. Despite the heavy bombardment the city had suffered at the beginning of the war, life remained almost normal. In spite of broken windows and houses burnt or collapsed, the city bustled with activity, complete with public transportation. Prices had skyrocketed, but almost everything was available. The Jews were not yet forced to wear the yellow star.

We came to an empty apartment owned by Uncle Wolfe and Aunt Zivia, who were away. Uncle Wolfe had been stranded in Denmark, cut off by the war. His wife Zivia had fled to the Russian side with her two daughters. We shared the apartment with Uncle Avigdor, another of my mother's brothers, and his wife and two sons. They too were refugees.

Life in Warsaw was more pleasant than in Plonsk. Half a million Jews lived in this city—the largest concentration of Jews in all of Europe. Even though it was also under German occupation, there were few Germans around.

Several days after our arrival the Germans ordered all the Jews in Warsaw to wear white armbands with a blue Star of David. Jews were again hunted in the streets, and we witnessed a repetition of the Plonsk pattern.

I, however, never wore my armband. I tried to stay off the main street—the side roads seemed somewhat safer. Though I was always alert, I had several near misses. Before leaving the courtyard of our house, I always peered through the gate to see what was happening. If there were no armbands visible, it meant a hunt was on.

Mothers with strollers were often the couriers of news.

One day while walking along Dluga Street with Musio, we were aware of a strange sound behind us. A woman with a stroller passed us, and without a glance, whispered, "Be careful! They're hunting on the corner of Dluga and Leszno." We immediately changed our course.

Just before eight o'clock every night the streets exuded frantic activity. People rushed home before curfew began. Anyone caught outdoors after that hour was beaten at best, and sometimes shot.

The adults in our family spent the evenings playing cards as all of us youngsters watched over their shoulders. One of the uncles somehow even managed to keep us supplied with halvah and chocolate.

Once, looking out of the window I saw an SS man catch a Jew and beat him viciously until he fainted. I was appalled to see that the whole performance was done so that another soldier standing nearby could photograph it.

Beating without cause or provocation was common, but killing for no reason hadn't, to my knowledge, yet begun in Warsaw. Official announcements, threatening death to Jews for trying to escape, or avoiding work, or for being caught after curfew, were pasted on the walls to scare the population and to enforce total obedience and subservience. There was no ghetto at that time, however, and Jews could live and move freely throughout the city.

When the Germans took over Warsaw, many Jews escaped to Russian-held territories. To our surprise, some of them returned, saying the conditions they experienced there were so bad that they preferred to be home in Warsaw with their families. It was hard for us to understand that. We told them to wait until they got to know the Germans, then they'd know what bad really was! We continued to plan our escape to Russian-held territory.

The Bug River was the border between German and Russian occupied territories. People were smuggled across the river in both directions, but every day it became more difficult. Those living near the border and familiar with the terrain made a living of smuggling people across for money—lots of money.

There were many disasters. Some people paid but were never taken across. Others were led straight to German or Russian patrol guards. If the Russians caught them, they were returned to the German side. Germans who caught them would beat them, or strip them naked, and send them back to the Russians. Back and forth, back and forth. Some were killed. The people either managed to be smuggled through eventually, or met their death there.

We tried but couldn't find a guide, so with Uncle Avigdor we decided to move to Sieldce, a town near the border between the two territories. Rumors had spread that it was easier to find guides there. Cousin Micha took our horse and cart, and all our meager possessions to Sieldce, and we were to follow by train and meet him there.

The next morning all of us who were wearing armbands removed them and we took the tram to the train station in Praga, a suburb of Warsaw. The two families—ours and Uncle Avigdor's—numbered eight people. We waited at the station for about six hours, in constant fear of being recognized as Jews. Jews were forbidden to take the trains, so when we saw a German our hearts sank. Eventually the train arrived. We bribed the conductor to let us into a freight car to Sieldce and climbed in.

By evening we arrived safely in Sieldce. We paid heavily for an unheated room in someone's house, where we all slept together. It was now mid-December, and bitterly cold.

There were very few Jews left in Sieldce. Most of them had gone over to the Russian side of the river. Uncle Avigdor found a guide, and moved his family into the guide's house. Our family stayed on in the icy room. After the first frost the river had partially frozen and no boat could cross, but the ice wasn't yet strong enough to enable us to walk across. So we were stuck.

It was decided that Uncle Avigdor and his family would go with their guide on December 27. We, having found another guide through a go-between, would leave on the following day. Our guide, however, began to demand more money than we had agreed upon. What choice did we have? Our lives depended upon him. On the twenty-eighth, before nightfall, horse-drawn sleds took us to the border. It was totally dark by the time we reached the last village near the border, and came to the home of our guide. We waited there until midnight, which was when we were supposed to cross. The guide sent one of his daughters to distract the German guards by flirting with them. He and his second daughter led us.

The ground was covered with snow, but we were warmly clad. Our guide led us along the shore, trying to find a safe place to cross. We were all carrying bundles, the last of our possessions. We eventually reached the spot where we had expected to cross, but the river hadn't frozen over yet. So we plodded on in the snow, heavily laden, exhausted. Finally we reached a spot where the river was completely frozen. At the guide's instruction, we all hid behind bushes until the patrols, on both the German and the Russian sides, passed. Then we quickly started across the river. The guide led the way and tested the ice. It creaked under our feet and at one point almost cracked under Musio. It was frightening. In the still of the night, each creak sounded incredibly loud, and we were sure a patrol would hear us.

We finally reached the other bank, Russian-held territory. There was an open field, and the nearest village was about half a kilometer away. We began to run, looking back all the time to see if we were being followed. After about two hundred yards we sat down to rest. Luckily, we managed to spot a Russian patrol passing about five hundred feet away, before they spotted us. We didn't dare breathe. We were motionless. To them we must have looked like bushes. When they were out of sight, we started to run again to the village.

It had been prearranged that we would spend the night at one of the farmhouses, and the following morning the farmer was to take us to the town of Semiatic, four miles away. Trustingly, we gave the last payment to our guide, and he disappeared into the night. After knocking and banging for admittance, the farmer, from behind barred doors, told us he wouldn't let us in because he was afraid. We didn't know what to do. If a passing patrol were to spot us, we would, after all our efforts, be turned back over to the Germans. Utterly desperate, we kept banging loudly on his door.

Frightened that someone would hear and understand his involvement with smuggling people across the border, he eventually opened the door to us. He shoved us into a dark room, and after a lengthy negotiation agreed to take us to the next town at dawn, as previously arranged, but at double the price. The farmer's children amused themselves by shouting into our dark room that they could hear the patrol coming for us, which made me sweat with terror, and my clothes became totally drenched. In the morning we discovered that my father's fur coat had disappeared, as had mother's purse with all our money. Desperate, we created a row, threatening to expose them. The farmer returned our stolen possessions and demanded that we leave, or else he would call a patrol. On a sudden impulse, with the bravado of youth, I stepped forward and forcefully told him that unless he fulfilled his promise to take us to Semiatic, I myself would go to the Russians and tell them that he personally had brought us across the border. We might then be sent back, but he would surely be shot.

Another lengthy discussion followed, another increase in pay demanded, and he finally agreed to fulfill his side of the bargain. In order to avoid attracting attention, however, he insisted that we leave half our belongings behind, to be brought to us the following day. My brother, my father, and I were told to go to the main road. The farmer and my mother would come in his wagon and pick us up. Impatient to get going, we agreed to everything.

So, on December 29, we arrived at the Russian-held town of Semiatic. It was a typical little town. Most of the houses were built of wood, the higher-class ones of brick. There was no running water, and outhouses could be seen in the yards. Electricity was connected for several hours in the evening. In the center of town was a market square with nicer homes, some shops, a church, the town hall, a police station, and even a school. There was no public transportation. People used horses hitched to sleds or rode horseback. An occasional truck would come by.

The first stage of the war was over for us—we had escaped the German occupation and arrived destitute in Russian-occupied territory. All our property remained in Raciaz. Most of our money had gone to pay our way. But we had no regrets. We asked around for someone who could put us up, and were directed to a kind Jewish shoemaker named Mendel, who admitted us into his home. We rejoiced to see streets with no Germans around.

4

IN SOVIET-OCCUPIED TERRITORY

December 29, 1939–June 21, 1941

We removed all our possessions from the cart and moved into the room allocated to us by Mendel the shoemaker. He was hospitable enough, and had a brother-in-law in the Russian militia who could arrange everything for us—for a fee, of course. Before letting the farmer go, we told Mendel how he, the farmer had treated us. Mendel threatened to report the farmer to the Soviet authorities unless he returned the rest of our possessions.

After a brief rest, we went outside. It was exhilarating to breathe the fresh air, to walk the streets without fear of Germans, to feel free and equal. We walked along singing for joy. We had broken out of hell. My mother was especially happy and hopeful. We hadn't seen Soviet soldiers yet, just the local militia in civilian clothes with red armbands.

The first Soviet soldiers we encountered, the border units, in white fur coats and peaked hats, made a favorable enough impression. We felt truly lucky and decided to celebrate our new-found freedom by going to the movies. I didn't understand a word of the Russian film, but enjoyed it anyway. Life seemed so beautiful.

I spent a very restless first night in Semiatic and found in the morning that my body was covered with little red spots. I asked my mother what the little black insects were that were jumping all over me. She identified them as fleas, which I had never seen before, but for a long time to come they would be a constant presence in my life.

Our host the shoemaker had several children, all of them filthy, all of them busy catching their fleas. The constant sound of his wife nagging and the children bickering was hard on the nerves. The children were expert thieves, as well. Their lifestyle was totally alien to me, and very disturbing.

On the day of our arrival there was a devaluation of the Polish zloty and the only official currency became the Russian ruble. That left us utterly penniless. We had to sell some of our possessions in order to buy food.

My father and Musio took the train to Bialistok, a nearby town, to find my aunt Rujia and to borrow some money from her. Mother and I remained to wait for the farmer to return the last of our belongings. Mother cooked. Despite everything, we were satisfied just to be free.

The farmer returned with some of our things, claiming that the Soviets had confiscated the rest. We now had more to sell. Still waiting for Father and Musio, we spent the evenings walking around town. My multilingual mother, who was fluent in Russian as well, began to teach me the language. Mother asked a Red Army soldier what life was like in the Soviet Union. He said that life was good and there was plenty of everything there. Of course we believed him.

On January 1, 1940, Father and Musio returned with some money and we left by train for Bialistok. We thought we might find work and stay there in safety.

It took us two days to cover the short distance, in an unheated train with broken windows. It was snowing and bitterly cold. The train spent more time standing than moving. We were transferred from train to train, waiting indefinitely each time. Food was unavailable but at every station the national drink "kipiatok"—boiling water—was awaiting us. We spent all night at the town of Czeremsze, where we first saw a unit of the regular Red Army (Soviet army). Scruffy soldiers wore peaked hats and shabby padded jackets, each one in a different shade of khaki—there was no uniformity of uniforms. Some wore shoes, others had a sort of cloth footwear. Their bayonets were tied to their rifles with rags. The soldiers appeared hungry. They slept on the dirty ground. The officers were slightly better dressed. There was a tremendous contrast between the bedraggled Soviet soldiers and the immaculate German and Polish ones. But they were decent to us.

We finally reached Bialistok and met Aunt Rujia and her family. We found Kozak, our accountant from Raciaz. He had left Raciaz by train with my Uncle Shlomo and headed to the eastern part of Poland. As that region had been occupied by the Soviets on September 17, they fell under Soviet occupation and had never even seen the Germans. Kozak now held a job as an accountant for the Soviets, earning 400 rubles a month, hardly sufficient to subsist on. We stayed in Kozak's apartment. We found out from him that Uncle Shlomo worked at a lumberyard in nearby Lyda and felt bitter toward the Soviets.

My responsibility each morning was to get bread. I had to wait in line for four or five hours to buy one two-pound bread. I soon became an expert at cutting into the line closer to the door and saved myself hours of waiting.

There were still some privately owned restaurants and shops in Bialistok. We sometimes ate at a Jewish restaurant, when they had something to serve. The shops were almost bare because the Soviets bought up everything. They took whatever they wanted and set their own prices. We couldn't find work in Bialistok and decided to leave.

Throughout our wanderings, our choice of places was dictated by the whereabouts of numerous relatives scattered throughout Poland, whom we could count on for help. Our plans kept changing, however, based upon where we thought we would find safety and the availability of work.

We decided that Father and I would go to Rovno, which was where my father's nephew Avram lived. If we could find a means of support, Mother and Musio would join us.

In mid-January we left Bialistok. The train schedules were irregular and unreliable, and the stops at the various stations along the way were long and tiring.

When we finally arrived at Avram's house, he received us warmly. Working as chief engineer in a big yeast factory, he was quite comfortable financially. His wife worked there too. Life in

vno was easier than in Bialistok. For one thing, bread and work
ere more readily available.

Avram promised to use his influence in helping us get settled,
jobs, and to enroll me in high school. He couldn't do enough
We cabled for Mother and Musio to come. I passed my en-
ms and was admitted to the high school. After all the wan-
uldn't believe that we were actually beginning to settle
g back over the four and a half months since the Ger-
land, and our wanderings began, I had seen more
than I had during my entire life. We had lived
bin, Plonsk, Warsaw, Semiatic, Bialistok, and
in each place that we could resume a more or
. Would Rovno at last offer us a semblance

and Musio arrived. Because of the un-
were frostbitten and for a while she had
or's care. But our mood was elevated.
Musio was going to take a course in
f promise.

ble burst. Avram came home with a
ets were rounding up the refugees and
unknown destination. No one knew
aware that refugees were staying with
cked up, so he hid us in a part of the
, the authorities came looking for us,

ng for refugees at the train station, that
traveled and went to the next town, where
led out. From there we intended to take the
been we heard that Uncle Avigdor had set-
t the Jewish refugees in Rovno had all
strange s to labor camps in Siberia.
ing for th shivering in an unheated station in a
We took tire of 40 degrees below freezing, wait-
looking out ich, not knowing when it would come.
tside on the platform in the bitter cold
here were so many people waiting that

unless we pushed our way in when it came there would be no pl
for us.

Finally the train arrived. Thousands of people spilled out of t
depot and rushed toward the train. Shoving and pushing, t
stronger ones more successfully, people climbed in. Holding han
so as not to lose each other, we pushed together. But the mob m
aged to tear us apart. Father and Musio disappeared. I was still ho
ing on to Mother. I wasn't strong enough to break through to
train, and saw that there was no way we could get in by contin
on in this manner. In desperation I climbed over people's head
the while holding Mother's hand, while she elbowed her
through the crowd.

This was how we got in. We went from car to car until we
Father and Musio. We also found a place to sit. The conduct
to throw us out because we didn't have the proper tickets.
long bargaining session, accompanied by shouts and curses,
got his bribe and let us stay. That night we arrived at Bara

We left our belongings at the station and went in sea
uncle. Baranovich was covered in a thick blanket of snow.
the address but Uncle Avigdor and his family had left t
eral days before. Relatives of Uncle Avigdor's wife were i
ment and allowed us to stay there overnight.

We again had to continue looking elsewhere to s
cided to go to Oszmiany, where another of my fath
Hershek, lived.

In the morning we were back at the railway sta
waited for twenty-four hours for the train. Two da
rived at Hershek's home. He and his wife extende
ity to us and the warm house was a most welcome
freezing conditions we had experienced during th
son was my age, and that was an extra bonus fo

The border between Soviet-occupied territo
was somewhere between Oszmiany and Vilna. So
town several miles from Vilna, was under Sovie
Vilna was now part of Lithuania, an indepen
by, but not occupied by, the Soviets. Vilna had
belonging to Poland and a prominent center

During February and March we revived

any. Hershek and his wife took excellent care of us. I walked around town observing the Soviets, listening to their beautiful songs. Even today, whenever I hear these songs, they bring back fond memories of Oszmiany. I went skating with Hershek's son, and enjoyed every minute of it. Hershek's wife Liza was a dentist, and he was a dental technician. During the day he began to train me in his profession. At night I went to high school and also began to study Russian. My life was full. Each member of the family had his own responsibilities. Mother was in charge of the kitchen. Musio started looking for a job. Every morning at 5 A.M. all the men went to stand in line for bread. After standing for three or four hours, each man was rationed two pounds. Once each month, sugar was available, but it took eight to ten hours of waiting in line to buy just a pound.

I didn't particularly want to be a dental technician, so Hershek arranged for his neighbor to train me in photography at his studio. I enjoyed that more. Musio was sent to Baranovich for three months to study bookkeeping.

Father got a job as assistant manager in a lumberyard in Smorgon, a town about eighteen miles from Oszmiany. Mother was supposed to move to Smorgon with Father, and I was to stay on with Hershek in Oszmiany because Father's salary of 400 rubles a month was barely sufficient for two people. Also, there was no feeling of permanency in his job. One could be fired at any moment because someone else wanted the position and gave the boss a bigger bribe. If that happened, we would all have to move again, and my life would have been disrupted for nothing. Meanwhile the family would have to be split, and that saddened and worried me.

Uncle Shlomo suddenly surfaced in Oszmiany. He was doing pretty well at his job in Lyda, but was full of complaints and rage at the Soviets, calling them liars and cheats. We soon discovered how right he was. His purpose in coming was to plan crossing the border to Vilna in Lithuania with us.

We had heard rumors of the possibility of getting visas to Japan and China in Vilna and crossing the Soviet Union by train to the Orient. Years later I found out that some people had actually managed to do just that. We found a guide who was willing to take us across the border. We contacted my parents and Musio, and they came back to Oszmiany.

Uncle Shlomo went back to Lyda to collect his things and was to return in four days. We were supposed to leave for Vilna on the day following his return. We waited for a whole week and Shlomo never showed up. He simply disappeared. Father went to Lyda to look for him and found no trace of him. We decided to delay our departure again. Mother then went to try to find him, but with no results. Years later we learned that in Lyda a Soviet militiaman had observed that Shlomo had several nice suits which he coveted, so he informed the NKVD (later to be known as the KGB) that Shlomo was against the Soviet rule and wanted to escape. When my uncle went to collect his belongings, he was nabbed and sent to a Siberian labor camp.

Meanwhile Lithuania was annexed to the Soviet Union and all the escape routes were thus closed to us. So we went back to our previous occupations. My parents returned to Smorgon, my brother to Baranovich, and I, the only one in the family to stay in Oszmiany, continued to live with Hershek, and to train and work in the photographer's studio. I was even promised a salary. I was excited at the prospect of getting my first 200 rubles, and planned how I would proudly present all that money to my parents.

I missed my family desperately, especially my mother's kindness and encouragement.

In late March, three weeks after I started working at the photographic laboratory, some chemicals splashed into my eye, and my vision was impaired. I couldn't use that eye at all. The local doctors didn't know what to do for me, and they decided that I should go to Bialistok to see a specialist.

I left Oszmiany for Bialistok and went again to Aunt Rujia. She took me to one of the best-known eye specialists, another refugee. He immediately recognized the problem with my eye and out of sympathy for a fellow refugee charged very little for his care. In ten days my vision improved considerably.

With my eye swathed in bandages I set out to go back to Oszmiany, and stopped on the way to visit my parents in Smorgon. But my grandiose plans to present my parents with my first hard-earned salary were foiled because the money had gone for the medical treatment.

In Smorgon I found out that, in my absence, a new law was enforced which forbade refugees to live close to the old borders, and since Oszmiany was close to the Lithuanian border, I was not allowed to return there. I was forced to stay in Smorgon, a typical small town, which was still smothered in deep snow. My training in the photographer's lab was cut short. But I was back with my parents!

My father meanwhile had lost his job, so mother, after a great deal of effort, found work as a bookkeeper. Mother had never worked before and certainly was not a qualified bookkeeper, but her natural common sense and intelligence made her good at the job in a very short time.

My parents were living in a tiny room rented from a Jewish wagon driver. It could only hold a bed and a table. At night I put a plank on the table and slept on it. After work mother cooked and did the housework. Having missed my parents so much during the weeks of separation, I was happy to be with them and the small room, bedbugs and all, was heaven to me. Mother's cooking tasted to me like the best gourmet meals possible. I waited for her at work during her lunch break and walked her home in the evening. That was the highlight of my day. We always had so much to talk about. Whether we discussed the future, or some film we had seen, or remembered our relatives and our life in Raciaz, or even just acted like a couple of kids pretending to be some fictitious characters, she was easier to talk to than any of the friends I ever had. Her love and care and support for me were so great that despite the difficulties, I was happy.

Though I was under the legal working age of sixteen, I felt the need to get a job and help out with the expenses. I tried several places but my age and lack of profession and experience made it very difficult. Finally, I wound up in a photography cooperative. When the Soviets had taken over the area, they had immediately organized all the independent professionals—carpenters, shoemakers, bakers, photographers, etc.—into cooperatives, headed by an organization called Prom Soyuz. Six local photographers had brought their equipment and set up the cooperative.

I bluffed my way into the cooperative, saying I'd had two years of experience. The place was very busy and shorthanded because everybody needed pictures for all the various new identification papers required by the Soviet authorities, so I was taken on for four nights as a temporary assistant at 20 rubles per night. I was supposed to develop pictures, but I was totally unfamiliar with the work, my only experience being the three weeks I had spent as an apprentice in Oszmiany. On the first night, the man I worked with started to test my professional knowledge but I covered up my ignorance by saying that I had previously worked on a different type of equipment. I began to develop the negatives, but the pictures weren't coming out right. I was in a sweat, scared that he would find out that I had bluffed my way in, so I tried stalling for time.

Since it was very late at night, I managed to convince my boss to go home to sleep, and promised that by morning all the work would be done to his satisfaction. As soon as I was left alone, I began experimenting. A large pile of destroyed material accumulated before I finally hit upon a way of developing the photos. At dawn my work was done—not the best quality but acceptable. Exhausted and sweaty, with all the ruined pictures tucked into my jacket to conceal the amount of paper I had wasted, I went home. I had survived my first night at work. Every night from then on there was an improvement in the quality of my work, and at the end of my four night trial period I asked for a permanent job.

It was early May, 1940, when I was accepted into the cooperative and became a full-fledged productive member of Soviet society. I looked forward to the salary, which would help my parents, and set to work with optimism and youthful energy. My job in the laboratory was to develop negatives, print, and enlarge pictures. Within a few weeks I became an "expert." We were now seven photographers. I was the youngest and the only single person. The others had previously owned their own studios and had families to support.

The official salaries for the employees were set in the following manner: Of the total net income of the cooperative, two thirds was to be taken by the Prom Soyuz (Industrial Cooperative). The remaining third was then divided among the employees. My salary was set at 13% of the employees' share. The Soviet regime didn't consider this system exploitation of the worker. It was explained to us that we workers should be proud to give up two thirds of our earnings because it went to our own workers' government, whereas the workers' money taxed by capitalist governments went to the capitalists who exploited the workers. It was hard to swallow that propaganda. The average photographer made 250 rubles a month, whereas it required a thousand rubles to support a family of four. An unskilled worker earned roughly 200 per month. A manager earned 750 a month, but managers had access to things unavailable to the rest of the workers, and were in a position to barter with other managers for food, clothing, and so forth.

We officially charged 10 rubles per picture and delivery took three to six months. Efficiency was hardly an issue that needed to be dealt with. The fluidity and flexibility with which money and commodities changed hands had nothing to do with official Soviet systems. Luckily for us, even photographs were a trading commodity. Because I photographed the manager of the shoemakers' cooperative in three poses and delivered the pictures within one week, I got a pair of shoes in exchange. The same system worked for clothes and other necessities. Very quickly I learned how everybody at all levels "supplemented" their income under the Soviet regime. They invested all their ingenuity and creativity in finding ways to cheat the government and each other of money and goods in order to survive. Those who were caught were imprisoned. A popular joke at the time divided all the citizens of the Soviet Union into three categories—past, present, and future jailbirds. A worker living alone and having to support himself had no time to stand in line for bread and other necessities. Without bribes and other forms of manipulation during working hours, he could not get along. During lunch break one could go to a workers' kitchen and get lunch for 5 rubles, but lines were so long one could rarely get food before having to be back at work. Workers extended their lunch breaks unofficially, came to work late and left early, in order to be able to take care of their most basic needs. The government caught on to this practice, and a new law was enacted. A worker who was late once by more than twenty-one minutes, or three times by ten minutes, would stand trial in a people's court for "progul" (truancy). The punishment could be a 25% salary reduction for three to six months, or, in recurring cases, three to six months of hard labor in a work camp, which was worse than prison.

Acquiring clothing was another problem, even if one managed to save enough money. Items arrived in the shops infrequently and in very short supply. Immediately long lines of people formed to buy them but only the first in line could get what was available. There was no selection of style. In one instance, after a long wait, I managed to get into the store and happily bought shoes. Suddenly I realized that what I got were two left shoes. When I complained to the salesgirl, she told me that was all she had and I'd better hang on to them in the hope that the next supply would bring right shoes, regardless of style or color, and I would then own two pairs. I never did get the right shoes.

The Soviet propaganda always depicted the working classes of other countries as hungry, deprived, and exploited. But when the Soviet soldiers occupied eastern Poland, they found stores full of food, clothes, shoes, watches, and other items, which the working class was buying without lines or restrictions. This baffled them and shook their trust in the validity of the stories they had been led to believe all their lives. But when asked by the local population about the conditions in the Soviet Union, the soldiers always said, "Oh, yes, we have everything, even matches."

I once jokingly asked a soldier who came to have his picture taken whether in the Soviet Union they had "kadahat," the Hebrew word for the plague. Not understanding the word but assuming it must be something good, he said, "Oh, yes, even more than you can get here."

In mid-June Musio finished his accounting course in Baranovich and joined us in Smorgon. He got a job as chief accountant in a savings bank. Mother got a better job in the "Raysoyuz," the county headquarters for unions. I continued in the photography cooperative. Father stayed home and stood in lines. He was frustrated at not being able to support his family. Even with three incomes for four people, we could barely manage. But we moved into two rooms in a slightly better house. Besides cooking and cleaning in the evenings, Mother waged an all-out war on the bedbugs by pouring boiling water on the walls and bedboards, which brought temporary relief. Except for my father, we were all content.

We made friends with some of the local residents. I met some youngsters my own age, mostly high-school students, and my social life picked up. I fell in love with the non-Jewish pharmacist's daughter, Halina, and that autumn I went through all the excitement and turmoil of a young boy in love. I even began to enjoy Russian films and activities. My mother knew of my infatuation, and gently teased me about it. She didn't treat it very seriously, because of my youth. It certainly was a minor issue compared to the crises the family kept going through.

The Soviets continued to round up refugees in the big cities and deport them to Siberia. But since we were productive residents living in a small town, we were not touched. My mother cried when she showed me a postcard from Aunt Rujia, who had been deported from Bialistok with her husband and eleven-year-old son. At the time, it seemed the worst possible fate. We didn't have a clue of what was awaiting us.

We still lived in a state of insecurity. If anyone, for whatever reason, signed a declaration claiming he was against communism— "counter-revolutionary"—he was sent without trial or explanation to Siberia or to jail, depending upon the severity of the charge.

After I had been working and improving my skills steadily for about half a year, a new Russian apprentice named Ivan was sent to us. His father, Colonel Kovalsky, was in charge of all the industry in our county. Since everybody in our cooperative was afraid of Ivan, he was dumped on me as my assistant in the laboratory.

Ivan was slightly older than I, friendly and direct, and he soon became my friend. In the darkroom he told me of his life. He had grown up in Moscow and recalled nightly roundups of his neighbors, including his playmates, who would disappear without a trace. Later those very people who had taken away his neighbors would in turn be rounded up and sent to Siberia. Nobody could guess who would be considered counter-revolutionary. Anything as minor as telling jokes against Stalin or the communist regime could be used as a reason for arrest. Ivan's father Colonel Kovalsky was spared and became the Soviet military attaché in Berlin. Ivan, however, remained in Moscow with his mother. During his father's absence he was caught stealing and was jailed but was released after his father's intervention. He also told of his uncle, who had been sent in the 1920s to organize farming cooperatives, called Kolkhozy, and was killed by farmers who opposed the plan. Ivan's stories taught me a lot about the tricks of surviving in the Soviet regime.

Prior to his arrival, we had worked out a system which seemed fair to us, though not necessarily to the authorities. We declared only half of our earnings to the government and divided the rest amongst us. When Ivan joined us, we were afraid that he would find out and denounce us. When I got to know him, I suggested including him in our scheme. We did just that, and he kept silent.

After a while, at one of the quarterly meetings of the cooperative, Colonel Kovalsky appeared and suggested replacing the manager of our cooperative, the senior photographer in our group. To my surprise, he proposed me as the new manager and said that one of the reasons for his choice was that being so young, I hadn't yet been contaminated and corrupted by capitalism. I suspected that another reason was that I was friendly with his son. He put it to the vote by asking, "Who opposes?" Of course, no one dared to, so he announced that I had been voted in unanimously. That was how I was introduced to the election system in the Soviet Union.

I came home upset. I was not yet sixteen and had no idea how to handle my new position. I discussed my promotion with my mother, and got some advice from her. I spent the night agonizing about what I should do.

The next morning I assembled everyone at work and told them that since I was the least experienced in photography and in management, I would give up my right to the extra cut from the income which I was now entitled to as manager. I appealed for their cooperation. At first they were suspicious. Gradually, as they realized that I genuinely meant what I said, I had no problems and we worked in harmony.

We worked five days a week and then had a day off, which meant that I was off on a different day each week. Every cooperative ran on a different schedule. On one of my free days, which fell on a Sunday, Ivan and I invited our girlfriends out. We decided to surprise the girls by bringing a camera. I was in a hurry, and instead of neatly cutting off a piece of film from the large roll which we received from the factory, I tore off a strip and inserted it into the camera.

That day in the countryside with Halina, Ivan, and his girlfriend was one of the most enjoyable days that year. The autumn day was crisp and sunny. The leaves were turning. First we showed off our expertise with the camera and took many pictures. There was a wooden bridge over a creek, and we photographed each other on it. We brought a picnic basket and ate under the trees. Ivan had his harmonica with him, and he played sentimental Russian songs. We sang. The problems of the past two years were far away. The future looked bright. I had a job; I was already a manager at this early age. My family was with me. My girlfriend was in love with me. I was happier than I had been in a long time. Life was beautiful.

We found a secluded spot and split with Ivan and his girlfriend. Halina and I kissed, caressed each other, and swore eternal love. This was the first time I really explored a girl's body, and felt her exploring mine. We were very excited, but didn't allow ourselves to go all the way. We went home in the evening, and I was in such a state of bliss that I wanted to treasure it. I wanted to share it with my mother, but was embarrassed.

The next morning, just as Ivan and I were developing our film, we were called out of the darkroom. Two men in civilian clothes identified themselves as NKVD—secret police—and demanded to see the film that we had taken on our outing the previous day. They closely examined the wet film which we had just developed, and then arrested us. At their headquarters they put Ivan and me into separate cells and started interrogating us. Accusing me of being a Western spy photographing military objects, they produced their evidence—a picture of Ivan and the two girls standing on a ten-foot-long wooden bridge spanning a creek. I had taken that picture. Because the film was torn at the edges, it was an indication, according to them, that more photographs of other places of strategic and military importance had been taken and passed on to enemies of the Soviet Union. They told me Ivan had already confessed and given them all the details. I was therefore advised to tell them whom I spied for, and who received the photographs.

I couldn't convince them that I was not a spy. They took me back to the lab, where I showed them that the tear in the film fitted exactly the tear in the remaining roll. Even then they refused to believe that there were no pictures other than those they saw, and they continued grilling me for two days.

At first I took the whole incident lightly, but as time went on I was getting worried. Suddenly on the third day I was brought out of the cell and with no explanation whatsoever Ivan and I were released. Later I found out that when Colonel Kovalsky discovered where his son was, he approached friends in high places and our release was arranged.

My family meanwhile had been trying desperately to find out why I was being interrogated by the NKVD, and to find ways to get me out. When I suddenly walked in the door, they were overjoyed.

Several months went by uneventfully. The Soviet work schedule was changed to six working days, and Sunday was the day of rest. However, because Sunday was the busiest day for photographers, our day of leisure was on Monday.

Sundays were designated as the time for taking pictures of soldiers. They came in droves, entire units at a time, with their sergeants and officers. Sometimes the lines were half a mile long. Each soldier was allowed two poses, one full length and the other a close-up. Because their uniforms were scruffy, we had two sizes of clean caps and uniforms, as well as a rifle and a pistol, which each soldier could borrow. Some of them tried to coax and bribe us for additional poses, but we had to refuse. The only exceptions were the officers.

Every day we deposited our official earnings in the bank. We drew our salaries once a month. My job, on the first of each month, was to get the money from the bank and divide it. Of course the money was never available until at least a week later and I had to waste a lot of time standing in line. As manager I felt it my responsibility to do something about it and asked for a meeting with the Soviet director of the bank. He had a bad squint. Coming straight to the point, I offered him six photographs on good pre-war Belgian paper, and promised that his eyes would appear in focus. In exchange, our cooperative was to get our salaries on the first of each month, without standing in line and delays. He agreed. We retouched his pictures, and he never looked so handsome in his life! He was happy, and I never had any further problems getting our money from that bank on time.

Peasants would come in with chickens, eggs, and other produce in exchange for photos. When someone brought home-made vodka, it was usually drunk on the spot, which was how I got drunk for the first time, when I wasn't yet sixteen. My friend Ivan filled a mug of vodka for each of us. Being manager, I was handed the first mugful, which I couldn't refuse without losing face. I took the foul-smelling liquid, closed my eyes, and gulped it down. I became so drunk that I needed Ivan's help to struggle home and face my shocked mother. I was too sick to get out of bed for two days.

We received another postcard from Aunt Rujia addressed from the labor camp in Siberia and began to send parcels of food and clothes to her regularly. We also received a card from Uncle Shlomo, consisting of one sentence: "I am better off now because I am in the hospital." It was sent from a detention camp, where he later died.

My father took on any job he could find and for a while worked as a night watchman. All the collected income in our family was handed over to Father, and he did the shopping and paid all the expenses. We wanted him to feel that he was head of the family. Mother worked hard at her job but still managed to make our surroundings a home. Musio was so successful at work that he became deputy to the bank manager, a Soviet by the name of Popoff. One of our greatest pleasures was going to the movies together, though the films were mainly propaganda, extolling the wonders of the regime. On Friday nights we lit candles and had a Sabbath meal. We discussed our dreams of starting a new life in Palestine after the war. We met the new year, 1941, with the hope that the war would soon be over.

My social life centered around the movies and Sunday night parties with Halina and friends. On Mondays, my days off, I liked to sit in on trials at court. I particularly enjoyed the alimony cases. It was quite common for country girls to have babies out of wedlock, and the new Soviet law permitted any unwed mother to claim child support from the father of her child. In one case a girl brought in a man, claiming that he was the father. The man insisted he had never set eyes on her before. The prosecutor's summary was short and to the point. "Comrade Stalin said that every child should have a father. As there is no other man said to be the father, I claim that this man is the uncontested father." The judge accepted the prosecutor's view.

In the spring of 1941 we heard rumors of the possibility of war between Germany and Russia. We saw Russian troops moving through our town toward the German border and by June the flow

of soldiers and military equipment was growing steadily. Knowing
the German obsession with expansion, I felt war was imminent.
Again my life focused on the fear of war, though there was no official indication of such a possibility.

Selim Sznycer (the author) at the age of fifteen after he was chosen to manage the photography cooperative in Smorgon, USSR, where this picture was taken. The medal he is wearing was a typical award for productivity and efficiency.

Selim's parents, Hannah and Shmuel Sznycer, during their honeymoon in Warsaw, 1918.

A family outing in Yablona, Poland, 1930. Selim is in the first row, extreme right, with his father sitting behind him. Musio is at the left end and Hannah stands in the back, next to the baby.

Selim and girlfriend Halina (third and fourth from left) with friends in Smorgon, 1940. This is the photo which landed Selim and Ivan in jail for three days!

5

UNDER THE GERMANS AGAIN

June 22, 1941–February 14, 1942

Rumors of German forces concentrating along the border began to circulate daily. We kept asking each other for news, but nobody knew anything.

On Sunday, June 22, 1941, I went to work as usual. Hardly any customers came in that morning. In the early afternoon someone told us that the Germans had attacked the Soviet Union and war had started. We rushed outside to ask other people what they had heard. The rumors were confusing. Finally it was confirmed. Molotov, the Soviet foreign minister, delivered his radio message to the people, saying that at 4 A.M. the German horde had crossed the Soviet border and started bombarding our cities. Justice being on our side, it was inevitable that we would win the war, he said. Compared to other propaganda speeches I had heard, this one was weak and unconvincing. But that was the only information we had and it was broadcast over and over again. We found it odd that this most important announcement was not made by Stalin himself.

In confusion, people started running about, trying to get more information. Later in the day, I heard German planes flying overhead. They strafed the town center with machine guns for a short time, not doing much damage but making sure we knew that the war was really on. It brought back all the memories of when the Germans attacked Raciaz, and with horror I thought of being caught

We traveled all day, non-stop. Along the way we met some friends from Smorgon—the Kupper and Levkov families—and they joined our group. We found out later that the train we had tried to get on was bombed and never reached its destination.

We reached Ilya at nightfall and stopped to give ourselves and our horses a rest. The following morning we went on toward the old border, only to find the road barricaded and guarded by Soviet border police. No one was allowed through. We were told to return and to fight the Germans. We decided to try to cross the border by a different route, which led us through some remote villages and woods. After Poland was divided between Germany and the Soviet Union in 1939, this region, which was once a part of Poland, had been occupied by the Soviets. The farmers hated and resented the Soviets for taking over their lands and trying to organize them into Kolkhozy (co-operative farms), and resisted the program. They also blamed the Jews for everything—for communism, for poverty, and used this as an excuse for expressing their hatred of them.

There was chaos all around, no one in charge, no one to prevent looting. The farmers took this opportunity to attack anyone they could. The fleeing refugees, largely Jews, were vulnerable and easy targets.

At one of the villages, farmers stopped us and started to take away our possessions. We tried to resist but they attacked us with sticks, rakes and sickles, calling us murderous Bolsheviks. "You are trying to run away, but we won't let you. You must pay for your crimes toward us." Two armed members of our group began to shoot. The farmers stopped attacking but did not leave. They began to throw stones at us, still blocking our way. I felt helpless and lost, with nowhere to turn. At that moment German airplanes flew overhead and began bombing. The farmers ran, looking for cover. We took this opportunity to whip our horses and flee to the woods. It was ironic that the German planes saved us from the local farmers.

Heading toward the border, we met groups of Jews escaping from a nearby village who told us that the very same thing was happening there. Bands of farmers were rampaging on the roads. There were rumors that the Germans were near Minsk, and we were surrounded. So we decided to turn back to Ilya.

One member of our group, a tall, bald, middle-aged attorney

named Zilberstein, was a German Jew who had fled from Germany to Poland and, later, when the Germans occupied Poland, had escaped to the Soviet side. Now he was on the run again with us. He said he wasn't able to take it anymore. We stopped at a well to get water for ourselves and for the horses. Just as we were about to leave, Zilberstein said he wanted to get more water. He walked back and before our eyes threw himself headlong into the well. We tried to save him, but when we pulled him out he was already dead. The fact that he preferred to kill himself rather than face the Nazis again for the third time affected me terribly. I was shaken by the thought that this man knew the Nazis, and that the future to him seemed so horrendous and unbearable. And here were we, possibly going to be under Nazi rule again.

During the night-long journey through the woods back to Ilya we heard cries of people being attacked by the farmers in nearby villages. Trying to avoid them, we lost our way several times. Finally we were back at Ilya. The Soviets had already fled the city, and the local population was looting. A vacuum of authority had been created, and the people took advantage of it.

Some of the fleeing Soviets returned to the city and tried unsuccessfully to restore order. They too had tried several times to leave the city but had to return each time because they found that the roads to the Soviet Union were cut off by the Germans. When we tried to get a true picture of the situation from the authorities, we were told that everything would be all right. We kept hearing artillery fire from all directions. Several times German planes flew overhead and shot at the town, but did not do much damage.

On Saturday of that week larger groups of Russian soldiers passed through town. This frightened the looters somewhat. Many in the population began to eagerly await the Germans' arrival, in the hope that at least some order would be restored.

A local Jewish resident took us into his home on the edge of town. Beyond his house were fields and woods. We all took turns at the window, on the lookout.

Sunday morning, while Musio was on guard at the window, he shouted that he could see German tanks coming. I rushed to the window and recognized the black swastikas. A tank stopped almost directly in front of our house and I clearly saw the smirking face of

the soldier sitting in the turret. A group of Soviet soldiers started
running through the fields toward the woods. The Germans saw
them and opened fire with the tank gun and machine guns.

The Soviet soldiers were gunned down. The house rattled from
the shooting. When the shooting stopped and more Germans arrived, we saw a shocking spectacle—local Polish and Belorussian citizens running toward the Germans, welcoming them with flowers.
Girls blew kisses at them, and everybody behaved as though their
saviors had arrived. This was how I saw the Germans again, on June
29, 1941—my sixteenth birthday.

A new phase of our lives began, which proved to be the most tragic
of all. We had premonitions of horrors to come. Having no friends,
no means of support, and no reason to remain in Ilya, we decided
to return to Smorgon, where we hoped to find people we knew and
to recover some of the possessions we had left behind. We got back
on our cart with the last of our belongings—a few changes of
clothes, some basic utensils, and blankets—and started on our way.
The main road to Smorgon passed through Vileika, the capitol of
that county. We decided to bypass it and took side roads until we
reached a small town, Kurzeniec, five miles from Vileika. The Kupper family, a father and two sons, Grisha and Mulek, who had lost
their mother, were still traveling with us. We stopped in Kurzeniec
to give our horse and ourselves a rest, and to try to get some food.

A poor Jewish harness-maker named Yankel agreed to take us
and the Kuppers in. His children unharnessed our horse and took
it into the fields to graze. There were no Germans in Kurzeniec. Occasionally Germans on motorbikes would pass and if they saw the
local population looting the stores and cooperatives, they would disperse them by shooting into the air. That seemed to keep some semblance of order.

At sundown the harness-maker's son returned crying from the
fields and told us that some local hooligans took our horse, and that
he himself barely escaped from them. As we had no other means of
transportation, we decided to wait out the looting. We expected the
Germans to bring order to the town and we would then be able to
find a way to get back to Smorgon.

We spent a week in fear of the gangs of hoodlums who broke into Jewish homes and robbed, beat, and vandalized. One of these gangs broke into the house where we were staying, armed with sticks, iron rods, and knives. Luckily, Yankel knew the leader and begged him to spare us all. It worked and they left.

Yankel's family, which consisted of his wife, two sons, a baby daughter, and his old parents, all shared a room with a wooden floor. He agreed to let us stay in a second room, with a mud floor. The four of us and the three Kuppers settled into it. We draped a piece of cloth in the middle of the room to create a bit of privacy between the two families.

Despite the very close quarters, we got along well with Yankel's family. We appreciated their kindness in sharing their home with us perfect strangers. There was no bickering, and we tried to be helpful to each other in small ways.

Kurzeniec was a town of some two thousand people, over half of whom were Jews. The rest were Belorussians and Poles. The borders between the various East European countries shifted with unpredictable frequency. In regional wars, parts of Belorussia (one of the republics of the Soviet Union) became Polish, and vice versa. The lands belonging to Lithuania and Latvia switched hands. The villages and towns around the borders consisted of mixed populations of Poles, Belorussians, and Lithuanians in varied proportions, who lived in relative harmony. As the Soviet Union expanded, these small countries came under its rule. The thread binding this medley of ethnic groups was their deep resentment of the Soviet occupants. The Germans, pushing their way eastward through Soviet-occupied territory, incorporated their loyal followers, especially from Latvia and Lithuania and the Ukraine, into their auxiliary forces.

Most of the Jews in Kurzeniec were artisans—shoemakers, bakers, blacksmiths, tailors. There were also doctors, pharmacists, teachers, shop owners and farmers. The Belorussians were mostly farmers. We found the relationship between the Jews, the Belorussians and the Poles in Kurzeniec congenial. The center of town was the market square, where the town hall was situated. Yankel's house was on Miadzol Street, a short walk from the market square.

Some Jewish families living near Yankel gave us food, so we were not hungry. My mother had immediately made some friends.

Among them were the pharmacist Gvint and his wife and daughter Rivka. An instant closeness developed between us and the Gvints. They were kind and helpful, and shared our Zionist ideas.

In early July, a week after our arrival in Kurzeniec, the first German commandant came and began to set up the new occupation regime. The commandant, a white-haired army officer, and twenty soldiers immediately organized the local police force and issued the first orders—all the Jews were to assemble in the marketplace. Rumors began to circulate that all men between the ages of fifteen and sixty would be taken to work. People were afraid to ignore the order so everyone, including us, appeared. Grouped in fours and surrounded by armed German soldiers, we stood there for an hour. Trucks arrived, and we were sure they were meant to take us away. Another hour went by and nothing happened. Then the Commandant, accompanied by several officers, came out, picked out a translator from among us, and gave a short speech.

The gist of it was that we were to work for the Germans. The Jews would have to select their own representatives to form a Jewish Council called "Judenrat" which would receive and enforce orders directly from him concerning Jewish matters. As of that day we were all to wear a yellow patch with the letter "J" on the left side of the chest. We were all supposed to show respect by bowing to anyone wearing a German uniform. Jews were forbidden to be on the sidewalk and had to walk in the street, like horses. They were also forbidden to take the train. They were not allowed to associate with non-Jews. Curfew would be enforced. Then, to our relief, we were dismissed.

The Judenrat was elected, and an Austrian Jew named Shatz, who spoke fluent German, became the head. Whenever people were required for work, Shatz was notified. The Judenrat had a list of all able-bodied men, who took turns working. This was at least a better system than being grabbed in the streets at random.

The Judenrat also had to ensure that Jews supplied accommodations, baked cakes, made ice cream, and provided other delicacies for the Germans. The women worked as servants, cleaning the soldiers' shoes, doing their laundry, and other chores. Each group of the German occupying forces—the SD, the Gebietskommissar, the gendarmes—made their own demands and requisitions, almost like supermarket shopping. The Judenrat tried to fulfill these orders, in the hope that gratifying them would stave off atrocities.

On the outskirts of Kurzeniec was a transit camp for Russian prisoners of war. Groups of prisoners were marched in, stayed for a day or two, and left for the next camp. Musio and I, along with other people, worked for the Germans in this camp, cooking, cleaning the dilapidated barracks, digging new holes to be used for latrines, and doing other jobs in preparation for the next batch of prisoners.

We were always hungry. Due to my mother's tremendous drive and ingenuity, however, we were able to get some food from our Jewish friends. They kept us from starving. Bread and potatoes were the chief staples of our diet.

During the High Holidays in September 1941, all the houses of prayer were full. My father attended services from morning until night in a building in the courtyard where the Gvint family lived. Though I was not religious, I began to participate in the prayers. I wanted God's protection for me and my family. I will never forget the fervor of the praying figures, wrapped in their shawls, packed into the room, bowing and pleading with closed eyes. The cry in their voices sent chills over me. Surely God would listen!

Despite the hardships, we tried to observe all the rituals of the holidays. On Simhat Torah, the last day of the High Holidays and a day of joyous celebration of the Torah, we saw Yankel talking outside the house to a policeman he knew. The policeman led him away. We sneaked out to our neighbors to find out whether anyone knew of any unusual happenings in town. There we heard rumors that Jews accused of being communists were being arrested. Very troubled, we returned home and tried to console Yankel's wife and parents.

Shortly thereafter, a German officer accompanied by soldiers and policemen entered the house and made us all line up in the yard. The house was searched. We didn't know what they were looking for. Then the officer told us that the soldiers would lead us away to the police station. My mother stepped forward and, in fluent German, asked the officer why he was arresting us. Astounded, he asked how she knew the language so well. She told him that she had studied German at school and during World War I had many German friends. He asked whether we were related to the family living in the house. She explained that we were refugees, and that Yankel's family had kindly given us refuge. He ordered her to go back into the house and to take her family with her. She immediately took us and the Kuppers, with whom we had gone through so much, saying they were family too.

The soldiers took Yankel's entire family away—the wife with the infant in her arms, the two sons, and the old parents. The grandmother pleaded in vain to be allowed to get some warm clothes for the baby. We tried to find out what was happening. Where were they taking Yankel and his family? Who else was taken away? Why?

Fifty-four people, entire families, were brought to the police station and later taken out of town. One ten-year-old boy returned the next day and told us what happened. They had been taken to the nearby woods. At his father's urging, the boy found a moment to slip undetected behind the trees and hide. He watched from there. The men were given shovels and made to dig mass graves. Then everyone was shot. Yankel was so strong that it took seven bullets to kill him. His wife died with her baby daughter in her arms. As soon as the victims fell, the policemen and some of the spectators stripped off their clothes before shoving them into the grave. The boy lay down in a hole and covered himself with leaves. He stayed there until everybody left, and at night came back to Kurzeniec. The Jewish community was shaken by this first mass murder, but tried to console themselves into believing that it happened only to those Jews who were identified as communists.

Our family continued to subsist on charity in Yankel's house. My family moved into what had been Yankel's family's room, and the Kuppers remained in the other one. We were devastated by the murders of our kind host and his family, and deeply grieved their deaths.

The dominating figure in the Kupper family was the older son, Grisha, who was a lawyer. He was in his thirties, selfish, unpleasant, and constantly abused and humiliated his old father and younger brother Mulek. We twice saved the father from suicide. He tried to hang himself because he felt that he was a burden to his sons. Once, Mulek walked into the room just as he was trying to attach a rope to a hook in the ceiling, and stopped him. Very upset, Mulek told us about it. After that we were aware of his depression and were alert to any unusual sounds emanating from the room when Mr. Kupper was there alone. The second time, after a particularly unpleasant scene between the father and Grisha, my mother and father were in the kitchen when they heard a thump on the floor. They rushed into the room, and saw that old man Kupper's neck was in a noose hanging from the ceiling and that he had just kicked the stool from under himself. They immediately cut the rope with a kitchen knife before he could harm himself.

We provided all the food and the Kupper family contributed nothing to the household. Grisha accepted everything as his due, and all he gave was criticism. Old man Kupper and Mulek, however, were grateful for our help. I asked my mother why she did so much for them when Grisha was so thankless. She said that since she had taken it upon herself to help them, she was doing her best. She felt sorry for them for losing the mother, and told me we were lucky to have our family intact. She softly added, "Please, God, keep it that way until the end."

A Pole of German descent, named Matros, a schoolteacher by profession, was made town mayor. This liberal man managed to help some Jews. My mother appealed to him in Polish for help. Most of the population spoke Belorussian, and the Jews also spoke Yiddish. Few of the townsfolk spoke Polish. In the ensuing conversation, the mayor, impressed with her intelligence, eloquence, and personality, promised to do his best.

He indeed helped us. He put my mother in charge of the distribution of bread to the Jewish population. Bread was rationed, four ounces per person per day, and Jews were supposed to get theirs in a separate store. I helped my mother with the distribution. Through this job we got to know all the Jews in town. I became familiar with all the names and the quantities each family was entitled to. I found out that it was not customary to identify people by their family names, as many families were related and bore the same name. Rather, they would be called by the first name together with the father's first name (Pinhas Ziske, meaning Pinhas son of Ziske). Some were identified by their profession—like Shmulik the shoemaker.

Every day we brought the bread from the bakery to our Jewish shop for distribution; ten rations per loaf, and several extra loaves for wastage while slicing. We learned to slice the bread exactly, to minimize waste because the extra bread could be used by us. That enabled us to have enough to eat and even to trade for other necessities, as money had no value and people bartered for everything. Whatever we had we shared with the Kuppers.

Although six weeks had passed, I still hadn't recovered from losing Yankel and his family. I could still see the grandmother and the children at play. I could still hear their voices. On November 21 I was at the bakery with my mother, waiting for the daily supply of bread when the deputy Gebietskommissar (county commander) Hendel arrived at the market square with his gendarmes and began grabbing and beating the Jews who were passing by. He was notorious for this kind of senseless cruelty. Since our home and the bread shop were across the square from the bakery, we could not reach home to hide. So together with the bakers, who were all Jews, we began to run through the side streets toward the fields and woods on the outskirts of town. Along the way people peeped out of windows and asked what was happening in the square. When they heard that the infamous Hendel had arrived from Vileika and was brutalizing Jews, they poured out of their homes and joined us. The group grew. We hid in the woods in the cold all day. By evening we were half frozen and ravenous. We heard the Germans on the roads. My mother and I, huddled together for warmth, worried about Musio and Father. When it was dark we crept back home.

We found everybody there safe, and they told us that Hendel and his men had rounded up the Jews they could find in the houses and herded them into the square. They ordered everyone to undress and searched their clothes for gold, silver and other valuables. Then they searched the houses. For six hours they kept the naked men and women outside in the cold. Obviously disappointed in the poor loot, the Germans told Shatz, the head of the Judenrat, who was also in the square, to immediately bring more gold, and only then would the people be released. Shatz brought more gold, and the people were allowed to go. This was not the first time that the Germans demanded valuables from the Judenrat, who would collect from the Jews and pay up. This time, in addition to the normal procedure of collecting, they had decided to frighten and humiliate them.

The winter was bitterly cold, but we managed to trade bread

for warm clothes. I continued working with my mother at the store until the beginning of December, when my father took over my job.

Mother had long and frequent discussions with Matros the mayor. She asked him for safer jobs for her sons, and he took Musio and me to work at the town hall. Musio became a bookkeeper and I a messenger boy. I didn't wear the identifying Jewish patch. The policemen, knowing I worked for the mayor, didn't touch me. This was certainly a safer place to work, since each time the Germans came to round up and beat the Jews, my brother and I would hide in the municipal building. No one imagined there would be Jews there.

Musio was admitted to a group of Jewish youths who were in touch with some escaped Russian prisoners hiding in the surrounding villages. Our friend Zalman Gurevich, handsome, tall, and full of self-confidence, was one of the organizers and leaders of this group. The common aim of this group was to organize a partisan unit that would leave for the woods in the spring, to fight the Germans. The plan was a secret that was hidden even from our families. Musio told me about it and swore me to secrecy. He told the group that as a messenger I could help, and I was included. I was moved by Musio's confidence and faith in me and proud to participate. I fantasized about stealing arms from the Germans and fighting them.

The secret meetings of the Jewish group were sometimes held in the town hall, to which both Musio and I had the keys. The cache of arms we acquired—some stolen, some bought from villagers— were stored in the attic of the building, unknown to anyone in the town hall. It was the safest place we could find.

One day a German open military vehicle, somewhat like a jeep, pulled up in front of the town hall as I was standing on the steps. A group of German officers got out and asked where the mayor was. I showed them the way and went back outside. In the glove compartment of the car I saw a Parabellum revolver. I wanted desperately to steal it for our group, but it scared me to think that the Germans would notice it missing and would suspect me. I wavered for several moments. Almost of their own accord, my hands reached out for the revolver. I looked around and saw nobody. Taking a rag, as though about to clean the car, I dropped it over the revolver, looked around again, and grabbed the bundle. I tucked it into my belt, under my overcoat. I was afraid that if I tried to run I would arouse suspicion. If I walked nonchalantly back to the town hall, however, it would look like I finished cleaning the car and was returning to my post. My heart thumped wildly as I walked into the building, to the room where my brother worked.

I approached him casually and whispered in his ear, "I stole a revolver from the Germans who are here. It's under my coat. What shall I do?" He looked around. Luckily no one else was in the room. "Give it to me, quick, I'll hide it somewhere," he said. I handed him the wrapped revolver and he quickly hid it in a drawer. He urged me to invent an errand that would take me out of the building and not to return until the Germans had gone. I told another messenger boy that I was being sent to the flour mill, and quickly disappeared.

Later Musio filled me in on what transpired after I was gone. He went into the mayor's office and found it empty, as the mayor was at that time in conference with the Germans in another part of the building. Musio quickly removed the revolver from his drawer and hid it behind some books in the mayor's office. Half an hour later the Germans left. Minutes after, they barged into the mayor's room, furious, shouting that a revolver had been stolen from their car. The mayor swore that nobody there could have done such a thing, and suggested that they search the premises and the employees. He said, "You can start by searching my office." The German officer answered, "We don't suspect you. You are our true ally. But try and find who did it." The mayor hinted that it might have been the partisans. The Germans frisked several of the employees and then asked where the partisans could have come from. They were pointed in a certain direction, jumped into the car and left. After the mayor went home, Musio took out the revolver and hid it in the attic with the rest of our cache.

At work I was able to hear the radio and to take home the German newspapers. The German propaganda was of course full of optimism, promising that within two weeks Moscow would be taken. Hitler made a speech, claiming that the Germans were on the outskirts of Moscow, Leningrad and the Danube Basin. "The army is only waiting for my orders, and Russia will collapse." But the offensives on Moscow and Leningrad failed. The papers then praised the heroic efforts of the German army holding up in the bitter Russian winter against the enemy hordes.

On December 8, we heard that the United States had entered the war against Germany and our morale hit an all-time high. America, the symbol of strength and democracy, would surely vanquish the Germans and save us. We were going to live!

The good news spread by word of mouth. Speculations and predictions all pointed in one direction—Hitler was going to lose the war! The only question was how long it would take. My mother translated the news to us from the German newspapers. Reading between the lines, we gathered that the Germans were very upset with this unexpected turn of events. The propaganda until that date rarely attacked the United States, but now the U.S.A. became the target of German outrage.

At about this time the German army began to suffer increasing setbacks, and as they did, their behavior toward the population worsened. General Brauchwich, who gave the order to retreat from Moscow, was discharged. As the army retreated we saw how unprepared they were for the bitter Russian winter. The soldiers were dressed in autumn coats and garrison hats. They began to confiscate furs from the people and requisitioned all the horses and sleds.

From the flow of Russian prisoners of war who were brought to the transit camp just outside town, we could also gauge the outcome of the battles. At first there were tremendous numbers of prisoners. Jews who were forced to work in that camp heard stories of the cruel treatment of the POWs. Some nights up to half of them met their death by starvation, beatings, or murder. Some attempts to escape succeeded. We later found out that during the first months of the war, between three and five million Russian soldiers and officers surrendered and were taken prisoner. The treatment they received was so horrendous that they decided it was better to escape and fight. In December 1941 the flow of Russian prisoners decreased noticeably.

The year 1942 began very sadly for us in Kurzeniec. In his New Year's radio speech to the German nation, Hitler said that the Jews were out to destroy Germany but that the Germans would destroy them first. People began to debate whether this speech was just for the sake of propaganda. But I believed he meant every word of it.

That day, two Jews in our town had been killed by Sheringkevich, one of the cruelest Belorussian policemen. He was leading a group of Jewish workers to Vileika, where the Gebietskommissariat was located. He was drunk and for the sport of it shot two carpenters.

Life went on in permanent fear, and the struggle for food continued. Mother still dealt bread to the community and my brother and I held on to our jobs. I was frequently sent to bring provisions to the town hall. Naturally, I found ways to hide some to bring home. One of the most precious commodities was salt; it was used as a scale for bartering, almost instead of money, since salt was essential to people as well as to livestock.

Our underground group continued to function. Our main aim was to acquire weapons, ammunition, maps, and all the other equipment we would need when we joined the partisans. When we acquired a rifle or a revolver from a peasant, we had no way of knowing whether it worked. Whatever we bought or stole was hidden in the attic of the town hall. On one occasion, when I was carrying a rifle concealed in a sack of hay on my back toward our cache, I was stopped by a policeman who wanted to take me to forced labor. With my heart in my mouth, I coolly showed him my identification card proving that I worked as a messenger for the mayor and explained that the hay was for him. He let me go.

Our routine changed with the arrival in nearby Vileika of a group of SD (Sicherheitsdienst, the Nazi Security Forces) who took over Jewish matters from the Gebietskommissar. We found out that the same happened in other eastern territories occupied by the Germans. Although they did not wear black uniforms, we called them the Gestapo, knowing they were different from the regular army. Though they were dressed in army uniforms, the skull insignia on their hats and black ties identified them.

In mid-February, the Judenrat in Kurzeniec was ordered to provide ten workers for the SD. At that time nobody really knew who the SD were, or why they came. Ten men went to Vileika. Four days later they were back, some alive and the rest as corpses.

On arrival at Vileika, they had been ordered to clean and prepare living accommodations for a larger group of workers that was supposed to come. When they finished the job, they were gathered in a courtyard and told that they would get their pay for the work.

Then they were beaten with sticks and whips until they collapsed, unconscious or dead. An electrician was ordered to climb up a tall ladder to change an outdoor bulb. When he was standing on the ledge, they removed the ladder, and laughingly told him that his payment was to jump down. He broke both legs in the process. The workers were told that the SD was there to "take care of the Jews." Then all the survivors in the group were ordered to take the dead and wounded and go home. This was our introduction to the ways of the SD.

When further orders were given to provide Jews for work, everyone was terrified but had no choice. Every day a new group was sent, and went through similar experiences. Luckily no one else was killed at that time.

Our only consolation was that the war wasn't going their way. The German papers described very heavy fighting and the vicious resistance by the Soviet army. Whenever there was mention of retreat, it was described as straightening of the frontlines. At home we spent hours trying to analyze and interpret every move and change at the front. My mother was the most optimistic one and constantly tried to read something positive between the lines. She encouraged us to stay hopeful that the end of war was not too far away, and that we would all return to a normal life.

We heard rumors of the frontlines moving close to us. I dreamt of finding the Soviets in town, and the war over.

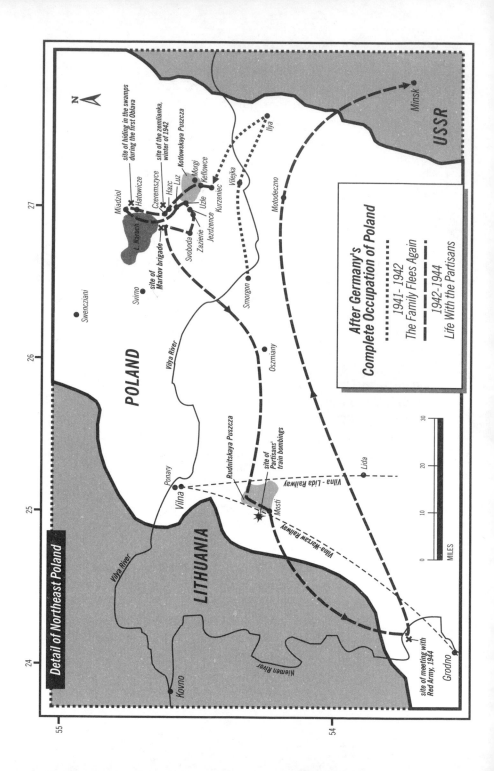

Detail of Northeast Poland

N

POLAND

USSR

LITHUANIA

Vilya River

Niemen River

Swencziani

Svirno

site of hiding in the swamps
during the first Oblava

site of the zemlianka,
winter of 1942

Kotowskaya Puszcza

Miadziol

Hatowicze

Czeremszyce

Hazc

Luz

Morgi
Keflowce

Uzle

Kurzeniec

Svoboda

Zazierie

Jezdzence

site of
Markov brigade

L. Naroch

Vilejka

Ilya

Smorgon

Motodeczno

Oszmiany

Vilya River

Ponary

Vilna

Rudnitskaya Puszcza

site of
Partisans'
train bombings

Mosti

Vilna - Lida Railway

Lida

Vilna-Warsaw Railway

site of meeting with
Red Army, 1944

Grodno

Kovno

After Germany's
Complete Occupation of Poland

.... 1941- 1942
The Family Flees Again

– – – – 1942-1944
Life With the Partisans

MILES

0   10   20   30

6

UNBRIDLED SAVAGERY

February 15–September 8, 1942

In February the first group of SD arrived for a visit in our town of Kurzeniec, led by Inspector Egof. He was arrogant, tall, and broad-shouldered—exactly what Hitler would have considered a typical Aryan. He understood Russian; we learned that he had spent several years in the Soviet Union before the war. The town and the surrounding roads were covered in snow, and the SD arrived by sled. They came to call on the mayor, and I was in the hallway when I saw Egof in a Russian fur hat with his tall boots shining like mirrors. He held a whip in one hand and in the other a leash leading a huge dog. He began to question the mayor about the Jews—what they did, and what they were contributing to the war efforts of the Third Reich. He wanted to see the head of the Judenrat and I was sent to bring him immediately.

Shatz rushed into the room and I remained at my post in the hall. Egof put in an order for boots, furs, poultry, and other things. When Shatz returned within the hour with the items listed, the SD departed without any incident, and we all breathed a sigh of relief.

The next time Egof appeared, a few days later, he wanted to see personally where the Jews worked. Again Shatz was called to show the whole entourage around—the SD and the local gendarmes. By noon Egof completed his tour and then returned to some of the places he had been and coldly shot thirteen people, commenting to his group, "This one is already too old, and out of the kindness of my heart I will do him the favor of killing him." I knew most of the people because of my work distributing bread, and hearing about it was almost as bad as personally witnessing it. In another place, he said it was a shame to waste bullets on Jews and took a chair and killed a man with it. Shatz had to stand there and watch this performance. After that Egof demanded the best food available for his lunch. He then ordered cats to be brought to him. While he was eating, Haim-Zalmen, another member of the Judenrat, ran through the town yelling, "Bring cats and save yourselves. Egof wants cats!"

Before Egof had finished his lunch, there was a sack full of cats which Haim-Zalmen had rounded up. While he was eating, Egof entertained himself by shooting the cats one by one as they were pulled out of the sack.

During his visit Egof wrote down the names of the ten most attractive young women he had noticed. He told the Judenrat to bring them to the town hall in the evening. The petrified women arrived and awaited their turn entering his room one at a time. It was dark there, and a revolver was lying on the table. I don't know what transpired inside. All the women came out crying, but at least they survived.

After this second visit to Kurzeniec, Egof became the terror of the town. Whenever he was said to arrive, everyone hid wherever they could. Each time he made fresh demands for gold and other valuables. If he was satisfied with what he received, he left without killing anyone. If not, there was always a number of dead.

Many of the Kurzeniec Jews worked in the town of Vileika, where the SD headquarters was established. Some of them walked to work and back every day. The more skilled craftsmen lived in a labor camp in Vileika and everybody thought that they were the privileged ones who would not be harmed, as even the SD was using their skills. Whoever could, tried to get into that group.

All the Jews had to work, and each one felt that a job which was appreciated by the Germans would be his security. Though sex between Germans and Jews was strictly forbidden, many Germans had Jewish women whom they called their "personal slaves."

March 1 was Purim, a Jewish holiday that celebrated the defeat of a cruel emperor who tried to kill all the Jews centuries ago. We dreaded the Jewish holidays, which the Germans frequently marked by staging horrors. On that day, the Jews who worked in Vileika left Kurzeniec in the morning as usual, but returned immediately, saying that the whole town of Vileika was surrounded by SD forces, obviously in preparation for something horrible, and they were turned back. Panic struck our town. People with family in Vileika began frantically trying to find out what was going on. Though fear gripped everyone, some of the people hoped that this was just a new tactic for taking possessions and scaring the Jews. But others feared that something dreadful was happening.

At noon, Hillel, a Jew from Vileika, appeared in town, utterly confused and incoherent. With difficulty he explained that at dawn he had heard shots and, looking out the window, had seen SD rounding up all the Jews from house to house. Even those who showed working permits were taken away.

Hillel escaped through backyards and side streets into the fields and found the town surrounded. He couldn't explain how he managed to avoid getting caught and reach Kurzeniec. We all knew something was happening to the Vileika Jews, but what? We could only speculate. By evening several more people managed to escape and reach us, but they didn't add any more information. The only news we heard was that trucks were taking the people to an unknown destination.

For the next two days no one was allowed to go to or from Vileika, and we heard nothing more. On the third night a man named Duvid sneaked into Kurzeniec. His face was bloody, his clothes torn and wet. His speech was quite garbled, but he still managed to tell what had transpired.

Most everyone in Vileika had been killed—men, women, children, infants. They were brought in trucks to the local prison courtyard, where they were stripped of all their possessions. The Gebietskommissar then arrived and selected several personal servants and the best craftsmen. The rest were led, in groups of six, behind the prison building where a mass grave had been dug, and made to stand facing the grave. Behind them, six SD shot each one in the back of the head with a revolver. Those who didn't fall into the grave were pushed in by the local policemen who surrounded the execution area.

Because the ground was frozen hard, snow was shoveled to cover the corpses. Duvid was shot too, and fell into the grave. But at night he regained consciousness. He pushed off the snow and the corpses that lay on top of him, crawled out, and dragged himself to Kurzeniec. The bullet that he got in the back of his head miraculously came out through his mouth without damaging his brain. He recovered from his wound and left Kurzeniec. A few months later we heard that he was caught in another roundup and killed.

This was the first mass murder in our area. The Nazis even had a name for such systematic exterminations of entire towns: "Aktion." We Jews called it "akzia." Prior to this Jews had seen pogroms, where villages were looted, homes destroyed, and spontaneous violence and rape were perpetrated on Jews by vicious groups of anti-Semites. But it was totally beyond our comprehension that a civilized nation in the twentieth century would be capable of taking an entire community—the workers who served them, the children, women, young and old people—and systematically murdering them for no other reason than that they were born Jewish. We reasoned among ourselves that there were millions of Germans living in the United States and millions of German prisoners of war in the Soviet Union who could be used as a deterrent. Besides, these crimes could not be concealed or tolerated. Didn't the murderers sense that they would eventually be punished?

We couldn't allow ourselves to believe what we heard. To believe it would be to know that we were utterly helpless. It was winter, and we had no escape. My mother still had hope that somehow we would be saved, and because of her optimism people rallied around her.

A few days later Hendel, the deputy Gebietskommissar, came to Kurzeniec and demanded that the Judenrat turn over to him two hundred more of the best craftsmen to be transferred to Vileika, where a ghetto was being established for them. When the craftsmen left, with Shatz among them, total gloom settled over Kurzeniec. The feeling was that the craftsmen were removed because they were useful to the Germans, and that the next mass murder was scheduled for Kurzeniec. All those who had friends among the local farmers sought refuge with them. We were among those with nowhere to go. We stayed on in Yankel's old house.

The weapons that our little resistance group had collected were distributed to the members in order to resist and kill as many Nazis as possible before they could murder everybody. But there weren't enough arms for all of us, and Musio and I didn't get any.

It is difficult to convey the helplessness and desperation of waiting to be killed with no escape. We had to do something. We decided to build a hideaway. The whole family worked together, to construct a double wall in the attic. For lack of materials it wasn't the best job, but at least we were doing something. One of us was always on the alert at the window to warn of any suspicious activities and to give us time to hide. My parents held up pretty well under the constant strain, as did Musio and I. The two of us vowed not to fall into Nazi hands without resistance. I chose the largest kitchen knife and secretly began to practice using it.

We slept in our clothes. I found it extremely nerve-wracking to stand watch at the window at night. The slightest movement I saw seemed to indicate that the SD were coming and it would fill me with terror. An entire week went by and, since nothing further happened, the tension began to ease up. Our group put their arms back in the cache.

Just as we began to feel more secure, other news came. There were rumors of a massive massacre in Ilya.

A few days later several survivors reached Kurzeniec and confirmed the rumor. The SD, with the aid of the Lithuanian militia, surrounded the town and began an akzia. All the Jews who were caught were shoved into the synagogue and it was set on fire. Those who tried to escape were shot. Selected craftsmen, however, were singled out and sent to Vileika, the same ghetto where the Kurzeniec craftsmen were.

It was becoming obvious to us that the massacre in Vileika was not an isolated incident, as some people had tried to believe. This was a systematic elimination of Jews, town by town.

After the war I found out that the 150 members of the SD who had their headquarters in the town of Vileika were part of the Einsatzgruppe, which was established for the sole purpose of exterminating Jews and other people considered undesirable by the Nazis. At the Wannsee Conference in January, 1942, which was headed by Gestapo and SS leader Himmler's deputy Reinhardt Heydrich, a plan was worked out for the "Final Solution." This name was given to the program of total extermination of European Jewry. In addition to the existing concentration camps, extermination camps would be established. Four Einsatzgruppen were also formed. The most vicious members of the SS volunteered to join this group and received special training in mass murder. Some of their commanders held Ph.D. degrees. They were taught how to gather people in isolated areas, how to select the best places for killing them, how to transport the people to these spots, and how to murder and bury them quickly, meticulously and efficiently. And they were taught how to conceal their intentions until the last moment, so that the people wouldn't resist. The prior constant humiliation, beatings, physical and emotional torture, and sporadic killings were aimed at breaking the spirit and the will, and bringing the Jews to total submission. That would prevent any possibility of organized resistance. The Jews could then be led docilely to their demise.

At the time, we were totally unaware that we were part of a major scheme. We attributed the behavior toward us to the winds of the war. We thought that as the German victories decreased and their military efforts failed, they were letting out their frustrations on the Jews.

Fear and tension reached new heights. We wondered which town would be next. During the next week of relative calm, my mother did her utmost to build up our faith in the basic decency of human beings, even the Nazis, and our hope this nightmare would stop. There were no options open to us, and the only positive thing in our lives was hope.

Life in our town was getting progressively more difficult. The cruelty of the visiting Nazis and local police increased. Sheringevich, a resident of a nearby village, was the most sadistic of all. When the SD arrived in Vileika and took over the responsibility for the Jews, they also took charge of the prison, and it was there they found Sheringevich. He had been put in prison by the Gebietskommissar for killing two Jewish craftsmen while leading them to work. As the SD did not consider this a crime, they let him out and put him in charge of the prison. Sheringevich's methods of torture were performed so thoroughly that the Nazis elevated him to the post of executioner for the SD. He visited Kurzeniec regularly, where he was known to many of the Jews from previous times. He would demand gold, watches, clothing, and other valuables, and would catch and beat up anyone he could get hold of. His very presence in town struck terror.

One day in March, while I was out on an errand for the mayor, I saw Sheringevich arrive in his sled at the marketplace. All the Jews suddenly vanished from sight. I didn't want to arouse suspicion by running, especially since I didn't wear my "Jude" patch. I walked along briskly back to the town hall and stayed there all night.

The next morning I found out that after he visited his mistress, he went on a spree. He entered Jewish homes and wherever he found people he killed them. I was at the town hall at the time, and unaware of what was happening. There were thirty-two murders to his credit that night. He took the women and children outdoors and, dancing around them, sang, "Pray to your God, and see if He can help you. If I decide to kill you, even your God won't save you." Then he killed them, some by shooting, some by stabbing, and some by beating. In one home he found a woman with her infant. He became excited and claimed that it wasn't humane to shoot babies, so he grabbed the baby by his feet and smashed his head against the wall while the mother helplessly looked on. He then shot the mother.

Sheringevich had respect for the local Jewish doctor, who had treated him before, and didn't harm him. But he bragged to him about his bravery and success in executing the Jews of Ilya. He had perfected his skills in shooting and managed to kill three people with one bullet. And instead of killing children one by one, he had them thrown into a mass grave and then he would toss in one grenade to do the job. The SD admired and praised his efficiency. I myself witnessed him abusing an elderly man, smacking him until he became blind and fainted.

Most of the Jews in Kurzeniec were becoming apathetic and resigned to their fate. Our young group, however, didn't utterly lose hope, and looked for a possibility to resist.

In mid-March another shock shook the town. At dawn trucks full of SD moved through Kurzeniec toward Dolhinovo, a small town not far away. A few days later we found out that another massacre had occurred there. This akzia took two days, after which those who managed to escape were allowed to return to live within a ghetto which was established there. This was different from the way they had handled the massacre in Ilya. There was nothing predictable about the SD's dealings with the people. In each town, they used variations in their tactics to confuse the victims.

Whenever we heard of a massacre in another place, the whole town of Kurzeniec panicked again. My mother wouldn't give in to apathy or despair, and her strength rubbed off on us. With renewed energy we started building a better hide-out, a big double wall in the log barn adjoining the house. We managed to get the necessary material but had to be very careful not to be seen building. There was no ghetto in Kurzeniec, and some of the neighbors living on our street were Belorussians and Poles. We knew through experience they could turn on us at any time. Even our Jewish neighbors must not become aware of what we were doing. Because of the secrecy, the work progressed slowly, but when it was finished it really looked quite professional. The wall, which we built of logs, was hardly distinguishable from the original structure. Through a camouflaged opening in the roof we could squeeze between the two walls into a space about two feet wide. We and the Kuppers could stand there in single file.

Pesach, or Passover, was approaching, and we were afraid of whatever surprises the Nazis had planned for this holiday. A few days before the Seder, which marks the start of Pesach, we saw Jews running from the marketplace, whispering that the SD had arrived in town. We immediately hid in our shelter and stood there until dark. When we didn't hear any shots or commotion we came out stealthily. The SD had departed. They had come to hang a peasant for robbing the homes of dead Jews; they considered all property of the Jews as belonging to them. Sheringevich was the hangman, and many officials came to participate in the occasion, which was duly photographed. The corpse was left hanging there for three days.

On the night of Seder in April 1942, Mother tried to retain the traditional Seder ritual. The meal was made mostly of potatoes. Instead of wine we drank tea. The windows were covered with sheets to prevent anyone from looking in and we took turns peering out. This was the saddest Seder in my life. The festivities that for generations symbolized the celebration of the Jews' freedom from slavery, found us in a worse situation than our forefathers had been in in Egypt. We read the Hagaddah with unbearably heavy hearts.

At midnight we heard noise. Carts were going by full of people we couldn't identify, surrounded by Germans and police. They were heading in the direction of Vileika. In the morning we found out that the SD and the police had chosen this night for an akzia in a very small town where only two hundred Jews lived. Most of them were killed.

My parents continued working in the shop, distributing bread. Musio and I still worked at the town hall. My father turned to religion more fervently than ever and put himself completely in the hands of God. Every morning at four o'clock he went to pray at the "shtibel," a room allotted in one of the homes for congregating for prayer. I, on the contrary, was disillusioned and gradually moved further away from religion. I couldn't accept the idea that if God had any influence on human behavior He would have allowed such atrocities.

We kept hearing news of the war. Things weren't going well for the Germans and we hoped that the Soviets would break through the front and take Kurzeniec before the Nazis would succeed in exterminating us all.

It became warmer and the snow began to thaw. Musio and I started secretly preparing to go into the woods with our resistance group. This was a major decision, as we would have to leave our parents behind, not knowing how or if they could survive without us. Our own lives would be forever changed. But we felt that this was the right decision—that our only chance of survival would be in the woods. The hardest part was not being able to share our plans with our parents at this stage, when all along we had shared all our thoughts, feelings, and hopes.

We began gathering non perishable food and other essentials for survival in the woods. The plan was that our group of twenty young Jewish men would join twenty escaped Russian prisoners of war who were hiding in the surrounding villages, and would form a partisan unit. Anybody who had weapons was considered a partisan, a resistance fighter. Zalman and two other of our men met secretly with the Russians to formulate detailed plans of action. The Russians insisted that we deliver our arms and supplies to them and then join them a few days later in small groups, in order to avoid suspicion.

While our group of emissaries was with the Russians, they all chanced upon a German patrol, and in the skirmish that followed, several of the partisans were killed, among them two young Jewish men from our town. The Germans didn't know where these people came from, and ordered the villagers to bury them. A villager recognized one of the boys as the son of Zosky, from Kurzeniec. He came to the father and demanded money to keep silent about the identity of the boy, and got it. The story spread like wildfire through the town and fear of German reprisals overtook the Jews of Kurzeniec.

Our group decided to stick to our plan, however, and proceeded with the arrangements in utmost secrecy. But somehow some of the mothers found out and objected to their sons' departure. The secret slowly leaked out.

My parents were divided in their reaction. My father was against it. He felt that death was even more likely in the woods than in town, and if it was bound to come, we should all be together. He said we had no right to break up the family. A heated argument broke out between Musio and Father, and for the only time in his life, Father slapped Musio's face. Mother wanted us to go and fight for our survival. She believed our chances would be greater, and that we shouldn't stay behind on account of them. She said their lives were almost over anyway. She was only forty-seven years old. My father was fifty-two. And she said that since we were young we should try to survive, fight, and take revenge for all the Jews killed.

My brother and I were determined to become partisans and fight the Nazis. We planned that as soon as we reached the woods and organized the unit, we would build an underground bunker and then return to get our parents.

When information of our group's secret plan reached the Judenrat, they called several of the young men in and notified them that they knew of our intention to become partisans and the identities of those involved. They forbade us to leave the town. Fearing that if the Nazis found out there would be terrible repercussions against all the Jews, they threatened to notify the authorities if we insisted on following through with our plans. Our families would then be taken away by the SD. They did not accept the young men's explanations that the Nazis didn't need an excuse or provocation in order to exterminate Jews. Look what they did in Ilya, Vileika and elsewhere.

We were faced with a terrible dilemma. If we left, the Judenrat might fulfill their threat, and we would be directly responsible for the death of our parents. We couldn't take our parents with us because our Russian compatriots insisted that only the young people come. When we shared the news with our parents, mother said we should leave in spite of all, but father felt differently. Our intention was to fight the enemy, and if we were killed, we would at least die fighting. Emotionally, however, we couldn't do something that might directly cause the death of our parents. The group felt the same way, so we delayed our departure temporarily, until we could leave unnoticed.

Although our weapons were so hard to get and conceal, we agreed to turn them over to our Russian compatriots. At least these precious arms could begin being used to fight the enemy. We were promised that when we joined the group we would get our arms back.

After a period of relative calm, the fears in our town began to subside somewhat. People wanted to trust the words of the Gebietskommissar of the ghetto in Vileika that nothing would happen to those who worked hard and diligently. Food was becoming more scarce, but we managed by keeping some of the bread from the store and by stealing some provisions from the town hall.

Mother worked very hard. In addition to her job, she cooked for seven people at home, a very complicated task. Someone had to climb into the oven and light the wood which we had chopped. Mother then shoved a heavy iron pot into the oven with a long paddle. Positioning the pot was quite an art. Too close to the fire would burn the food; not close enough would leave it uncooked. The pot had to be turned occasionally for even cooking. The Kupper family was still living with us, and continued to do nothing to help with the housework. Mother had lost so much weight she was almost unrecognizable. But she laughed about it, saying that all her life she had tried so hard to lose weight by dieting, and now she had a lovely figure with no effort. Her indomitable spirit and love of life did not desert her. Our friend Rivka Gvint, a young and impressionable teacher, used to come to visit us and usually left saying, "Now I have accumulated a supply of moral strength that will sustain me for the next few days."

Spring came and turned into summer in Kurzeniec. The German morale improved with some victories on the Eastern Front, especially those approaching Stalingrad. Our hopes that the Soviets would come and save us dissipated.

One day, as I stood at my usual post in the corridor of the town hall, a truck brought a number of SS to town. The officer of this elite Nazi fighting force entered the building and went into the mayor's office. A few minutes later the mayor rushed out of his room. He pointed right at me. I was petrified, certain that the Germans were about to take me because someone had told them our plan. Then the mayor spoke to me. "Go to the neighboring village with the SS as their interpreter."

In an instant I was in the truck with the SS soldiers, moving toward the next village. I sat there silently looking at the murderers—well-fed, jolly, rosy-cheeked, each armed with a machine gun, a pistol on his belt, and whip in hand. Suddenly the truck stopped and I was told to get down and sit by the driver to direct the way. I didn't know my way around the villages. But I knew I had better do something quickly or else I would arouse suspicion. I picked up the map by the driver's seat, found my bearings, and began to direct the driver. After a few wrong turns we arrived at the village.

I went from house to house with the SS. They demanded horses and carts, butter, cream, eggs, lard, and other provisions. With my limited knowledge of the German language, I translated what I thought was being said. Every peasant who wasn't quick enough in obeying orders was lashed with a whip.

I had never seen the Belorussian or Polish farmers so subdued and submissive, terrified of angering the Nazis. I didn't pity them a bit. These were the kind of villagers who continuously terrorized and robbed the Jews. Now it was their turn to see this side of the Germans, with whom they had been cooperating. The spread that was laid before the SS included food that I hadn't seen in a long time. I ate slowly, trying to disguise how hungry I was for such delicacies.

During the conversation at the table, one officer described the intense pleasure he got from beating people until they bled. Another officer expressed his revulsion, whereupon the first one said, "You

have probably never experienced what I am talking about. Try it
and see for yourself." I sat listening and realized I was actually star-
ing into the darkest depths of human nature. The scariest thing was
that he was exposing not only his own personal capacity for pure
evil, but that of most of the Nazis. When we got back to Kurzeniec,
we saw a Jew with the yellow patch in the street. One of the SS expressed surprise that there were Jews still around. He was sure that
they had all been disposed of. I dreaded to think what would have
happened to me had they suspected that here was a Jew sitting
among them.

They let me off at the town hall. I rushed to tell the mayor that
I had returned and asked him to try not to send me on such missions again.

At work, I tried to listen in on the conversations of the visiting
German dignitaries. Despite my limited knowledge of the language,
I managed to piece together bits of information and to get a clearer
picture of the Nazi tactics in dealing with the Jews. At first the Nazis
tried to cover up their real intentions by saying that they were aveng-
ing partisan attacks, or retaliating for the killing of a German in the
vicinity. Eventually they stopped pretending that they needed an excuse for exterminating entire Jewish communities.

Our resistance group finally decided that the time was right to
go into the woods and join the partisans, despite the Judenrat threat.
We couldn't acquire any more weapons. The local population was
afraid to sell to us, and the Germans were more alert.

Our plan was to leave in small groups. Musio and I were to depart with the first group, on the night of September 9. We were going
to cross the railroad tracks and enter the forest beyond, where we
were to meet with an established partisan group. After getting ourselves organized, we would return to fetch our parents. Detailed
plans had been laid weeks ahead. Mother helped us with our preparations, and this time my father did not object.

A few days before our scheduled departure, Mother went to a
fortune-teller. She refused to say what had been prophesied for her
and Father, and only told us that Musio and I would survive. The
optimism that had sustained her until then suddenly disappeared
and even she began to doubt the possibility of survival. It was unnerving to see her lose hope. She desperately needed our moral

support, and although Musio and I tried our best to give it to her, our parents both became nervous and edgy. Mother seemed to have a premonition of doom, though all the Jews had been assigned work for the next two months and were confident that until the completion of the jobs nothing would happen. Musio and I were also relying on these two months; it would give us enough time to come back for our parents.

7

THE END OF KURZENIEC

Wednesday, September 9, 1942

The day before Yom Kippur, the Day of Atonement and the holiest day in the Jewish religion, I was awakened from a deep sleep by someone tapping on our window. Our neighbor Doba was there to warn us that something was happening. My mother told me that Father had gone at 4 A.M. to pray at the synagogue. We dressed hurriedly. Shivering, my mother said, "We shall not survive today." I had never before heard such words from her.

In the back yard we met some neighbors, whispering, trying to find out what was happening. Dawn was breaking. A thick fog had settled over the town. We could see vague forms moving several feet away, and heard the heavy trod of German soldiers passing along the street in front of our house. Voices speaking German. The Kuppers had come out with us and decided to hide in the double wall in the barn. My mother, my brother, and I chose not to. We couldn't see ourselves dragged out like hunted animals if the Nazis found us. We preferred to run through the fields toward the forest.

Everyone dispersed, but we waited about fifteen minutes, hoping that Father would return. When there was still no sign of him, we squeezed through the wires surrounding our backyard and ran crouching through the wheat fields. The woods were three miles away. The fog was still heavy and we couldn't see ahead of us. We began to hear shots coming from different directions—from the encountered. Now our last route of escape was being closed off. With the sound of the German patrol growing louder, I felt death getting closer and closer to me. Scenes flashed through my mind of Germans catching me, torturing me, killing me, burning me. I was so gripped with terror that I literally felt my hair standing on end. A voice shouted within me, "I must save myself!" My mind was racing. "Maybe I can break through the German chain," I thought. "If I am meant to die, I'd rather be killed trying to survive than waiting passively."

Death seemed just minutes away. Once caught it would be all over, but until that moment I wouldn't give up. Desperately searching for a way to save myself, my mind went blank. My movements were guided by desperation alone. I crawled under a nearby bush, deluding myself that this was a source of protection.

Musio saw me lying there, with my legs sticking out. "Selim, have you gone crazy? They will find you here immediately!" He dragged me out. Seeing the dazed look in my eyes, he slapped me and shook me violently. In a snap I came back to my senses and realized the foolishness of my action.

We all began to run to our left, back toward the non-Jewish section of the town. Along the way we tried one barn after the other, but they were all locked. I clutched the kitchen knife I had grabbed when we left the house that morning, and assured myself that even if caught, I would try to take my captors down with me.

The patrol was already very close to us. We continued searching for a route of escape. I suddenly spotted a barn door with a latch but no lock on it. This was it.

Beckoning to the others, I rushed to the barn. We silently opened the door a crack and squeezed in, closing the door behind us. The barn was stacked high with hay and wheat. We climbed about fifteen feet to the top of the bales and burrowed ourselves down on the other side between the hay and the wall. The last one up tried as best he could to cover up our tracks. Minutes later we heard the German patrol, accompanied by the local police, near the barn. They were asking some shepherd boy whether he had seen any Jews hiding around. He replied that he had seen some running, but didn't know where they had gone. I heard the barn door creak open and German voices inside. I held my breath. The door closed again, and the barn fell silent. From the time I was shot at, I guess the episode couldn't have lasted more than a few minutes. The patrol departed from the area.

Suddenly we heard sirens. I didn't know then the significance of it. My watch showed 6 A.M., only one hour since we had left home. A lifetime of experiences I would never forget crammed into one horrendous hour.

We found out later that the sirens were their signal to start the akzia, in which the Jews were dragged from their homes and brought to the town square. Up to this stage of the akzia, they only killed those who resisted or tried to escape.

We sat in the barn for six hours, not moving a muscle or exchanging a word. But the walls were rather thin, and I could clearly hear what was going on outside. Since there was nothing happening beyond the wall, I was beginning to hope that maybe I was wrong. Maybe they were only rounding up the Jews for work. Then I heard the sounds of people on the run, and a German voice shouting, "Halt!" Then shots. Then pained screams. Then silence. But it didn't last long. I recognized the voices of a family I knew—mother, son, and two daughters, begging and pleading for their lives. The SD responded with wild laughter, and shots. The younger daughter, who was still a child, was evidently kept for last, to witness the execution of her family. I heard her terrible cries, as she was being dragged toward the marketplace. She screamed curses at them and demanded to be killed right there on the spot, with her family. To think that a child of about ten—a child just beginning her life—would want so desperately to die with her parents! She wasn't granted even that. I heard her screams fading in the distance.

Guessing at what was going on, I kept thinking about my father and mother. I sat there biting my fingers, forcing myself to keep from doing something rash, like bolting from the barn to search for them.

That afternoon, someone silently entered the barn. Minutes later, he left and we heard the click of a lock on the outside. The farmer must have sensed our presence. All our efforts to conceal our tracks had been in vain. I was afraid that he had gone to inform on us. Why else would he have locked us in, if not to prevent our escape?

In low whispers, we consulted each other, and decided that we would not give up without a fight. We climbed out of our hiding places and on to the top of the piles. Armed with picks and farm tools that we found in the barn, we prepared ourselves to jump down and attack anyone walking in.

We lay there tense. Time dragged. Until dusk nothing happened, so we assumed that the farmer didn't plan to turn us in after all, and our tension slackened. Toward evening I smelled something peculiar. I couldn't figure it out. Suddenly it dawned on me. It was the smell of burning flesh! It was getting stronger and stronger as we lay there in silent horror. Nobody wanted to be the first to express what was in all our minds. But I couldn't escape the knowledge that the Nazis were burning people! Is my mother there? Is my father there? I was sweating, and an extreme weariness overcame me. I didn't want to think. I didn't want to feel. I didn't want to face the reality. But my thoughts wouldn't leave me. Waves of guilt swept over me for being alive.

Night fell and the shooting died down. We began to discuss ways to get out of the barn and reach the woods in the safety of the darkness. We tried silently to break through the planks of one of the walls, but the barn was so solidly built that we couldn't. We couldn't manage to pry open the door, either. Unintentionally, however, we made some noise, and suddenly saw a beam of light directed at the building. We heard a machine gun open fire. We climbed back in the hay, and lay still.

Before dawn we heard some movement and the click of the lock. The barn door swung open, letting someone in, and then closed. We heard whispers, and figured that the farmer or a member of his family had come there with a girlfriend. We thought of pouncing on them and trying to make our escape. I gripped my knife and crept along the hay in the pitch dark. Suddenly I fell off the bale and hit the floor. Jumping up instantly I began to look for the enemy but couldn't see anything. I ran to the door and tried to open it, and was surprised to find it locked. My hand touched another person and I was about to stab him, when I realized that it was Zalman. We kept finding others in the dark. Zalman caught the hand of someone, and cried, "Who are you?" No one answered. All we heard was the frightened chatter of teeth. Then we understood that it could only be another Jew. Zalman asked him in Yiddish, "A Yid?" and a soft reply came, "Yes."

It turned out he was Zalman's uncle, and from him we found out that the peasant who owned the barn, Ignalia Biruk, had saved him and his children by taking them out of their hiding place and bringing them into the barn. It was a tremendous relief to know that the farmer was not a threat to us.

At dawn the door opened again, and the farmer entered. Since we were no longer scared, we revealed ourselves to him. He asked us to leave the barn as soon as possible, and we promised to go the following night. He would leave the door unlocked for us.

In the light of morning, shooting resumed from several directions. We waited impatiently for every long hour to pass. At noon the door suddenly opened, and the farmer loudly told us that the town was burning and demanded that we leave his barn immediately. He worried that if the barn also caught fire, and we ran outside to escape, the Germans would accuse him of hiding Jews. I peeked out through the door and saw that the flames were far away, but the fields were full of German soldiers and policemen. We would have no way of eluding them. We firmly refused to leave then, but again promised to do so as soon as it was dark. He reluctantly agreed.

We later pieced together the events that led to the fire in the town. An elderly Jew named Zuska and his wife were in hiding in the attic of their house and on the first day of the akzia the Germans did not find them. On the second day, when the couple saw through the cracks what was transpiring at the market square, they poured kerosene over themselves and the attic and set it afire. The flames that demolished their house spread to adjoining wooden buildings, and the whole neighborhood caught fire. It took the Germans and the police a few good hours to gain control of the fire.

When at last night came, we began to prepare for our departure. Zalman's uncle refused to join us. He said that he had no chance of surviving in the woods with his children.

Around midnight, when all was quiet, we exited the barn, one at a time. In single file we crossed the fields and headed for the woods. From afar we saw the fire that brought the smell of burning bodies.

Without a sound we departed our town of Kurzeniec. At one point we thought we heard footsteps, and we fell to the ground. After waiting a few minutes without hearing anything, we got up and went on our way again. After about two hours we reached a small forest and sat down to rest.

I was suddenly aware of hunger and thirst, and it occurred to me that we hadn't eaten or drunk in two days. We began to look for farmhouses near the woods. We knocked on the door of the first one and begged for food. We were given some bread and water.

Sitting there in the woods, we heard the snap of branches. We jumped up and tried to hide. Suddenly we saw Shimke Alperovich, one of the men from Kurzeniec. He had been hiding there. When he heard our voices, he came out to join us. During the akzia he was hidden by the mayor in the town hall, and like us, on the second night, he sneaked out into the woods. He told us what he had seen and heard.

On that Wednesday at 4 A.M., the SD troops, with the help of Ukrainians serving in the German forces, completely surrounded Kurzeniec, and with their Lithuanian and Latvian auxiliary units entered the town. Exactly at 6 A.M. the akzia began, with the men going from home to home, from stable to barn, from building to building. They rounded up all the Jews and herded them into the market square, which was heavily guarded by SD. Machine guns were aimed at the people from all corners of the square. The Germans were very thorough in their search for hideaways, double walls, cellars, and lofts. Anyone trying to escape was shot on the spot. The Gebietskommissar arrived at the marketplace to watch the show and took this opportunity to pick out some pretty girls and artisans to be taken to Vileika. Then came the head of the SD and he did likewise. At about 3 P.M. trucks arrived and were loaded with twenty people in each truck. They drove out of town. Every few minutes they returned and took on a new group of people, accompanied by shouts, shoving, and beating.

The Jews were taken to the outskirts of town and into fields near some empty barns. Each group was ordered to undress. Their names and ages were meticulously recorded. They were then shoved toward the barns, where a semicircle of their executioners were waiting. When they reached the barns they were shot at from all directions.

The petrified people ran every which way in a frenzy, trying to dodge the bullets, until they were all killed.

The second group of arrivals was forced to pile the corpses into the barns before they in turn were killed. When the piles of bodies were too high, the victims were made to climb atop and were shot there, in order to save time. The local policemen helped with the process and those who were especially vicious were given the honor of being allowed to shoot. Behind the murderers were tables laid with food and drink, so that every once in a while they could refresh themselves. When the barns were filled sufficiently high with bodies, they were set on fire.

The luckier ones were those who died from the bullet shots. The wounded ones were burnt to death. The succeeding groups were made to stand by the burning barns, then shot, and the groups following them were forced to shove them into the flames.

In addition to the systematic orderliness of their scheme, the murderers had time to play little games, like forcing a son to push his wounded father into the fire before he in turn met his death. Some mothers were forced to throw their dead or wounded babies into the flames before they were shot. Many victims had become crazed and merely stared blankly by the time they were pushed toward the fire. As this process probably took longer than anticipated, the next batches of living people were shoved into the next empty barn and, when they were packed in, the doors were closed and machine guns shot them down through the walls. Then the barn was set afire and anyone trying to escape was shot.

The mayor of the town had been brought to the site to witness the proceedings. When he came home he was so shocked that he beat his head against the walls. This was what he had described to Shimke, whom he had hidden in the town hall.

One thousand and forty Jews met their death in this atrocity. Their only remains were bones, teeth, and other bits that did not burn.

8

IN THE WOODS

September 12, 1942–End of September

Dazed and weary, we sat in a little forest about three miles from Kurzeniec, located between the main road and the railroad tracks. The woods were too sparse to conceal us properly, but it was a good fifteen miles to the nearest large forest and we needed a rest. Several more people straggled in, including Rivka Gvint and her mother. Her father had been in the synagogue praying with my father when the horror began. Now there were ten of us, four of whom belonged to our resistance group.

One of the men told us of the role some of the town's non-Jewish population had played in the akzia. Apparently they ran from home to home, looting whatever they could. Some stood near the execution site catching the less valuable clothing which the Nazis threw to them. Some actively helped the Nazis find Jews in hiding. After the akzia they kept looking for surviving Jews and turning them in. They looted and vandalized the Jewish homes, dismantled walls, floors and chimneys, looking for the gold that they had been told was hidden by the Jews.

Children also participated in hunting out the Jews hiding in the fields and other places. Even children who were once playmates turned in their Jewish friends. When they found one, they would run to the Nazis or the police and point out exactly where the "Jude" was hiding.

The synagogue was not safe from looters either. Two families who had been in hiding under its roof were discovered by a local looter. They tried to run away and he gave chase. When he caught up with them he turned them in to the police.

The majority of the local population was indifferent to what was happening. Ignalia Biruk, the farmer who hid us was one of the very few decent human beings in Kurzeniec who actually tried to save the Jews.

Several days had passed since the time we were supposed to meet with the partisans in the woods. We had to reach our liaison to find out exactly where the partisans were.

In between the towns were vast expanses of uncultivated land, with patches of dense or sparse woods. Solitary farmhuts were scattered near the edges of the woods or on the fringes of the towns and villages. Somewhere among them was the home of our liaison to the Russian partisans. We needed to reach him. Zalman, who had met our liaison several times, and Musio went to find him. The rest of us stayed behind.

They returned with the news that the partisans had waited for us on September 9, as planned, then left for an unknown destination. They might be coming back shortly. Though we were reluctant to stay where we were, we decided to wait for a few days until we knew for sure whether the partisans would be returning.

Throughout the day we lay under the trees, covered with branches, afraid to stir. There was nothing to eat in these sparse woods. That night hunger and thirst began to torture us, so four of us went out to search for food in the surrounding farmhouses. We never knew which farmer would be kind and helpful, and which one would turn us in to the Nazis. We had no choice but to take the risk. It was pitch dark and on the way we got lost. We wandered around all night, getting thirstier and hungrier.

Before dawn we came upon a secluded farmhouse and knocked on the door. A woman opened it and we begged for something to drink and to eat. She said she only had some cold potatoes and water and she let us in. We all followed her toward the kitchen, with me bringing up the rear. The first room was used as a pig sty, with a trough of filthy water along one wall and scraps of food on the sawdust-covered floor. A number of well-fed pigs stood around and lazily eyed us as we came in. I was so thirsty that the sight of water overwhelmed me. I dropped down on my knees and started to lap up the pigs' filthy water in the trough. Then I got up and went into the kitchen with the others. The woman gave us some potatoes and clean water, and we left.

We found our way back and shared the potatoes and water with the rest of the group. Exhausted, we lay down under some bushes and fell asleep.

In the morning we were awakened by the cracking of twigs. Instantly alert and tense, we huddled under the bushes, trying to be invisible. The footfalls neither approached us nor went away. We realized that these people had sat down in one spot so we decided to crawl out and investigate. Creeping closer we saw a number of people trying, like us, to hide among the bushes, and understood that these too were Jews. We found relatives of Zalman and Rivka Gvint. It was a very emotional meeting.

A whispered conversation, soft sobs, and their stories. They had survived in a hiding place they had built in their cellar. They heard the Nazis searching their house but were not discovered. On the third night they left their hideaway and reached the woods. They had news of some of the families—who had escaped and who were massacred. No one knew anything about my parents. We had suspected that this was a total massacre, but had dared to hope that it was not so. Their confirmation of what had transpired came as a shock, but we still held on to the hope of finding our parents.

One of the men in the group who had escaped knew a farmer. That night we all went to that farmhouse and the farmer supplied us with food for the next few days and promised to bring more to us in the woods. Afraid to have us seen around his house, he was nonetheless a good man and we felt we could trust him not to betray us.

Back in the woods, we could not light a fire for fear that it would expose our presence. It began to rain heavily, day and night. We were drenched and had no place to hide. Our supply of bread and cooked potatoes dwindled.

Zalman and Musio left again to find our liaison and came back with the disturbing news that the partisans had not returned. According to the grapevine, they had gone east for the winter. Having only recently begun to organize themselves into units, the partisans from our area were short of arms, and more than half of them had only sticks for weapons. Old rifles from World War I which had been hidden by the farmers, and the arms we had given them, were the main weapons of the groups. They evidently felt that it would be safer for them to spend the winter in the east, where the partisan movement had grown considerably.

The rains stopped. We were so soaked that despite the danger we lit a fire to dry off and warm up a bit. Musio tried to dry his feet by the fire. The next morning he could not stand up—his legs were numb. Gradually he regained some feeling in his legs.

Our friend the farmer continued to bring us food and kept us informed of the latest developments in Kurzeniec. The Nazis were still finding Jews hidden in bunkers and elsewhere, and killing them on the spot.

Musio and I decided to return to Kurzeniec at night to see for ourselves whether anyone had survived in the hiding place we had built. We hoped that Mother had somehow returned after we separated in the wheat field and was still hiding there, not knowing where to go. She would need our help. Obsessed by the idea, we disregarded the danger we might encounter. I wanted Musio to remain behind because of the difficulty he still had walking, but he was as passionate as I was and immediately got up. He said, "You see, I can walk. We'll go together."

On a very dark night about a week after the akzia, we set out for Kurzeniec. Crossing the fields we arrived at the first houses. From there, crawling through the wheat fields, we made our way toward the yard of Yankel's house. It was totally silent. We decided to check out the barn first. Hearts beating, we tried the door and it opened quietly.

Shutting the door behind us, we went toward the double wall we had built and found the opening. We called softly to our mother, saying "we are here," but there was no reply or movement. I crawled through the opening and found the hiding place empty. We then tried to locate the spot where we had hidden our few valuables, to dig them up. We found the spot, dug with our hands, and found nothing there. We tried to believe that our mother had somehow returned, taken the gold, and fled. Wouldn't that mean that she was alive somewhere? We decided to go into the house to look for traces.

Stealthily approaching, we found the house stripped of doors and windows, and total destruction within. Aside from Father's torn fur coat we found nothing belonging to our family. We stood in the rubble; there was not the slightest indication that a week ago our family had lived here.

We went into the yard in despair. To our left was our ravaged home, ghostlike. Beyond that we saw low flames occasionally flare up from the nearby barns. The smell of burning flesh permeated the air, still smoldering a week later. I tried to push away the recurring thought that this smell was all that was left of my parents. I was becoming dizzy and losing touch with reality. I forced myself to think and not to let my emotions dictate my actions.

To our right was the house which had previously belonged to our neighbor Doba and was now occupied by several Bieloruss and Polish policemen. We heard music and women's laughter. The murderers, alive with happiness, were celebrating their glorious success in killing Jews. The only thing I longed for at that moment was a grenade to throw into that house. We had nothing.

Suddenly the side door opened and a policeman came out and urinated from the top of the steps. We threw ourselves to the ground and held hands to stop each other from doing something reckless, like attacking him barehanded. For an instant, through the open door, we had a glimpse into the room. We saw drunken policemen pawing the girls, shouting and singing. Then the door closed and it was dark again.

We crawled back toward the woods. At a distance beyond the town, when we were out of immediate danger, Musio suddenly fell and was unable to get up. His legs gave out as shock overcame him. We sat there silently for a while. Slowly, with my help, Musio began to crawl. Resting every so often, we finally reached the woods at dawn. We sat apathetically with our group, unaware that it had started to rain again.

Gradually the lice that had accumulated in our wet clothes began to bother us. We hadn't removed our clothing in many days. No matter how many lice we caught, there were still more.

We were constantly on the watch for anyone wandering around in the woods. Our friend the farmer came in a panic to warn us of an "oblava" (the Russian word for "roundup,") which was the

German system of surrounding and combing through the forests in search of Jews and partisans. Forming a human chain with the help of the local police, they would go into the woods, closing in and cutting off all possible routes of escape. Such operations usually took as long as a week or ten days.

We scattered through the woods and camouflaged ourselves as well as we could among the trees. Nothing happened. The farmer had also told us of rumors that there were groups of Jews and partisans hiding in Kotlowskaya puszcza, a huge almost impenetrable forest about twenty miles away. The puszcza was part of the Naroch Forests surrounding the enormous Lake Naroch.

That night we decided that three of us would go to the Kotlowskaya puszcza to check out the terrain, see how safe it would be, and see if there really was anyone else there. Then we would return and, depending on what we found, lead the rest of the group to the puszcza.

Shlomke was familiar with the area and would lead the way. He was an educated man in his thirties, single, and blond with blue eyes. At nine o'clock that night we set out. Bypassing Kurzenice, we followed the main road for about seven miles. Then, crossing fields and avoiding villages, we continued toward the puszcza. This was my first experience in making mental notes of the landmarks along the way, in case I would need to find my way back.

In the morning we arrived at the forest and, after searching for several hours, we found a camp of Jewish families. We were told that there were about a hundred and fifty Jews from surrounding towns and villages who had escaped the akzias and were hiding in the puszcza. There were no partisans there.

Shlomke found some relatives there and decided to stay. The third member of our group wanted to go deeper into the woods to look for his relatives who he heard had survived and were in hiding there. It was up to me then to decide what to do. I was unsure that I could find my way, but knowing that Musio was waiting for me, I decided to try it on my own. After a few hours of sleep I was prepared to set out.

Shlomke described the route to me again. Equipped with a stick and my trusty knife when it got dark, I left for the small woods near Kurzeniec. All my senses were alert. When I was unsure of the way at some point, I would sit down and force myself to remember the landmarks. I was driven by the additional fear that if I made a mistake I would fall into German hands. Alone at night in unfamiliar territory at the age of sixteen, I was scared. With even one other person it would have been different. As long as I was inside the forest I felt somewhat secure. I wasn't afraid of the bandits in the forest, since technically I was one of them. But when I reached the road along the fields, and so-called civilization, there was danger.

The moonlight showed me the way clearly, but exposed me as well. For hours I walked along the tree-lined road, expecting Germans to appear at any moment. I saw a German in every shadow, and with every rustle of a tree I threw myself on the ground. Eventually realizing that at that rate I would never make it to Musio and the group by dawn, I knew I had to control my fear. I decided to hide only if Germans appeared on the road. If they came in vehicles or on horseback, I would hear them from afar, I reasoned. If they were in ambush, I would have no way of escaping them anyway, so fear and panic would not help me. I pulled myself together and started walking briskly. When the shadows of the trees stirred and seemed like people, I just went on my way. For reassurance I began to hum softly. It helped.

At dawn I reached my group in the little forest. Everyone was still asleep. When they awoke and saw me alone they were amazed that I had found the way on my own. We decided that at night we would start moving toward the puszcza from which I had just returned. After the strain of the past two nights, I was exhausted and I slept for several hours. I needed strength to go through the same trip again.

When darkness fell, we set out. Musio still had difficulty walking. Propped by a cane on one side and one of us on the other, he moved slowly along, stopping frequently. At first the group waited for him each time, but eventually they went ahead to avoid danger and left us alone. I wasn't concerned as I knew the way. Musio suffered great pain but kept on going. His state was worsening and he began to crawl. I did not have the strength to carry him. We had no food or water. I wanted to pass through the open roads and fields before dawn and to reach some woods, where we could lie in hiding during the day. We finally managed to reach some small woods which were about seven miles before the puszcza.

Making our way between the trees we came upon a path, which we followed cautiously. Suddenly we chanced upon a small hut, well camouflaged, and a Jewish family hiding within. They had escaped from one of the surrounding villages and, being very familiar with the area, subsisted by begging for food from kindly neighboring farmers. They shared some potatoes with us. Musio could hardly move by then, and I was exhausted. We spent the remainder of the day resting there.

By nightfall I could see that Musio was in no shape to continue walking, and asked the family to allow him to stay on with them for a few days. I was afraid that if I stayed with Musio we would lose the families I had met in the puszcza. So I decided to go on to the puszcza to find them, and then return for Musio. Unwillingly, Musio agreed. I was given a few potatoes to take with me. The son of the family decided to join me and at night we set off.

After several hours we arrived at the dense forest without any mishap. We went deeper into the puszcza, looking for paths or other signs of people having passed through. We followed a path for about a mile and came upon a camp—some huts made of twigs, a couple of bonfires, potatoes baking, and several Jewish families trying to keep warm and dry by the flames. These were people from Kurzeniec and the vicinity. Since I had helped my mother distribute bread in the town, most of them recognized me. I thought for sure somebody knew what happened to my parents but nobody could give me any information. I asked them all to ask anyone who would come there in my absence. Horrifying as it was not knowing any-thing, at least I had a glimmer of hope.

I spent several days with these families and got to know their daily routine. At night those men who had some money went to the villagers they knew and bought food. Those who had no money sim-ply begged or scrounged. The women and children usually stayed behind. During the day everybody stayed deep in the forest, where it was so dense that people had to chop their way through.

One evening I was sitting by the fire when a newcomer came up. I recognized him as Antoshka, who had lived in the house to our left in Kurzeniec. He was a simple and uneducated fellow. He recognized me too and when he greeted me, said, "Your parents were killed. I saw with my own eyes how your mother was led away."

The suddenness of it took my breath away. I couldn't respond, or ask any questions. I didn't cry or show any emotion, but total emptiness overcame me, and with it a complete unawareness of my surroundings. I sat in this state for a while, not hearing any more of the conversation around me. Gradually my senses returned, and with them the realization that my parents were no more.

My mother, so warm and full of life, the sustainer of our morale, was no longer alive. No, that can't be true. It's a lie, a mistake. I can see my father and mother, they are next to me. I vented my anger on Antoshka for bringing such false news to me. I rose and moved away from the group. Sitting alone under a tree, tears began to flow, and an agonizing physical pain filled my chest. I don't know how long I sat there. At some point someone came up to me, brought me food, and tried to console me. I don't remember what they said. Thanking them for their concern and help, I got up and left.

For hours, not knowing where I was heading, I wandered through the woods and fields. Suddenly I realized I was entering the woods where I had left Musio. I began to think again. What should I do? Musio is so ill, if he heard what I had heard, his state might worsen. I decided not to mention anything for the time being, and to pull myself together. I tried to act as though everything was normal.

As I approached I could see the fire, which had almost gone out. Everyone was asleep in the hut except Musio, who lay dozing by the embers. As soon as he heard footsteps he woke up with a start and asked, "Who's there?" I said it was me. He threw some twigs on the embers, and flames flared up. Then he saw my face, and asked me what had happened. I didn't answer and he persisted in his questions. I could only say, "They're gone."

I sat down next to him. Wordlessly we embraced and cried. After a while Musio asked, "Is that true? Can it be? Why?" "It's a lie." I said, "To us they will always be alive, with us. I can see them looking at us and protecting us."

Musio said, "That's right, Selimku, they will always be with us. Our mother guided us until now and will continue to do so. We now have nothing left in our lives. Our main mission is to follow

Mother's last request: to save ourselves, take revenge on the murderers and their helpers, and to tell the world what happened."

We both vowed to fight, to avenge their death, and to try to survive. But if we were killed, we would die fighting.

We stayed with the family in the small forest for about a week longer, while Musio gradually recovered. At night we went out into the fields to dig for potatoes, which we roasted over the fire. That, and water, was our daily fare.

When Musio was able to walk we left for the puszcza. By then I was very familiar with the route. At a nearby village we stopped to beg for food, and a kind woman gave us some hot potato pancakes. This was our first hot meal in weeks.

In the puszcza we rejoined our friends' camp and built our own shelter of branches. The Jews in the puszcza had scattered and joined other camps which were several miles apart. Each family and group built their own shelter out of branches, and several groups shared a campfire. Night was the time to go to the villages to beg or steal food.

We found out that the Kupper family, who had shared our home and hideaway in Kurzeniec, were in one of the camps not far from us. We were happy to hear that and set off to find them. We greeted each other warmly and sat down to hear their experiences.

On the morning of the akzia, when Musio, Mother, and I ran away into the fields, the Kupper family hid behind the double wall which we had constructed in the barn. All throughout the akzia they stayed there. The Germans searched the house and the barn, but it never occurred to them that it was possible to hide between the walls.

Apparently a local boy found my mother hiding among the wheat in the field. He disclosed her location to a local policeman, who took her away. At about nine that morning the Kuppers heard the policeman bring my mother from the fields to the house. They heard her plead with him in Polish to let her escape. He promised her that the people were being taken to work and advised her to take some clothing and food with her. She went into the house, and they didn't hear anything more.

Two or three days later, at night, when it was quiet, the Kuppers left their hiding place and made their way toward the forests.

They met other Jews who were familiar with the way and arrived at the puszcza with them. They learned from one of the people there that my father was taken away at six in the morning, with a group of men who were praying in the synagogue. This was one of the first groups to be led to the marketplace. When my mother was brought there later in the day, she met my father there. They went to their death together.

The Kuppers and other friends who knew my mother told us we should be proud to be the sons of such a special woman who had helped so many people in those terrible times. But in spite of all the details we heard, we still could not accept the fact that we would never see our parents again.

We decided to stay in that camp and to build a shelter with the Kuppers. After all we had gone through together, they were the closest thing to family that we now had. Hungry, not knowing our way around, we asked to join some of the groups who knew how to reach villages where we could beg for food. They refused, telling us that if too many people were begging around, the farmers would stop giving food.

Musio and I had no choice but to strike out on our own. Since old man Kupper and his older son Grisha were sick, and the younger one cared for them, they couldn't go to the villages for food. At night Musio and I took empty sacks and went in the general direction of the villages. We followed paths and cart tracks for several hours until we reached our first village. We lay down for a few minutes to listen for sounds of danger, then went from house to house, softly knocking on windows and begging. "Kind housewife, please give us something to eat. We are hungry."

Many of them handed us some potatoes or slices of bread, a bit of salt and even an occasional egg. After several hours, with our sacks full, we retraced our steps and were back in the camp before dawn. It was such a relief to sit by the fire, roast our potatoes and eat our fill. We shared our food with the Kuppers.

Rivka Gvint and her mother also joined our camp. They were in much the same predicament as us. Nobody wanted to include them in their forays for food, so we offered to take Rivka with us on our next nightly expedition. She came with Musio and me, filled her sack with food, and we set off back to camp. Walking in single file deep inside the puszcza, we suddenly heard a rustle. We hit the ground behind a small ridge. We saw some movement from the side, and then eyes blazing in the darkness. Realizing that this was a wolf, we held our breath and lay still, hoping it would not attack us. When my eyes adjusted to the darkness, I noticed that there was a whole pack of wolves passing us on our left. They were either unaware of our presence, or not hungry. When they were gone, we got up, shaken by the incident and suddenly aware of yet another dimension to the dangers of the woods. We returned to camp.

We continued our nightly routine, which was becoming more difficult and dangerous. The peasants nearby were beginning to resent our presence and demands, and that forced us to venture out to distant villages.

We gradually adapted to our new lifestyle in the forest. We learned to cook potato soup and to be creative in finding ways to stretch out our meager supplies. Winter was coming and it was getting colder by the day. We had very little to protect us from the elements. I had the thin coat that I had escaped in and Musio did not have even that. At night we slept on the ground by the fire, back to back for mutual warmth. We kept the fire going all night for warmth and to deter the wolves, which we heard howling in the distance.

The lice multiplied, and our faces and hands were the only areas in our bodies that were free of their bites. There was no way we could wash or change our underwear. On sunnier days we would remove our undershirts and engage in a frantic hunt for the critters. That didn't help for more than a few minutes. Then the tickling sensation of something crawling on the body would begin, before the biting started. We were covered with scratches.

By the light of the fire, our camp looked unreal, like a painting—scattered shelters built of twigs and branches set in a dense forest, broken buckets and rags strewn around, and ragged people sitting with hands stretched out to catch a bit of warmth from the flames.

Most of the time we sat around silently. Occasionally a heated discussion about our future would erupt. How would we survive the harsh snowy winter which was coming, when we would not be able to go to the villages for food? The Germans would find it easy to follow our footprints straight to the camp and to capture us all. We had no weapons. Even the peasants coming into the forest for wood could track us down and kill us or betray us. Our endless discussions led us nowhere, and hopelessness took hold of the camp. Our days centered around trying to fill our empty stomachs and fighting the lice.

Musio and I tried to keep looking for solutions. We were determined not to succumb to apathy.

The Kuppers had some gold. We had nothing. We proposed building a common underground shelter—a "zemlianka." With their gold we could buy a supply of food, and maybe miraculously we could wait out the snow. The Kuppers began to stall, probably fearing that we would try to cheat them of their gold. Their fears were so totally groundless and insulting, after all that our family had done for them, that we decided to leave them.

9

PREPARING FOR A HARSH WINTER

October–December 1942

It was already the beginning of October, and the severe Polish winter would soon be upon us. Musio and I tossed more ideas around about how to survive until spring, and came up with something that seemed like a feasible plan. We concluded that the best solution, especially during the snow, was to be in a place which was totally secluded. We would have to find a spot far away from the camps of the other Jews, a place where even the villagers normally didn't go. We would build a zemlianka, camouflage it, gather enough food for the entire winter, and hibernate like animals, not going out or being in touch with any human beings until the snow thawed. We would buy some of the supplies and beg for the rest. We needed someone with some money and who knew the area to join us. We suggested our plan to several older and more experienced people, but they laughed at our preposterous scheme.

It was only about six weeks before the first anticipated snowfall. Normally, one night of begging would keep us supplied with food for two days. But the villagers were getting tired of us, and their offerings began to decrease. We decided to move further away from the puszcza and look for a new place where nobody would suspect Jews of hiding. We were sure that the Germans were aware of the presence of Jews in the puszcza but were not eager to penetrate these dense forests just yet to hunt them down. We figured that once there was snow on the ground, the Germans would simply follow the footprints leading them to the Jews.

We tried to organize a group, and since the older men did not take us seriously, we approached the younger ones. After some heated discussions, three young men agreed to go along with us. These were the simplest, least educated men in the group, and they were flattered to be included in the plans of such "worldly and educated young men." My brother, who had graduated from high school, was considered an intellectual.

One of the men was twenty-year-old Shimon the blacksmith. A dark-skinned, wiry boy with curly black hair and a large nose, he was the son of the blacksmith from Kurzeniec. From the age of twelve, he had accompanied his father from village to village shoeing horses, and he was thus familiar with all the roads and byroads in the area. He had never been to school and could barely read or write even Yiddish.

The second man was Jeijze, about thirty years old, a merchant to whom money meant everything. He used to travel with his older brother from market to market in the small towns, dealing in old clothes. He was short, fair, and very agile—and he possessed some gold.

The third man was sixteen-year-old Zelig, Jeijze's nephew. He was fair, somewhat taller than me, with an elementary school education. He was kind, helpful, and strong, but not very bright.

Musio and I completed the group. One night in the beginning of October, Shimon led us out of the Kotlowskaya puszcza to a distant swamp in a smaller woods.

The rest of the camp thought we were crazy and suicidal but wished us well when we said goodbye. Nobody knew where we were heading. That remained our secret.

Our aim was to reach Hadzhicz Swamps, which were surrounded by large villages. Shimon knew that there were forests in these swamps, and led us there. It was a difficult trek. We each carried sacks with provisions. In some places we had to balance precariously on logs strewn across the marshes for crossing. At times we waded waist-deep in the muddy water.

There were isolated farmhouses set in clearings in the forests or in the fields near the woods. These farmhouses—"hutors"—were very simple, primitive huts built of logs. They usually consisted of two or three rooms with bare log walls and tapers set into the cracks. The bedrooms held wooden beds with straw mattresses and hand-woven linen covers, and frequently there was an icon hanging over the bed. A large, flat brick oven in the kitchen was used for cooking and baking, and also provided a warm place on which to sleep. It was also the only source of heating. Water was brought in from a well. The livestock were usually kept in a barn, but occasionally a room within the house was allocated for the pigs and chickens.

When we chanced upon a hutor we entered and asked for food. The farmers would usually give us some, and we noticed fear in their faces. We realized that these farmers were afraid of the "people of the night," which is what they called the unidentified folks who scavenged for food among them in the darkest hours. They didn't report us to the Germans, or refuse us food, not knowing what the repercussions would be.

Each night was spent walking, and toward dawn we would find a spot in the woods where we could spend the day sleeping and eating.

A zemlianka had to be built in some obscure part of the woods, partly under the ground, and partly above ground, camouflaged with branches to prevent detection. The entrance was usually low and one had to crawl in. The size of a zemlianka varied depending upon the number of people it would have to accommodate. It seemed the safest and most appropriate way of living in groups.

It took us five days to get to the forest where we wanted to locate our little structure. Before we selected a spot we wandered about, getting our bearings and familiarizing ourselves with the general area. We were looking for a strategic location, not far from water, but where we could dig down for about seven feet without reaching water level. We picked a little hill in the forest, adjoining the swamp. By the side of the hill near the swamp was a stream. The forest was not dense, and about half a mile away there was a trail leading to the villages. We saw that we were invisible from the trail. There were numerous dugouts and trenches all around which were remnants from World War I. This was probably where the frontline had been at one time. We assumed that because of the trenches, and the difficulty of carrying logs across them, the villagers would not come to this part of the forest to chop wood during the winter.

Musio and I tried not to overlook any detail and weighed all the pros and cons before we finally selected our site. We could not afford mistakes, as we were dealing with our lives.

First we made a basic plan for the zemlianka. Then we decided upon the type and amount of wood we would need. Musio's education in mathematics and physics enabled us to calculate the size and thickness of the logs, taking into consideration the weight of the soil which the roof would have to support. We kept in mind the extra weight of snow or rain-drenched soil. These were very elementary factors known to every builder, but we five young men who had never constructed anything had to rely only on our intelligence and common sense. Musio and I tried to remember all the knowledge about survival tactics which we had gleaned in our childhood from reading such books as *Robinson Crusoe*.

We built a temporary hut out of twigs not far from our chosen site to live in until our zemlianka was ready. We had no qualms about stealing the tools we needed for building ourselves a zemlianka. From farmyards we took axes, hammers, shovels, saws, and buckets for carrying water and for cooking. Begging and stealing were no longer humiliating or considered wrong in our struggle for survival.

We set to work, busy from dawn until dark. First we dug a pit seven feet deep, twenty by fourteen feet in area. Then we started chopping wood. We made sure not to chop within half a mile of our location and to cut the trees at random so as not to create a visible open space. We then covered the stumps with moss, so as not to leave any trace of our work. We dragged the chopped down pine trees, leaves and all, to our spot. There we sawed off the branches and cut the trunks to the required dimensions. We lined the sides of the pit with seven-foot high logs, close together and tightly packed with moss, to create the walls. On the four corners we hammered thicker logs into the ground, to support the roof. We placed two heavy twenty-foot long parallel beams on the thicker logs, and created a roof out of thinner fourteen-foot logs, packed with moss for waterproofing. We then used the soil we had dug out to cover the roof, which created a little dome. We camouflaged the area with grass and planted a few small trees on top. Facing the stream we cut an entrance in the wall, the size of a window. Then we dug a 7'x7' pit, four feet deep, outside the opening. To enter our little house we had to jump into the pit, and crawl in backward, lying on our bellies. We placed a small tree in the pit to disguise the entrance, and removed it when we had to crawl in and out.

"Interior decorating" came next. A third of the zemlianka was allocated for storing potatoes. The middle third was destined to be our sleeping quarters. We built a log bunk. It was going to be very difficult to sleep on, but we did not have the tools to make planks, so the logs were just nailed together. The other third was our dining room, bathroom and kitchen combined.

The actual construction took over two weeks. We worked nonstop, fourteen hours a day, and the physical effort was tremendous. Once a day we cooked a bucketful of potatoes. This was our only hot meal.

Several nights a week we did the rounds of the villages, acquiring provisions. We must have been the only ones in that area roaming by night to beg and steal food. They did not know who we were and we felt that they were afraid of us. Being the least Jewish-looking in the group, and able to speak Polish fluently, as well as Russian with a Polish rather than a Yiddish accent, I was the one who usually went inside the houses to beg. Though the villagers were more generous than in the puszcza area, we realized that we could not get all that we needed for the winter just by begging. We needed other tactics.

We made a master plan of the provisions we would need to enable us to survive underground for up to six months. We calculated the number of meals we would have, the amount of food per meal and everything else we would require. Our top priority was a stove for heat and cooking. We had to have a big supply of food to sustain five hearty young men throughout the long winter, and the choice of imperishables was very limited. We planned to amass potatoes, peas, flour, some lard, salt, and matches. Any extras of course would be welcome. Since bread would become moldy after a while, we couldn't store much. The plan was ready, and now the only problem was how to implement it.

While Jeijze was dragging one of the huge logs in the forest, his clothes got torn and the gold pieces he had been hiding fell out. We spent hours trying to find them, but it was hopeless. The gold that we had been counting on to buy food was lost to us forever. Rather than fall into despair, we started thinking of other ideas.

It was obvious that a change of tactics was essential. Our first step was to start stealing potatoes from the cellars in the yards of the farmhouses. At night we would creep into the yards, silently open the cellar doors, and one of us would climb in and fill five sacks. We each carried a sack on our backs for about seven to ten miles to the zemlianka.

One night, when we were almost back at our zemlianka, I stumbled under the load of the potatoes. I fell into one of the trenches and didn't have the strength to push the potatoes off of me and climb out. I began to cry with frustration. The other boys helped me out of the trench and we continued on our way. In a trancelike state, I covered mile after weary mile.

That was about a month before the first snow was expected and our food supply was not nearly adequate. Only the pile of potatoes in our storage area was increasing.

Sitting by the bonfire one night, a new idea occurred to Musio and me. I cut off the tops of my boots and sewed them into a holster. It took me a whole day to do it. Shaping a piece of wood to look like a Soviet Nagan revolver, which had a wooden hand grip, I stuffed it into the holster. It looked like an authentic revolver when I attached it to my belt. We then shared our plan with the others. We would no longer beg for food. We would demand it!

At first they were hesitant. They were afraid that the risk was too great. It took a bit of convincing but finally we all decided to give it a try. I would enter a farmhouse alone, and they would wait outside. I put on Zelig's boots and Jeijze's fur jacket and positioned a wide belt over it with my Nagan holster fully exposed.

At the first village I knocked on the door and demanded in Russian to be let in. My friends stayed outside—heard but not seen. I demanded certain basic foods from the farmer—potatoes, flour, peas, lard, and salt—and specified the quantities. He did not try to chase me away, but began to bargain about the quantities. He said he would not have enough left for his own needs if he complied fully with my demands. I generously agreed to leave him sufficient food, and to be satisfied with less. He ran out and began to bring the supplies according to our mutual agreement.

After this initial success, we all agreed that the tactic could bring in enough food to last the winter. With practice, we perfected our method. Zelig, who also did not look like the stereotypical Jewish boy, would enter with me, in his Russian padded jacket. A shape resembling a revolver bulged under his jacket as well. He did not open his mouth, because his Yiddish accent would have given him away.

Shimon, Musio, and Jeijze remained outside, each one carrying sticks made to look like rifles. They walked in front of the windows, but were careful not to come into the light. I developed a form of taxation. I would ask each farmer about the size of his land, the number of livestock and members of his family, and would tax them accordingly. They would argue and we would invariably reach a compromise. When we could no longer carry such quantities of food on our backs, we began to add a horse and cart to our demands. A peasant's most valuable possession was his horse, so we promised that we would release it when we had reached our destination and it would come back to him. It usually did. We would pile up the cart, take it to the edge of the forest, unload our provisions, carry everything to the zemlianka, and send the horse back.

The negotiations were full of tension. Confident on the surface, I quivered inside. I worked out a system of acquiring as much as I could without overstretching the limits and causing rage. And I tried to deal with the wives, who were more flexible, more frightened, and more eager to appease me.

When I saw their resistance growing, however, I would calm them by saying we knew they were fine people and did not cooperate with the Germans. I would then slightly decrease my demands on them. During the negotiations, I never disclosed any information and kept them guessing as to our identity.

We confiscated a black iron stove from one farmer. We also removed a window from a deserted house which enabled us to close the entrance to our zemlianka but still let in some light.

Every night we made a new list of our needs and tried to amass provisions accordingly. We were under constant tension, fearing that someone would discover how vulnerable we really were.

One time we ran into trouble. I knocked on the door of a house and was let in by a woman. Her husband, a mountain of a man over six feet tall was standing there. The woman answered my usual questions, and I started listing my requirements. Zelig stood at the door. While we were talking, the two sons, as humongous as the father, walked in from the other room and stood beside him. The three of them eyed me suspiciously and I felt they were not afraid of me. All knotted inside, I continued my demands, all the while wanting desperately to get away without showing them my fear. I heard the father say to his sons, "He is a Jew. I feel it."

I knew I had to do something immediately, before the situation got out of hand. Turning on him, I started shouting, "What did you say?" Seeing my anger, he said, "Nothing, nothing!"

I let out a tirade of Russian curses, going through my entire vocabulary. Then I added, "Did you think I didn't hear you say I am a Jew? You must be a German spy! I'll show you what we do to German spies! We'll shoot you all and burn down your house!"

Turning to the woman, I ordered, "Bring me matches, I'm going to burn your house down."

Had they only known what was in my holster, and how much I was bluffing! But the atmosphere in the room changed immediately. The huge men towering over me became smaller and smaller and begged for mercy. The woman became hysterical and started to curse her men. She pushed them into the other room and swore to me that these stupid men were not German spies at all. She pleaded with me not to burn the house. I said we would check to see whether they were German spies, and if they were, we would return.

Haughtily I turned away, spurning the food on her table, and with a last threat, Zelig and I left the house.

As time went on, a sense of safety set in, due to the quite orderly and routine acquisition of food. There were no further hitches. We became less careful.

Eventually Musio, Shimon, and Jeijze started entering the houses with us, because it was warmer inside, and they could share in the food that the housewives put before us on the table. But Shimon, with his black beard, stood out with his stereotypical Jewish look, and I noticed that the farmers were beginning to suspect our identity. They saw that, aside from my "revolver," there were no visible weapons on any of the other men. Their behavior toward us became less fearful and more aggressive.

By November our work on the zemlianka was almost over. We moved in and took inventory of our stock of food and stored all we had. We discovered that we had sufficient food and most other necessities to last us through the winter.

But we were short of matches. We had only one box. Musio and I suggested not going out any more. We would solve our problem by keeping the embers in our stove alive all the time. But Shimon insisted that we should go out just one more time, to get matches and a few other items. Tense and reluctant as he had been in the beginning, he had gradually become too confident.

At dusk on November 18 we left our zemlianka and headed toward the villages. The sky was slate gray, as though forecasting rain or snow. I had a feeling of foreboding, but after the last argument, when Shimon, Jeijze, and Zelig overrode us, I didn't want to broach the subject of staying in the zemlianka again.

Just as we were out of the woods, it began to snow heavily and turned into a windy snowstorm. Very quickly the ground was white. We decided to pass the villages where we were known and to go further away. I seemed to see eyes following us from the windows of the houses. And I was afraid that our footprints in the snow could lead the villagers straight to our zemlianka. Finally I suggested returning immediately to the zemlianka by a different route and by morning the falling snow would have covered up our footprints. Shimon insisted that since we were out already, we should get the matches, but he did agree to go into one of the isolated farmhouses rather than into the villages.

We went to one farmhouse and got two boxes of matches. I shoved them in the pocket of my jacket. The snow had covered the entire area so we decided to retrace our steps so as not to leave additional footprints. We were going quickly in single file. I led the way and Musio brought up the rear.

Around midnight, the storm was subsiding and the snowfall was lighter. We were on a tree-lined road between two villages. Suddenly shadows emerged from behind the trees and a large group of peasants flailing sticks and sickles came running toward us, shouting, "Kill them! Kill them!" It happened so quickly that we didn't have time to plan any action. I felt a heavy stick landing on my shoulders.

Rushing through the ring of men who tried to surround me, I shoved one who was trying to stop me and he fell to the ground. I began to run away. Glancing back, I saw four or five of them chasing me. They were careful not to come too close to me because they must have been afraid of my "revolver." I ran as fast as I could. I had no idea what was happening to the rest of my group. On the white snow I was clearly visible to the villagers. Two of them followed my footprints and the others tried to approach me from the sides.

Flashing through my mind were the stories of farmers hunting foxes with the first snowfall. They would chase the fox, approaching it from different sides, so as to confuse and disorient the animal. When it was exhausted, they would pounce on it and kill it. I felt like that animal. I kept running, tripping, falling into pits and ditches. They relentlessly pursued. I was exhausted, and tried to snatch moments of rest behind trees, but as soon as I heard them approaching I would start running again.

They would occasionally disappear from view and I would think they had given up the chase, but then there they were again, shouting encouragement to each other, closing in on me. After a few miles, I was beginning to lose my strength. I removed the holster with my "revolver," and my fur coat, and threw them under a tree. It made it easier for me to run. I began to stop more frequently, for longer rests, but would continue running when I heard them coming. I could see a forest, but it was still far away. I came upon an area of shrubs and hid. I was totally drained, and couldn't get up. There they finally caught me.

I saw five of them, coming at me armed with stones and sticks and knives, and was sure that this was the end. I could hardly get up, let alone defend myself. I started to get up when I saw a stick coming toward my head and heard the crack of it breaking on impact, but I felt no pain. I lost consciousness. When I began to come to, I slowly realized I was lying in the snow, beaten and helpless. I felt death moving closer. I heard my assailants planning to kill me.

Before my eyes I saw my mother, my father, Musio. I thought, such a senseless end—I had not yet done anything with my life. I hadn't fulfilled my promise to my mother. I hadn't even killed a single Nazi. Unconsciously, a shout burst out of me. That is when I screamed out in Polish, "I want to live!"

I managed to elude my captors after they had stripped me of my clothing, while they fought over who would get my fur coat (which they'd found) and my boots, once they killed me, and I ran naked through the snowy forest throughout the entire night with my underwear on my head. I reached the zemlianka just as dawn was breaking and found that Musio was the only one who had made it back. As my brother held my freezing body, we cried with the joy of seeing each other alive and relatively unharmed. Although my head and body were swollen from the sticks that had been used on me, I somehow managed to avoid frostbite—even on my feet! Musio showed me a gashing wound which he had sustained on his head. It was still bleeding so I ripped a strip of lining from an old jacket and bandaged the wound as best I could. Musio gave me coarse underwear to cover my nakedness and lit the oven. He made me get into my crude bunk, and covered me with everything we had in order to thaw me out.

While standing guard with an ax in case any intruders would find our hideaway, Musio told me of his experience. He was the last in line and when he saw us being attacked he turned around and ran. His long legs carried him fast, and only one of the attackers saw him and tried to catch him. He hurled a stone at Musio and hit him on the head. Musio fell. When the attacker came close, Musio jumped up, smacked him in the face, knocking him over, and fled. He too ran all night until he found his way back to the zemlianka. He barricaded the window and kept an ax within reach, with the idea that if someone would come to get him, he would defend himself until the end. He had no idea what had happened to the rest of our little group.

The next night, Zelig and Jeijze appeared and told their stories. They had managed to escape and elude the attackers. Hidden in a pile of hay by a hutor, they lay motionless for a day and a half. When all was quiet they returned to our zemlianka.

Only Shimon was missing. We were beginning to doubt whether he would return, but several days later he showed up too. His dark face was ashen and he had two bleeding wounds on his back. He had tried to escape the attackers but they caught up with him. They beat him until he fell on his face, unconscious. They removed his coat—the only valuable thing he wore—then stabbed him twice in his back and left him for dead.

When he regained consciousness, he began to crawl to the nearest hutor. Dragging himself to the barn, he lay down in the hay and tried to stop the bleeding by stuffing rags in his wounds. But he lost consciousness again. He woke up in broad daylight, to find the peasant's wife trying to dress his wounds. She had found him that morning when she came to fetch hay for her cows, and began to tend to him, not knowing who he was. He told her that he was a Russian-Georgian soldier who had escaped from a column of prisoners herded by Germans. He promised that as soon as he could, he would go on his way. He was fed and his wounds were cared for. He stayed in the barn for several days, until he regained some of his strength and the bleeding stopped.

Gratefully, he left them and returned to the zemlianka. When he undressed, we saw that his wounds had reopened. We bandaged him again with cleaner rags and made him lie down and rest.

Amazingly, we all survived this ordeal. I didn't even catch cold after running naked in the snowstorm all night. After some rest I was as good as new. Evidently circumstances dictate the way our bodies react to emergencies—and youth helps.

Reunited, the five of us settled into our routine. But the matches which we had gone out for were lost to us, together with my fur jacket.

About two days after Shimon came back we had another mishap. We were lying on the bunk and it was Musio's turn to cook. While he was stoking the stove with wood, some of which was still damp, the zemlianka filled up with smoke. Overcome with the fumes and feeling dizzy, he opened the window and tried to crawl out for fresh air. Halfway out he fainted and the rear part of his limp body slumped against the hot pipe of the stove, which normally routed the smoke out through the window. We jumped up and tried to move him away, out of the entrance, but he was stuck. It took a few minutes until we managed to drag him back into the zemlianka. Then Jeijze and I crawled out the window and, with Zelig and Shimon pushing from behind, we pulled his unresponsive body outside by his hands so he could get some air. Laying him gently on the ground, we began to rub his face with snow until he was revived. That was when we saw the terrible burns on his behind. The pain was agonizing, and we had no means of treating the wounds. We were even out of clean rags by now.

I ripped the lining out of his jacket and tried to rinse it. With this less-than-sterile bandage we dressed his burns. For a long time he could only lie on his stomach or stand.

We now had two patients on our hands—Musio and Shimon. Every day I changed their dressings. I tried to remove the bandages which stuck to their wounds by soaking them with hot water and jerking them off. I then applied cleaner rags to their sores. The lining in the jacket was running out, so the bandages got smaller by the day. I only hoped that the wounds would crust before we were left with no more material.

Thus we learned another lesson the hard way—through experience—from that point on we used only dry wood for our stove.

10

HIBERNATING IN THE ZEMLIANKA

December 1942–May 1943

After our brush with death on November 18, we decided not to go out of the forest until the snow had melted in the spring. I looked around at what would be our confining surroundings for the next six months. A log partition about 5 feet high, which separated the pile of potatoes from our bunk where we all slept side by side, served as a headboard. A layer of straw served as a mattress, and coarse blankets were our sheets and covers. If I wanted to turn in my sleep, I had to push the men on either side of me. Musio slept next to the wall. I was next to him. Then came Zelig, Jeijze, and Shimon. In the middle of the remaining area, closer to the exit, was our round iron stove. The only place where we could stand up was around the stove. These were very tight quarters indeed for five men. The metal exhaust pipe ran from the stove through a cut-out in the bottom corner of the entrance window, which served also as our only source of light. Then outside, in the ditch, the pipe bent upward to ground level. When we placed our camouflage tree in position, the pipe was not visible.

The pipe served a double purpose. In addition to drawing out the smoke, it provided indoor heating. Along the opposite wall were our sacks of provisions. Three large sacks contained peas. One large sack held wheat flour and a smaller one was full of other grain.

There was a big bag of salt. Onions and garlic hung over the sacks. Suspended from the ceiling over the massive pile of potatoes were bread rusks. Some pork meat and fat, which we preserved by salting heavily, also hung on hooks. We also hung some lamb and pork meat outside on the high branches of trees, where they froze. The freezing temperature preserved the food, and there was no smell which could attract animals—or humans. We had heard that garlic had healing qualities and was a good substitute when medication was unavailable, so we took to wearing a clove of garlic in a crude pouch around our necks, so we could chew on it if we were ill or wounded.

We had four metal buckets which we used for cooking and for bringing in and storing water. One kerosene lamp provided light at night, and we had three liters of kerosene. Our one remaining box of matches, three plates, several tablespoons, a knife, and a few old pots completed our kitchen.

We had to go down the hill to the stream for water. We found a ditch which we used for a toilet, and we covered our traces with snow or earth. When we couldn't go out, we used a special bucket with a lid until such time when we could empty it out into the ditch. An important chore was emptying the "bathroom bucket." It was done frequently, so there would be no stink added to the other discomforts we had to live with. We had some thread and needles, scissors, rope, a saw and an ax, a hammer and some nails, and even an old razor for shaving.

In order to preserve our matches, we kept a low flame burning in the stove until we turned in for the night. Just before going to bed we would cover the glowing embers with ashes. In the morning we would dig up the embers, blow them back into life, and keep them glowing until dark, when we used them to ignite the dry wood, which we always had on hand. The nights were long, from 4 P.M. until 7 A.M. We cooked twice a day, a bucket of potatoes and peas per meal, and as long as our meat lasted we threw in a piece. We also added some pork fat and salt. The meat and fat had been precut and divided into portions. After calculating all the provisions we had, the number of meals we would eat, and working out the menu, we figured that if we stuck stringently to our plan, we would have enough food for six months. We calculated that our supply of kerosene would enable us to keep the lamp burning two or three hours per day.

We took turns cooking, lighting the stove, bringing in water, and handling all the chores. We tried to go out for water only during snowfalls or storms, when the wind would sweep away our footprints. That meant we needed a constant supply of water, to be stored in buckets. Occasionally we ran out of water and had to risk going out, but we then tried to cover up our tracks by sweeping them with branches. That was the best we could do. We hoped that a storm would come before some people would. Snowstorms were also the time we went out to chop wood. We would gather a supply that would last for a fortnight or so, since we only had space to store so much.

The first rays of light coming in through the window woke us. We kept track of the days by carving a notch in the wall, with a larger cut for Saturdays. We cooked just before sunrise, and again at sundown, in the hope that there would be nobody around in the woods at that time to see the smoke. Until the cook of the day finally had the fire going, smoke would fill the zemlianka. The rest of the group would pull the blankets over their heads and breathe through the blankets, so as not to choke. When the food was ready, we opened the window to clear the air, and only then surfaced for the meal. We took turns eating, as we had only three plates. Occasionally we would leave some of the peas-and-potato concoction to be eaten later in the day.

This whole ritual repeated itself twice daily. The chef would announce the menu of the day, which varied in name only. We would have "Beef Stroganoff sans Beef," or "Soup of the Day." The evening meal was eaten by lamplight, to be distinguished from the morning meal, which was eaten by daylight.

We celebrated the Sabbath every week by making pancakes out of flour, and eating them instead of the rusks. When the stove was not being used for cooking, a plank of wood transformed it into a table. Right after the evening meal, we would put out the light, chat a while in the dark, and go to sleep. Our usual night lasted 12–15 hours. Our bones ached from lying all these hours on the round logs of the bunk. I became familiar with every curve of the logs.

Our attire never changed. We wore long coarse underwear which had several important attributes. First of all, it took up minimal space. Also, there was less of a place for the lice to hide in. But most of all, this was all we had to wear indoors. We saved our few coats to be worn outside.

Once a week we boiled water, stripped naked, and washed ourselves and our clothes. Only through the lack of soap did I understand the vital importance of that commodity, for a major source of our daily suffering was the scourge of lice.

Every day we removed our underwear, turned it inside out, and hunted for lice, in all the seams and folds. We would roast them over the stove, holding the underwear as close to the flames as we could without burning the cloth or our fingers. We would watch the lice falling into the fire and think we had conquered the menace. Putting on clean clothes after our weekly wash, we would hope to be free of them. One of the methods we tried was to freeze them out by putting the underwear in the snow overnight. We would bring in the underwear frozen stiff and put them on as soon as they thawed. But with all this creative warfare, the longest we ever lasted lice-free was an hour. Just as we were congratulating ourselves on the successful extermination of the pests, we would inevitably start to feel something tickling and crawling on our skin.

My legs were covered with sores. One day, after I put on the boots which we all shared for bringing water, the top of the boots got stuck to my open sores. It was so horrendously painful trying to remove the boots that I ended up cutting them open.

Every so often we would shave and give each other a haircut with our blunt scissors. We even had a contest for the best barber, which I never won.

We were living in cramped quarters with people we might not have chosen under different circumstances. It was most certainly a test of endurance and human decency. We adapted. They were simple, good-hearted men. There was no major friction or conflict, but neither were there any stimulating conversations initiated by them. We spent the long hours between chores and meals sitting on the bunk, daydreaming and talking. Musio and I were particularly interested in discussing the war, analyzing and predicting the outcome. The last news we had heard was in the fall of 1942, when the Germans had besieged Stalingrad, deep within Soviet Russia. Also, the German General Rommel had taken Africa, and the frontline was at El Alamein on the Egyptian border. The Germans were about to attack Egypt. They were successful on all the major fronts and it seemed as though the world was crumbling at their feet, even though there had been setbacks on the Eastern Front. Despite all of this, we tried to remain optimistic and to convince each other that eventually the tide of war would turn and the Germans would be defeated.

We drew a chessboard on the ground and used pawns made of potatoes. Musio was the uncontested champion. I learned a lot from him about the game. Musio talked to me about literature and history and became my private tutor, filling in some of the gaps in my education, which had been abruptly terminated when I was fourteen.

Our conversations would sometimes touch on our personal pre-war experiences. We would reminisce about our home in Raciaz and our parents, and Musio would talk about his high school in Warsaw. Jeijze would talk about his home town, the marketplace and his activities as a merchant. Zelig described how he used to help both his father in his shop and his uncle Jeijze in the market stall. Shimon told of his life in Kurzeniec, where he was born, and how, from the age of ten, he helped his father the blacksmith. They would walk from village to village, trading goods and shoeing horses.

We fantasized about what we would ask for if our wishes were granted. Musio and I imagined ourselves sleeping in a clean bed again, free of lice. We dreamed of living in Palestine, equal members of society in our own Jewish state. Jeijze and Zelig each wished to own a shop and become successful merchants. Shimon wished for a meal of twenty scrambled eggs with sausage and butter. He ridiculed our dream of a life without lice. He said it was not feasible. Lice had always been a normal part of life as he remembered it. They were there to suck away the bad blood within us, and without them we would probably not survive.

The heat of our stove began gradually to melt the bottom layer of snow over our zemlianka, and water saturated the soil covering our roof. The earth became heavy and we noticed that our roof was beginning to sag. Water began to drip inside. We tried to prop up the roof, but were not successful. We heard ominous creaking of logs and were afraid that one day the entire roof would collapse on us.

During the next snowstorm we went out into the woods, chopped down some trees and put up additional support for our roof. It helped. The roof did not sag anymore, but it became even more crowded inside.

One day in January 1943, we heard the sounds of shooting close by. We sat inside in fear. In about an hour it was quiet again. Later we found out that the Germans were combing the woods in search of partisans and the "night people." There were no signs of habitation in the area of our zemlianka and they passed us by. At the end of January we heard airplanes bombing the area. We could also clearly distinguish the sounds of artillery shots and, from afar, the echo of machine guns. We didn't know what was happening. Our thoughts fluctuated. The optimistic view was that the Soviets must be near, pushing the Germans away. The pessimistic one feared that this was another big siege carried out by the Germans. After a few days it quieted down and we remained in suspense, in the dark as to what had really taken place.

February was the coldest month. It snowed heavily but we felt more secure, knowing that our footprints would be erased immediately if we went out. We occasionally heard peasants in the woods, chopping trees. Sometimes they came close to our hideaway. We worked out a plan of action in case they discovered us. Luckily that did not come about.

Musio's and Shimon's wounds eventually healed and we were all well again, though pale from lack of sunlight and fresh air.

In March we began to make clothes from the rags we owned. We didn't have enough leather for shoes for all of us, so we substituted bark, string, and rags. Our confidence grew, and occasionally when the sun peeked through the clouds we ventured out. At first the unfamiliar fresh air tired us. Deep snow still covered the ground but spring was definitely in the air. Although we still had some food left in storage, we were rather fed up with the diet of peas and potatoes, and longed for some bread.

By mid-April the snow began to melt. After five months of hibernating underground in total isolation in the midst of a war, not knowing what had transpired, we decided to renew contact with the outer world.

We were careful to avoid treading on the patches of snow still lying on the ground, and headed toward the most isolated farms. We had grown so accustomed to the total silence in the zemlianka during the long months that even the crunch of our own footsteps on the frozen ground sounded loud and threatening.

At the first hutor we knocked on the door and asked for bread, which the farmer kindly gave us. We then asked him what was happening in the village. He quickly slammed the door on us. We met with the same response to our question at the next three hutors. The farmers looked at us as though we were ghosts or madmen. Our ashen faces probably added to that impression. We began to understand that something had transpired in the villages that we were unaware of. We returned to the safety of our zemlianka, upset and tired.

After two days we went out again, in a different direction, toward a village where Shimon had a friend. He went in alone and asked a few questions. We waited at the edge of the village.

His friend—a farmer—told Shimon that during the winter the Germans had faced several serious defeats. They failed to capture Stalingrad, and the entire Sixth Army there surrendered to the Soviets. In Africa, too, Rommel's army was chased far away from the Egyptian border by the British. Notwithstanding these problems, the Germans in Belorussia continued organizing roundups in the woods and the nearby villages. Most of the villages, including those we had asked about, had been totally burnt. Many of the men were killed, and the rest taken to work camps in Germany. The roundups and hunts in the puszcza which we had left took several weeks and, as far as he knew, most of the Jews were discovered and killed. Rumor had it, however, that in the woods near the village of Zazierie there were a number of Jews still in hiding.

Back in our zemlianka, digesting the news, we decided to go to the Zazierie woods to try and find any Jewish survivors. We camouflaged our hiding place. With mixed feelings, we left for good the zemlianka which had been our home and safety for five months. We suddenly felt exposed and vulnerable.

Shimon led the way. We reached a river and asked a farmer living on the banks to take us across, but his boat had a leak. He directed us toward a small makeshift bridge. The night was pitch dark. We walked along the bank of the turbulent river. The melting snow which had turned the ground to mud penetrated through our crude shoes and by the time we reached the so-called bridge we were soaking wet. We found a few stakes pushed into the ground, connected with narrow logs, meant to support fishing nets. The logs were entirely submerged in the rising water, and the trick was to go from one stake to the next, balancing on the narrow logs without falling into the water.

The current was very strong and pushed against our legs, making things even more difficult. Slowly and very carefully, step by step, we negotiated our way, all the while calling to each other to make sure no one had fallen. It took about an hour to go half way across the wide river. I slipped a few times, but managed to grab the nearest stake. Near the end of the "bridge," the water was not deep but the stakes were short, submerged in the water, and not easily visible. Shimon, who led the way, and Zelig, right behind him, both fell into the freezing water. We managed to pull them out and we all finally reached the bank safely.

The roaring water, the wind, the voices calling to each other in the night, the tension, and the effort to keep from slipping off the logs, all seemed somehow familiar. I tried to remember whether I had ever gone through this before, and finally realized that this crossing reminded me of something I once read in *Robinson Crusoe.*

As soon as we reached the woods, we lit a fire and tried to dry out. It was very, very cold.

The following night we went toward Zazierie and met a group of Jews and a few armed partisans roaming about the village. The Jews had built several zemlianka and formed a warm and close-knit group. Among them were some of our friends from Kurzeniec— young Shimon Zimmerman, who had been part of our little resistance group, and his girlfriend Riva, and Papa Pozner and his young daughter Hannale. They were overjoyed to see us. Everyone was sure that the five of us had been captured, as no one had heard from us since November. We decided to stay with the group.

Shimon Zimmerman was slim and wiry, active and resourceful. He knew his way around very well. Riva was petite and cute, very supportive of her boyfriend, bright and full of fire and energy. They were inseparable. "Papa" Pozner, in his forties, had lost his wife and younger daughter to the Nazis. Being older than most of the others, he was very fatherly toward us all, hence his nickname. He was very protective of his sixteen-year-old daughter Hannale, who was pretty, intelligent, and very reserved. They both had beautiful voices and introduced us to all the Russian and Yiddish songs. One of the pleasures of living within that group was hearing Hannale sing in her rich, warm voice, with her father accompanying her.

They told us what had transpired in their part of the woods that winter.

German military units had surrounded the forest and then entered with sleds and horses. The local peasants led the way. Systematically, they combed the area and shot any Jew they came upon. There were no partisans in the woods at that time. Of the hundred and fifty Jews hiding there, less than fifty managed to escape. This was similar to what had happened in other parts of the forest. The survivors broke up into small groups and spread out.

Here, in the Zazierie woods, we met our first real partisans. Initially, any random group of people with weapons who united in order to survive and to resist the Nazis were considered partisans. But these partisans were an organized force, fighting a different kind of warfare. We told them of our previous contact with the partisans in Kurzeniec and how we lost touch with them when they went east. They said they had heard of that group and that to the best of their knowledge, most of the group had been killed in combat around Minsk and the rest had dispersed.

We asked to be accepted into their unit. We were strong young men ready to fight. They replied that they only accepted men with weapons. In vain Musio and I tried to explain that we had given the arms we had acquired in Kurzeniec to the partisans who went east. Their answer was clear-cut. No one would be accepted without weapons. But where and how could we get them? Their commander came up with some clever "advice." "Take a stick, go to a German garrison, kill a German with your stick, take his rifle and come back to us. Simple, isn't it?"

Unable to convince him to take us in, the five of us decided to stay in the Zazierie forest.

Life in the woods now differed from life before the roundup in that the feeling of relative safety was no longer there. Panic struck each time there were rumors of Germans around. When we heard of an increased German presence in the area, we immediately expected a new oblava. An "oblava" was a siege where tremendous numbers of Germans surrounded the forest, entered it, and thoroughly combed the entire area, assisted by dogs, airplanes, and tanks. Without such force the Germans were reluctant to enter the forests because of their vulnerability to the partisans. Although the partisans were the Germans' main target in the oblava, Jews were an added bonus; all Jews found in hiding were shot on the spot.

A group of young men who had escaped from a labor camp in Vileika found their way to our camp. Most of them were originally from Baranovich, a town where the entire Jewish population had been crowded by the Germans into a small area, a ghetto, with very stringent rules and limits set on their freedom of movement. They told us of the liquidation of their ghetto. Most of the people were sent away, nobody really knew where. The stronger men were taken to labor camps in Vileika. Their job was to clear the areas around the railroad tracks of trees and other obstructions, to prevent partisans from being able to get within 1000 feet of the tracks without being seen. While chopping trees in the woods, they escaped. The Germans pursued them and recaptured and killed most of them. But this small group succeeded in reaching us.

Shimon, Jeijze, and Zelig decided to leave us and went back to the puszcza. People weaved in and out of each other's lives, meeting, parting ways, trying to find safety, not really knowing what was best. It was impossible to dwell on the sadness of parting from people who had shared such a long and difficult period with us.

Shortly thereafter, unfortunately, a new oblava began at the puszcza. The small group of partisans that were near there had disappeared, so the only people in the forest were Jews, most of whom were caught and killed. Jeijze was among them. We had no information about Zelig and Shimon.

We feared that the roundup would reach us too, and made plans to hide. Luckily, however, the oblava somehow bypassed our area.

11

PROVING OURSELVES TO THE PARTISANS

May–June 1943

Some of the men who had joined us from the labor camp in Vileika became an integral part of our experiences. Among them were Yacub, the Kudowitzky brothers Leibel and Boruch, their brother-in-law Kviatek, and Bonchak. I struck up an immediate friendship with red-haired, blue-eyed, freckle-faced Yacub. He was an electrician by profession. Yacub had an air of confidence and decisiveness about him, which made him stand out as a leader. Boruch was the older of the Kudowitzky brothers. He was short, wide-shouldered, with dark hair and eyes, and a hook nose. He was very smart and religious, and constantly quoted from the bible. Leibel was tall, blond with blue eyes, strong, and very much under the influence of his brother. They had both been butchers before the war. Kviatek was short, thin, stooped and dark-skinned. He was a whiner and complainer. Bonchak was a tailor and was tall, fair, thin, energetic, and strong.

Several groups of partisans came into the Zazierie woods; our aim was to be accepted into their units. These groups consisted mainly of Russian officers and soldiers who had escaped from German prison camps. We didn't know whether there were any Jews among them.

Our group went from one commander to another, but their reply was always the same. No acceptance without weapons. And there was no way we could get any. We didn't know any farmers from whom we could get a few rifles, and barehanded it would have been insane and futile to try to ambush a German patrol and get their arms. We had to come up with a better way.

Finally, in June, Commander Podolny of the "Istrebitel" (Destroyer) unit, agreed to send us on a trial mission. If we succeeded, we would be accepted by him. We didn't know then that he was a Russian Jew. Twelve of us were selected to go, including Yacub, Musio and me, Shimon and Riva, and the Kudowitskys. Yacub was made the leader.

The mission was to infiltrate the German garrison in Kurzeniec and to burn a factory which produced wooden rifle butts. I dreaded returning to the town where I had spent the longest and worst day of my life. We were also to cut the telephone poles between Kurzeniec and Vileika. Commander Podolny promised to provide us weapons for the mission.

We came up with a detailed plan and just before we set out we got our promised arms, if you could call them that. Yacub was given a revolver with one bullet. Leibel and I each got a German hand grenade. That was all. With those weapons we were expected to outfight the two hundred Germans and fifty local policemen stationed in Kurzeniec.

We were given the name of a peasant who was an informer for the partisans. When we found him, he told us of the exact location of the German guards and the police, and described their system of guarding. The German camp was situated at the end of town. The police were in the central market place. There were also sentries patrolling the streets. But, according to the informant, there were no guards inside the factory.

Taking into account the short nights in June, we planned to arrive within two miles of the town at dusk, and in the dark to skirt the town to the other side, where the factory was located. We had to go past a lumber mill which was well-lit and guarded by the Germans. We prepared cans of fuel and other flammable material to carry with us.

We arrived at the edge of the woods early and waited until 11 P.M. before heading for the town. It was a light, starry night—quite usual for that time of year. From afar we saw the first houses. We walked quickly, in single file and as silently as possible. We knew we had to cover a very long distance and be back in the safety of the woods before dawn.

We were about half a mile away from the lumber mill when suddenly searchlights streaked across the ground, flares were shot into the sky, and machine guns came alive. We threw ourselves upon the ground and lay motionless. Judging by the random direction of the searchlights and shots, we figured that the Germans didn't really know where we were, and if we were perfectly still it would be very difficult for them to locate us. We lay there for about two hours. Occasionally the lights circled and machine guns spurted their staccato outbursts. Finally all was still again. But by that time it was about 2 A.M. and dawn wasn't far away. It left us no time to accomplish our mission and we decided to return to the nearest woods.

About two miles within the forest we lay down to sleep, taking turns guarding. We decided to try to fulfill the mission on the following night.

As we were working out the details of a new plan, several of the men vehemently objected to trying again. They felt it was not only suicidal, but worse still, might get us caught alive. They claimed that even if we managed to arrive at the factory and set fire to it, we would still have to take the same route around the town, passing a main road and coming near the lumber mill. At these dangerous spots our route of retreat could easily be cut off, leaving us surrounded by Germans. We did not even have enough ammunition to kill ourselves.

Yacub and I insisted on going. We felt that at this point we should not back out. Musio wanted to join me, but I still remembered how his legs gave out on him the last time we went to Kurzeniec, and talked him out of coming. We asked for volunteers, planning to go alone if no one else offered. Shimon Zimmerman and two other men from Kurzeniec joined us. The five of us set off.

The remaining seven, including Musio, were to complete the other part of the mission by cutting down the telephone poles as soon as they saw the factory in flames. If we hadn't succeeded in burning the factory by 3 A.M., they would then begin to cut down the poles anyway. They had one grenade among them. We planned a meeting place in the woods after the mission.

We left the forest at dusk. It was dark when we arrived near the lumber mill. This time we crawled very cautiously and aroused no suspicions. We crossed the field and the main road quickly and safely. At the outskirts of town we removed our shoes as an extra precaution. Shimon knew the way very well and led us straight to the factory yard. We silently helped each other over the wall. The factory was a long and narrow wooden building stretching all the way to the main street, which was constantly guarded by German patrols. A row of houses stood along each side of the yard.

So far no one was aware of our presence. Shimon, armed with a stick shaped to look like a rifle, stood guard in the yard. He was to warn us in case of danger. We managed to pry open a window. Then, carrying rags, cans of kerosene and matches, we began to climb in.

Yacub went in first. I was sitting on the sill, prepared to jump in, when a piercing shriek shattered the silence. "Bandits! Bandits!" The sound of breaking glass.

The intensity of my fear—being right in the middle of a German garrison—left my arms and legs limp. My first impulse was to run away. I was sure that within the next few minutes we would be in German hands.

Yacub was the first to react. He dashed toward the voice, breaking through doors as he rushed from hall to hall. Seeing Yacub run, I jumped inside, holding firmly on to my grenade, and ran after him. I could clearly see him in the moonlight that was streaming in through the windows. I was just behind Yacub in the last hall when I saw him stumble and spin around. A man standing at the door had hit him with a club. I swung my grenade and hit the man over the head. The long handle of the German grenade gave me leverage and was perfect for this kind of blow. Yacub meantime regained his balance, grabbed the man from behind and got hold of his throat. The watchman was a large, strong man and tried to fight us off. Yacub stuck his revolver to the man's temple and said firmly, "We are not bandits. We are partisans. If you don't stop yelling we shall kill you."

The man instantly stopped resisting and pleaded, "I am only the night watchman. Please don't kill me." Yacub began dragging him back the way we came, all the while holding the revolver to his head.

I raced back to the other men, calling, "Come in and burn the building."

They jumped in, spread the rags along the wooden walls of the first hall, and poured the kerosene over them. I grabbed one of the cans and started splashing fuel on the walls. Meanwhile Yacub had dragged the watchman to that hall. When the watchman realized what we were about to do, he tried to shout again, but Yacub silenced him.

The fire we lit began to spread with incredible speed. The other men were already outside when I jumped out through the smoke-filled window. Thinking I was the last one out, I began running to safety. Suddenly I realized that Yacub wasn't there with us. I heard boots running and gunshots from the direction of the street. I ran back to the window. In the middle of the burning hall stood Yacub in his bare feet, his red hair in wild disarray, his shirt torn, still holding the watchman by the throat and aiming the revolver at his head.

I yelled, "Yacub, run! Everything is burning! Leave him! We are retreating! Run!"

Yacub shoved the watchman aside and sprang out through the burning window frame. He got slightly burned, but his clothes did not catch fire.

We rushed to the fields, retrieved our shoes and joined the other three men. We ran back the way we had come. Glancing back we saw the flames rising and spreading.

Gunshots, machine-gun fire, and flares were flying in all directions. Each time a flare lit the sky, we threw ourselves to the ground. Counting on the chaos around us, we ran across the main road, not far from the lumber mill. We hoped to be safely back in the woods by the time the Germans figured out what had happened.

In the forest we stopped running, put on our shoes and compared notes. Shimon told us that when the watchman started shouting, people in the nearby houses began peeking out through their windows, asking what had happened. Shimon told them, "Don't go out, don't open your windows. We are partisans. If you disobey, we shall shoot you." They quickly barred their windows.

Our other group was already at the appointed meeting place when we arrived. They had managed to reach the main road, then separated into pairs. When they saw the flames and heard the shots, they started to saw the telephone poles. Each pair destroyed two or three poles and then ran back into the woods.

It was getting light. We hid in the woods for the rest of the day. Later we heard people moving by cart nearby. When they began shooting, we figured they were Germans. We ran deeper into the woods and lay there camouflaged.

The following night Yacub, Shimon, and I went to a peasant loyal to the partisans, whom Shimon knew. He lived close to Kurzeniec. Shimon went into the house. We waited outside. A short while later Shimon came out with some bread. Back in the woods he told us a most incredible story.

The peasant told Shimon that the night before hundreds of partisans attacked Kurzeniec. The factory and part of the town were burned down. The Germans, seeing such a force, hid in their bunkers and fought fiercely from there. The fire spread rapidly because nobody dared to leave their houses or posts to put it out. The night watchman, who survived, had jumped out of the burning factory and testified that he was attacked by a large group of partisans. Nobody understood why a revolver was held to his head and yet he wasn't killed. If they had known that Yacub was saving the only bullet in his revolver for himself if necessary!

For me, this was the turning point in the war. For the first time in three years, instead of constantly being on the run, or hiding underground trying to survive, I had actually participated in an attack on the German war machine. This was the beginning of my revenge.

After a day of rest, we marched back in high spirits to the partisan camp. Uplifted by our success, expecting praise, certain that now we would be accepted as full-fledged fighters, we came to the headquarters of "Istrebitel."

Yacub went in to see Commander Podolny to brief him on the success of our mission. Within minutes he returned, accompanied by a different officer and several armed partisans. Our grenade and revolver were immediately taken away and we were given a lecture. The officer reprimanded us harshly. Though we had accomplished the mission, we had not acted according to orders. He said we were supposed to burn the factory, and not part of the town as well. It was reckless of us, and could be construed as "counter-revolutionary." He would be justified in shooting us, but as we did destroy the factory and cut the telephone lines, he would merely send us away.

We asked to speak to Commander Podolny and were told that he was not around. We tried to explain that we did not set fire to the homes, only to the factory. The fire had spread to the adjoining wooden buildings because the Germans and the local people did not come out to put out the flames. Had he really expected us to stay and put out the fire? The officer was annoyed that we dared to argue. He aimed his machine gun at us, as did all the partisans with him. He ordered us out of his sight before he changed his mind about not shooting us.

Bitterly disappointed and discouraged, we left. We later found out that this officer refused to have any Jews in his unit. At Podolny's request he had agreed to send us on the mission, certain that we would not dare go out on such a suicidal operation. This was to serve as further proof of his claim that Jews were cowards.

We returned to the camp in the forest of Zazierie and settled back into our routine. We stayed there for about a month. Some nights the men went to the villages to gather food. Hannale and Riva stayed in the camp and cooked.

One night five of us were returning from a village with sacks of potatoes. Hardly able to drag my load, I could never figure out how short and wiry Kviatek was able to carry more than I. We were exhausted but still going quite fast. Kviatek and I brought up the rear. I heard snoring. I looked around to see where the sound came from and realized that Kviatek was walking with his eyes closed, asleep and snoring. I called his name. He jerked his eyes open and asked, "What happened?" I told him, "You were asleep. You could trip and fall and hurt yourself." He said, "Oh, that's nothing. It was just a snooze. I always do it."

One day, a commander of a specgruppa partisan unit passed through our area. He came to our camp and said he needed guides who were familiar with the countryside to lead his unit on its missions. A "specgruppa" was a small unit created for specific purposes. The mission of this particular group was to acquire weapons from the local population. It was known that the peasants hid weapons which they had collected from retreating or killed Soviet soldiers in 1941. Because Shimon, Musio, and I were from this area, we were chosen. We were warned that this was a temporary assignment. Upon completion of the mission we would return to our camp and the specgruppa would go on its way.

This was the first time that I would be going into the villages with fully armed, experienced partisans. They were Russians, mostly ex-military men. I was with a group of fifteen, led by Suvorov, a short, stocky, bright, and ingenious man. He always seemed cheerful, but he had a sadistic streak in him.

Our first assignment was to acquire food. The accepted, though not popular, means of acquiring provisions from the peasants and villagers was called "zagatovka." Though sometimes simply requesting food was enough, often more forceful coercion was required. We would go from house to house getting potatoes, bread, butter, and lard. We could only carry hard-boiled eggs. I saw Suvorov and the other men, reluctant to leave anything behind, crack open fresh raw eggs and gulp them down. I was taught the most efficient way to make a small hole in the shell and suck out the contents. On the first night, overwhelmed by the abundance of food, I swallowed over twenty raw eggs. In one house I found and confiscated a basket with forty hard-boiled eggs.

On the way back to the specgruppa base, sitting down to rest toward morning, Suvorov asked me what was in the basket. Seeing the eggs, he grinned and said, "Oh, good. Let's have breakfast." He took out a pound of butter that he had confiscated, shelled and buttered the eggs and we began to eat. I barely managed to eat two eggs, having eaten twenty raw ones earlier. But Suvorov happily finished the remaining thirty-eight, and the butter! Satisfied, he was ready to go on.

Our system of zagatovka quickly became more sophisticated. When we entered a village, two partisans guarded at both ends. The rest of us, in groups of four, would go from door to door. I usually ended up with Suvorov and got to know the tricks he used.

We would start the evening with a good meal by first trying to find a well-to-do farmhouse and asking for food. Not wishing to make threats, Suvorov would ask politely. When it was served, he would ask for vodka. If he was not satisfied with what we got, he would take out his grenade and place it on the table. The frightened housewife would ask him to take the "bomb" away, and he would say in his most charming manner, "It doesn't want to leave the table. It wants to eat some good food and to drink vodka." Then we would all leave the table and walk toward the door. The poor woman, expecting the "bomb" to go off at any moment, would rush to bring us anything we wished for. We would agree to sit down to a good meal and Suvorov would reattach the grenade on his belt.

We asked for weapons at every house. The farmers usually denied having any. Suvorov would then demand to know which other farmers had weapons and where they were concealed. If he was not told, he threatened to confiscate everything the farmer had. It usually worked. We would be given names, but rarely told where the weapons were hidden.

We would then go to the mentioned peasants and demand their arms. Suvorov would shed his charming ways and turn into a roaring beast. He threatened to shoot them, to burn them, to take away their possessions, if they didn't hand over their weapons at once. If they still denied having any, he went to extremes. He would grab the peasant by the ear and as though aiming at his head, would shoot a bullet through his earlobe. When the poor man recovered from the shock and discovered that he was still alive, Suvorov would apologize that he had missed his mark and promised to do better with the next shot if the farmer didn't comply with his demand. By that time the peasant was usually ready to give up all his firearms.

In one case, all of us were sure the peasant was hiding his weapons, but none of our tactics worked. Calmly and stubbornly the farmer said, "Go ahead, kill me. I have no weapons to give you." Suvorov and another partisan led the man outside and ordered him to dig his own grave. We were told to keep his wife and children at the window to watch.

Suvorov positioned the peasant to face the grave and shot. The peasant fell in. Suvorov then called, "Bring out the woman, it's her turn now."

With that the woman broke down. She tearfully pleaded for her life and said she knew where the weapons were hidden. She led us to the cache. Under a pile of hay were two rifles which we confiscated. Reentering the house, the poor woman almost fainted upon seeing her husband sitting at the table. From the window the wife couldn't have seen that Suvorov had shot between the farmer's legs and pushed him into the grave.

Another time, a supporter of the partisans pointed out the house of a peasant who had been seen at an adjacent town entering the German police station on his way to the market. The suspicion that the peasant was a spy was strengthened by the fact that he attended church, which was against the Soviet government's principles. He had to be working for the Germans.

Going toward that peasant's house, Suvorov turned to me and said, "I am sure he is a spy. Let's kill him."

I asked, "How can you be so sure? Maybe the other peasant wanted him dead for his own personal reasons. Let's hear what he has to say." Suvorov said, "If he is dead then for sure he won't be a spy." After seeing my shock at this reasoning, he added, "But okay. Let's beat a confession out of him."

We went into the house and ordered the peasant to remove his pants and to lie on the table. Then with a long metal rifle cleaner Suvorov began to whip the man's behind.

The farmer screamed in pain, "Why are you beating me?" Suvorov hollered back, "What were you doing in town?"

The farmer at last admitted that he had gone to the police station to request a permit to visit a relative in another village. He swore that he was not a spy and had not given the Germans any information. He sounded convincing. Suvorov gave him another twenty lashes to make sure he would remember never to go to the police station again or else he would be shot.

During the time I was part of the specgruppa we managed to accumulate quite a substantial cache of weapons. In appreciation of our services Suvorov gave me a Russian rifle from World War I, without a butt but with several bullets. After cleaning it, and having a carpenter make me a new butt, I had a real working rifle. Musio received a rifle with a sawed-off barrel.

A rifle in the partisans was more than the most important possession one could have—it was a trusted friend, never to be let out of sight. A rifle could be the difference between life and a defenseless death. The only problem with my rifle was that it sometimes failed to eject the bullet case after a shot, and I had to stop to knock it out with the rifle cleaner before I could use the rifle again.

Our mission with the group was over. We parted warmly from Suvorov and the rest of the specgruppa, and returned to our comrades in the forest of Zazierie.

12

IN THE JEWISH OTRIAD

July–September 19, 1943

In the beginning of July, rumors circulated that in the puszcza adjacent to Lake Naroch a Jewish unit was being formed as part of the brigade of a Colonel Markov. Yacub and Shimon went to check the validity of the rumor, and to see whether we could possibly join them.

Colonel Markov, a non-Jew married to a Jewish woman, was one of the leaders of the partisan brigades formed in the beginning of 1943 in that area. Before the war he had been a teacher in Svenciany, a Polish town which was occupied by the Germans. In 1941, shortly after the occupation, all the intelligentsia, especially the teachers, were arrested. Markov escaped to the woods with several of his friends and colleagues. They managed to ambush the car of the Gebietskommissar of Svenciany. They killed him, his driver, and his adjutant and took their weapons. The Germans killed five hundred innocent citizens in retaliation.

Markov was joined by several escaped Soviet prisoners and communist officials from the surrounding villages and towns, and organized one of the first partisan otriads. An "otriad" was a single partisan unit. Gradually, young local peasants who wanted to avoid being taken into labor camps joined him too. As more and more people became part of Markov's fighting force, he reorganized them into several otriads, which were formed into a brigade. By the middle of 1943 he already had about a thousand partisans under his command. All the various units which had been formed by then were controlled by the partisan high command in Moscow. For his achievements Markov was given the rank of full colonel.

Officers with radio equipment were parachuted from Moscow or smuggled through frontlines to organize additional otriads and to coordinate operations. Each otriad was a separate fighting force of about eighty to a hundred and fifty people, with its own commander, a chief political officer called a commissar, a chief of staff, and platoon leaders. The bases of the otriads were miles apart.

Markov's brigade had a very poor supply of arms, consisting mostly of rifles and machine guns from World War I, hardly any heavy artillery and very few new submachine guns and automatic rifles.

Markov was personally known to a number of the leaders of the FPO, a Jewish fighting organization within the ghetto of Vilna. They contacted him through messengers and it was agreed that a group of armed Jews would escape from the Vilna ghetto and join Markov's brigade. Glazman, one of the leaders of the FPO, was the first to arrive with his group at Markov's headquarters. Markov agreed to form a separate Jewish otriad which he named "Miest" (Revenge), and make Butenias, a Lithuanian Jew, its commander. Glazman became the chief of staff, and Bomka, a Russian Jew, would be one of the platoon leaders. Shurka Bogen, an artist by profession, who came from the Vilna ghetto, also became a platoon leader.

Such was the setup that Yacub and Shimon found when they reached the newly-forming otriad. The unit was greatly in need of partisans with rifles who were familiar with the woods and the puszcza. Glazman gladly accepted Yacub and Shimon, and Musio and me with our rifles. As for the rest of our group, he agreed to take only those young men who knew the area.

Yacub returned to our base in Zazierie equipped with a horse and cart which he had acquired in some mysterious way. We packed our belongings and that night all of us departed for the Miest base in the puszcza.

We decided to smuggle in the girls and the older members of the group. Just outside the base Shimon had all those who would not be considered welcome get off the cart and he later sneaked them in unobtrusively. Musio and I hid our rifles in the cart, not knowing whether Commander Butenias would try to take them away from us. We drove with Yacub right through the main entrance to the base.

We were told to build ourselves a zemlianka and become a part of Bomka's platoon. When we saw that there were other partisans with rifles and Bomka told us that we could keep ours, we took them from hiding and stored them in our newly built zemlianka. Only about a third of the partisans had arms.

Not only was I now a true partisan with a rifle, but in a Jewish otriad, and appropriately named "Revenge" as well! I was proud and in great spirits.

One of the first and essential missions of each otriad was to acquire provisions. Because I had a rifle I was given the job of going to the nearby villages at night to replenish our supplies. Only three out of every group of ten going on a zagatovka had arms, both to fight off the Germans if necessary, and to scare the peasants if they did not cooperate with us.

The villagers closer to our woods were supportive of the partisans, though not necessarily by choice. Each otriad was allocated a specific area, and could only get food in the villages within those limits. In our designated area we would approach the village leader with a list of the supplies we needed. It was up to him to decide how much each villager was to give, and he accompanied us on our rounds. We then requisitioned carts and horses, loaded our supplies, and the owners of the carts drove us back to the edge of the woods. The peasants had to wait there while we took the wagons to our camp to unload, because the sites of the bases had to be kept secret. Then all the carts and horses were tied together and returned to their owners.

Further away, nearer to the German garrisons, the population was more loyal to the Germans, also not necessarily by choice. There, because it was not considered under partisan jurisdiction and not bound by any self-imposed partisan restrictions, any otriad was free to go on a zagatovka. Thus, in the villages near the German garrisons our pattern was different. A scouting patrol had to check that the area was clear of Germans and local police, then leave a small group on guard at both ends of the village. Most of the villages were built along one main road. Two groups, one starting at each end, went from house to house collecting food, clothes, and occasional livestock. The peasants protested, argued, pleaded, but were afraid to resist.

Additional groups of Jewish fighters from the ghetto in Vilna began to arrive at our base. One such group started out with twenty-five people, was caught in a German ambush, and only one person managed to survive. Our otriad increased in manpower but not in rifles or machine guns. Most of the people arriving from the ghetto carried handguns, which were considered personal defense arms, and not arms with which the otriad could face the Germans. We now had about a hundred and fifty Jews in our otriad, roughly ninety men and sixty women. We had some twenty rifles, several handguns, and a couple of submachine guns.

Markov's brigade had grown to six otriads, including ours, scattered throughout the puszcza. A special reconnaissance and scouting unit, called "razviedka" in Russian, was created as part of the headquarters of the brigade. It consisted of small groups of men stationed near the German garrisons around the puszcza. Their job was to immediately notify the brigade headquarters of all German movements in the vicinity, and to develop a network to spy on the Germans, which would help to guess their intentions.

One day the commander of the razviedka arrived on horseback and asked for people familiar with the Vileika area. Several men stepped forward and, after asking some questions, he chose Yacub, gave him a horse and a modern rifle, and off they went. Yacub was soon put in charge of the razviedka in the Vileika area, which contained the largest of the German garrisons. Stories of his exploits and his bravery became well known.

We had our contacts and informers in every village, even near the German garrisons. They were the first ones we approached when we arrived at night. Whenever a small group of Germans left the garrison we were immediately alerted and rushed to lay ambush. We succeeded in many cases to kill the Germans, and they gradually became reluctant to leave the safety of their garrison unless they were in large groups.

Several of the local police who had worked for the Germans saw the change in the tide of war and joined the partisans, bringing their weapons with them. They were gladly received in Markov's brigade, their loyalty unquestioned and all their past cruelties forgotten.

In August, one of the first successful missions by our otriad was accomplished by Glazman and six other partisans. They were gone for about two weeks, far from the puszcza, and blew up a German train. They had one confrontation with the Germans in which fire was exchanged, but they managed to return safely to our base.

As part of Markov's brigade, our otriad occasionally managed to get some more rifles. Since I was almost always included in these missions, Bomka, our platoon leader, allowed me to exchange my rifle for a newer and more reliable one. Besides being better equipped, the rifle also added to my self-esteem and to my stature as a partisan.

One night Glazman lined up all the armed men and led us to headquarters. There were other units assembled, and we were told that we were going to attack a German garrison stationed in Miadziol, a little town near the forest. The razviedka estimated that there were about three hundred Germans there. The plan was to reach the edge of the forest by the following evening and then attack the Germans at night. There were about four hundred of us armed partisans traveling on horseback, in carts, and on foot. I was one of those who had to walk.

We arrived near Miadziol as planned and rested up in the forest before continuing on. When darkness fell, we spread out and headed toward the town. Markov himself led the attack. When the order came, I ran forward, my rifle ready. The Germans started shooting at us with machine guns and rifles from within their bunkers.

We continued running until we reached the first houses and then opened fire. When we reached the police station at the main square, the policemen opened fire on us. We swept into the station and overpowered them, killing them all and taking their guns. Meanwhile the Germans stayed hidden in their bunkers and shot randomly from there. They didn't come out to attack us, so we left them there.

We were ordered to retreat and returned to the woods at dawn.

In addition to the arms, we managed to bring back clothing, food, shoes, and cooking utensils, much of which we could no longer get in the villages closer to our base.

Our casualties were two killed and several wounded. This first big partisan operation against a German garrison was considered a great success. We had proven to the local population that we were strong and that the Germans were afraid of us.

Several weeks later we heard from the razviedka that about fifty Germans had arrived at a nearby village and were confiscating the livestock. We immediately got our orders. Twenty-five from our otriad and twenty-five from another otriad united and ran to set up an ambush on the road the Germans would be using to return to their base. We chose a hill covered with trees and positioned our two machine guns on either side of the road. Camouflaged with leaves, we lay in wait.

I was exhausted, both emotionally and physically. The constant tension and fear had begun to take its toll. But the moment I spotted the Germans, the sense of danger put my entire being on alert. I clutched my rifle and focused my eyes to see every detail. Horses and carts with Germans atop, cows tied to the carts, Germans on bicycles in front and behind.

We were lying about fifteen feet apart. Unaware of our presence, the Germans drew nearer. I could hear them talking and laughing and told myself, "I've got to keep calm. I must aim at a German uniform and think of the revenge I promised myself."

After some of the Germans had already passed by me, our commander gave the order to fire, and he shot first. I pulled my trigger. Without thinking any more, I kept firing at any moving object. The Germans fled in all directions. We later found five dead. We took their weapons, the carts, the cows, and everything that was left behind, and returned to our woods.

When we were back in the forest we heard a tank coming from afar. This was probably a reinforcement for the German column we had ambushed. There were shots from the tank into the forest, but no attempt was made to enter. The Germans left the area at nightfall.

On another occasion we received orders to cut telephone poles and block off certain roads. Twenty partisans set out. It took us two

days to reach our destination. We chose a two-mile stretch of the
road that cut through the woods. Breaking up into two groups, we
started chopping down trees, so that they fell across the road. We
also set up ambushes with two machine guns. Two scouts on horseback on the lookout brought back orders and information. With my
rifle slung on my back I began to saw a tree with another guy. We
worked as quickly as we could, and I was drenched in sweat. The
noise of crashing trees sounded like cannon shots and I expected
Germans to appear at any moment. Working all night, we also cut
telephone poles and quickly returned to our base without encoun-
tering any Germans. We heard that it took the Germans two whole
days to clear up the mess we had created and to reopen the road.

Another mission was to burn wooden bridges on the main road.
We took cartloads of very dry hay, which we emptied under the
bridges and then ignited.

Some of the women participated in these operations. The rest
stayed in camp and took care of the other needs by cooking, wash-
ing, mending, and helping in any way they could. We had three
meals a day—pea soup and potatoes, and tiny portions of meat.

The zemlianka in which our otriad lived were built partly in the
ground and partly on top of the ground. Each hut accommodated
between thirty and fifty people. Bunks were built along the walls
and a stove stood at one end. It was hot and stuffy inside. We all
slept close together, lying on straw, covering ourselves with coats
and rags. Some of the zemlianki were for women only.

In our eternal fight against lice we built a version of a sauna. It
was a wooden structure with a door that could be firmly closed.
Large stones were heated from beneath until they were red hot. We
would go into it in groups of ten, close the door, and pour cold water
on the hot stones, creating steam. The higher we stood the hotter
the steam was. I tried to stand high up for as long as I could tolerate it, to be certain that my lice were cooked. I sometimes wondered
if I would be cooked before the lice. Part of the standard equipment
in the steambath was twigs. We would hold them high up to get
them really hot and then thrash each other with them. Painful as it
was, we had the feeling that this was opening our pores and cleans-
ing our skin. Coming out of the steam bath we were a sight to be-
hold. The grime combined with the ashes from the stones created

dark streaks on our red bodies. We would then run outside and rinse our bodies in cold water. This was a weekly ritual.

As mentioned, most of the members of our otriad were from the ghetto in Vilna. We heard terrible stories of what they had survived, and of the infamous Ponari, where the Jews of the ghetto were shot and buried in mass graves.

Musio and I developed a special friendship with a fellow named Moshe Markh. Somewhat older than Musio, he became like a brother to us. This short, bespectacled, balding man was resourceful, optimistic and had a rare sense of humor. He was highly intelligent and had been active in the Zionist Organization in the ghetto. He slept next to us, and we shared everything. Though we were in the same unit, however, we did not always participate in the same operations.

Our otriad successfully accomplished many missions. But being a Jewish otriad, we encountered anti-Semitism from the other units. There were incidents when our partisans were attacked by members of the other otriads, who tried to forcibly take away our weapons. They believed that since Jews didn't know how to fight anyway, we should give our arms to them. Chief of Staff Glazman complained to Colonel Markov, who replied, "Don't ever give up your weapons. Kill them or be killed, but never give up your arms to anybody." The veterans among us knew this rule. Some of the newcomers, however, though outraged, were intimidated and gave up their arms when ordered to do so.

Finally, Colonel Markov had to dismantle the Jewish otriad when he got instructions from the political head of the Bieloruss Communist Party. The explanation was that a separate Jewish otriad increased anti-Semitism, plus Jews were not officially recognized as an ethnic entity in the Soviet Union.

So two months after our otriad was formed, our commander assembled us all. Colonel Markov arrived on horseback with several of his aides. We were separated into groups: those with rifles; those with handguns; those unarmed; women; and the elderly. Moshe Markh had to go with the unarmed men. Personal relationships did not influence the fluidity with which groups were organized and dismantled. People were constantly being shifted around, parting, and reuniting. Though we were somewhat used to it by now, it was still very difficult to be separated from our friends. We had no way of knowing whether our separation from Markh was permanent, or whether our paths would cross again.

Our Commander Butenias left us. He had been sent to Lithuania to organize a Lithuanian partisan group. Chief of Staff Glazman was also absent, as he had left with a group of partisans to go to Vilna to bring more people out of the ghetto. So Platoon Leader Bomka was in charge of the otriad. Markov told us that he had decided to merge our otriad with a non-Jewish one. The new name would be Komsomolski otriad. Our new commander would be Volodka. He was one of the original friends with whom Markov had gone into the woods. A new commissar and chief of staff had already been appointed.

Those without weapons, along with the women, and the elderly, would work for the partisans in a newly formed support group. The partisans would supply them with food and other necessities.

At this point, a new commissar arrived with seventy partisans, only some of whom were armed. The new commissar and chief of staff were unknown to us. Judging from the medals they wore on their uniforms, they seemed to be Soviet military men.

Each one of us was called in separately to Markov and Volodka, and asked a few questions about where he had come from, how long he had been a partisan, and other pertinent information. His weapon was then inspected, and he was assigned to a zemlianka.

The eighty from our otriad who were picked for the new unit were divided into three platoons. Forty of them had handguns only. I had my rifle, and Musio had his sawed-off shotgun.

The seventy Russians and Belorussians who had arrived with the commissar were also divided into three platoons. When we got to know them better we found out that most of them were local Belorussians and some were former policemen who had been working for the Germans. Who knew if there were any spies among them?

Bomka was made commander of the razviedka. New platoon leaders were also selected. Shurka Bogen, the artist, who knew Markov from before the war, remained the only Jewish platoon leader. Even in the woods he managed to find the opportunities to sketch the images of partisans. The Belorussian partisans were given all of the command positions.

The commander of each otriad had absolute power over his people. He was the only judge. Discipline was stringent, and no one had the right to question orders. Disobeying an order was punishable by death.

An episode that took place in our new otriad several days later reconfirmed this absolute power. A Belorussian in charge of the guards accused two Jewish partisans of dozing while on sentry duty. They were immediately arrested, their weapons confiscated, and they were brought on trial before Commander Volodka. They denied the charge, but of course Volodka believed the sentry commander. They were sentenced to death and within ten minutes they were shot.

A week later Volodka ordered everybody, which really meant the Jews, to turn in all their valuables, such as gold, watches, and money, so that he could buy more weapons for the otriad. We were called to his headquarters one by one and had to enter unarmed. There, under the watchful eye of Volodka and to the accompaniment of verbal anti-Semitic attacks, we were searched and stripped of anything that was considered of any value. This felt more like being searched by Germans than by fellow partisans. Musio and I had nothing they could take, but the whole procedure was humiliating and infuriated us. Individually, none of us could do anything because any form of resistance would be called counter-revolutionary behavior by Volodka and punished by death.

Only on political issues did the commissar have the power to overrule the commander. Since anti-Semitism was definitely a political matter, we complained to the commissar about this disgraceful behavior. He just laughed and said, "We are collecting all this to buy arms for you. Knowing you would not willingly give up your possessions we had to take them by force."

The Jews never got the promised arms, and the valuables went to Volodka and his gang, of which the commissar was a part.

Several days later Volodka issued an order that all those with handguns, meaning the Jews from Vilna who had recently arrived, were to turn in their arms at his headquarters. In return they would get rifles. We advised them not to believe Volodka's promises. Some of them listened and hid their guns. The rest gave in their handguns and got nothing in return. After the war I found out that Volodka was court-martialed for these incidents.

The unarmed Jews from the previous "Miest" otriad, including Markh, were transferred to the other side of the base and were forbidden to come to our side. We were not allowed to go to them either. They were told that they could join our otriad as soon as more arms were available

Musio's shotgun stopped functioning and he gave it to a blacksmith in an adjacent village for repair.

Mor, a man from Vilna who had hidden his handgun and was not accepted in the new otriad, asked platoon leader Shurka, whom he knew from before, to intervene on his behalf. Shurka took Mor's handgun and went to Volodka, showed it to him and asked permission to take Mor into the unit. Volodka took the handgun into his hands, admired it, and said, "I shall see," and started to walk away with it. Shurka jumped toward him and tried to wrestle the handgun from Volodka. A shot rang out in the scuffle. Volodka fell, slightly wounded in his side. Shurka was immediately arrested by the chief of staff. We saw Shurka being led away under heavy guard to the prison zemlianka. Shurka—tall, blond, with a slight mustache—walked fearlessly and proudly, with the dignity of a leader. Several hours later, after Volodka's superficial wound had been treated, Shurka was brought before him. The chief of staff asked Volodka for permission to execute Shurka.

Shurka said, "Volodka, if you were right to take away Mor's handgun, I should be shot with this very same gun."

Volodka was silent for a few moments and then said softly, "Let him live."

13

THE OBLAVA

September 20–Mid-October, 1943

We heard that the Germans were gathering forces all around the puszcza, preparing for an oblava. Anybody they caught would immediately be shot. The oblava, which could go on for two or three weeks, was the action most dreaded by the partisans. Rumors circulated that the Germans were going to attack from Hatovici, a nearby village. We were ordered to be ready to move out at short notice, carrying as little as possible, and to bury the rest of our possessions in pits.

The hundred and twenty Jews who were separated from us were still not allowed to join us, but some of them managed to bribe their way back into our otriad.

By the afternoon of September 26 we were all ready to depart. Most of the other otriads had already left their bases. But Volodka's wife was about to give birth, and he wouldn't give the order to leave until the baby was born. Meanwhile we set up ambushes along the roads from Hatovici. Only a handful of partisans remained in camp with Volodka and his pregnant wife.

I and another partisan were sent to scout the area and hurried toward Hatovici, but before reaching the village we met several peasants running away. They told us that a very great German force was already in their village, with tanks, light artillery, and dogs. The Germans were grabbing all the cows, horses, and young men and taking them away in trucks.

We ran back to Volodka with this information. He saw no alternative but to retreat, and canceled the ambush. We were sent to brigade headquarters with the news.

Night was falling. We had to cross swamps in order to reach the headquarters. Several hours later, after losing our way, we finally arrived, only to see that something was amiss. There were no sentries. Nobody stopped us. We went to the bunkers of the headquarters and realized that the base was deserted. Some oil lamps were still burning, indicating that the people had only recently fled.

We set out back to our otriad. We arrived at midnight and the otriad was still there. It was pitch dark. We went directly to report to Volodka. He indicated which zemlianka I was to go to and await further orders. The Belorussian partisan who had been with me was sent to a different one. On the way I heard movement and asked, "Who's there?" I was surprised to hear a familiar voice. Musio came out from behind the trees and asked what happened. Where had I been? I told him. He said that when Volodka canceled the ambush he divided the otriad into groups—those with weapons and those without. The twenty partisans who had rifles were told to go into a specific zemlianka. Musio was excluded because his shotgun had still not been returned from repair. The rest were ordered to leave the base and to fend for themselves.

I took Musio's hand and we went toward the zemlianka where I had been sent. Sentries standing guard let us in. We found about twenty Jewish partisans with rifles. We sat there waiting for Volodka's wife to give birth. At about 4 A.M. she delivered a baby girl. We immediately got orders to move.

Volodka and several scouts rode on horseback. His wife and the newborn infant were in a wagon. The rest of us, including the Belorussian partisans, walked. Some of the Jewish partisans who were forbidden to join us infiltrated the group. Markh was with them. The others followed unobtrusively at a distance.

We arrived at the deserted base of the Chopayevsky otriad. Volodka again lined up all the Jews and separated the armed from the unarmed. When he tried to separate Musio and Markh from me,

I stepped forward with my rifle cocked and insisted that it belonged to all three of us. He came up to me and asked me to hand him my rifle, saying he wanted to see if it was clean. I pointed my rifle at him and said, "Colonel Markov told us never to give up our weapons to anybody. If you want my rifle, you must kill me first."

My face and manner made him pause. His angry face took on a smile and he said, "Fine, fine. You and your brother can both stay. But your cousin has to go." Markh told me to leave it at that, and left.

Volodka then tried to take away a rifle from an older man named Levitan, and a machine gun belonging to his son. These arms were meant to be given to several Belorussian partisans who were unarmed. Levitan and his son stood their ground and this time we were all ready to defend them. Seeing this, Volodka gave in.

Meanwhile, the group of Jews who had been separated from us and were following caught up and tried to enter the camp. Volodka shouted at them and when they refused to leave, took his machine gun and shot over their heads. He ordered the Bieloruss guards to shoot if the Jews came near again. The Germans had already entered the forest but Volodka was still busy with his plan to detach himself and his men from the Jewish contingent.

I was put on guard duty and when I returned I couldn't find Musio in our platoon. Asking around, I found out that he had been transferred elsewhere. Suddenly the scouts came riding up, shouting that the Germans were near, coming in great force. We were ordered to move out immediately and in five minutes were ready to leave. Musio was still nowhere to be found. I asked where he was, and the platoon leader said he was in the rear of the column.

Three scouts led the way, then came the platoons, the commanders on horseback, and Volodka's wife and child in the wagon.

We traveled quickly. The scouts knew the way and tried to lead us out of the woods before the Germans could completely surround the forest. In the afternoon we reached some swamps and stopped for a brief rest. I kept trying to find Musio. Out of nowhere Markh suddenly appeared and quietly lay down beside me. He wanted me to know that he and a group of our friends were following our otriad, but he had no idea where Musio was. Just as silently he disappeared.

We resumed our march. It was getting dark. The three scouts

who were always about half a mile ahead of us came galloping up, gesturing wildly that there were Germans ahead. Volodka ordered us to leave everything and to silently run into the woods, away from the road. After running for half a mile we spread out, and platoon after platoon formed lines of defense, facing the road. The commanders and Volodka's family stayed at the very back.

Darkness came quickly. Hiding behind a tree I tried desperately to see what was happening. If the Germans attacked, our chances of survival would be very slim. My heart was pounding. The thought flashed through my mind that if I were to be killed now, I would at least die fighting, rifle in hand.

We lay there for half an hour. All was quiet. The Germans were evidently unaware of our presence, so we went back on the road and continued on our way, following the same route the Germans had come from. We recognized their footprints from the marks of their boots.

We marched until midnight. By that time we had spent more than twenty-four hours on the go, without food or water and with only a short rest. From afar we saw flames. Villages were burning all around. I was sent out on guard duty again. As usual, the Jews were the first ones ordered to do that. It was a very cold night, and it began to rain. After two hours I was relieved.

Exhausted, I lay down in a ditch, covered myself with my coat and instantly fell asleep. I didn't even feel the rain filling the ditch and freezing over. When I awoke at dawn, lying curled up, hugging my knees for warmth, my clothes were frozen stiff. When I tried to move, a terrible chill rushed through my body. I climbed out of the ditch and began to run around to warm up. My coat had turned to ice, so I threw it off. My teeth chattered so that for an hour I couldn't utter an intelligible word. It took a long time to completely thaw out.

We moved on. After about seven miles we noticed that six men were missing—four of them Jews. These were the sentries on guard duty, whom the officer in charge had forgotten to notify that we were moving out. Volodka ignored the matter and we pushed on until late afternoon, when we reached the large swamps of Nevieshke.

After a short rest Volodka gathered us all and told us that according to the information he had, we were surrounded by Germans. They were inside the woods in large numbers and we could not fight them in any organized manner. We had to break up into small groups, each one going in a different direction, each one responsible for his own survival. The non-Jews who were well armed went with Volodka. The Jewish partisans went in a different direction. The rest went elsewhere.

In some ways it was a relief to be away from him. We had no idea what the right decisions would be or which direction to go, but we hoped that whatever happened would be for the best. There were sixteen of us. One of the men was familiar with the swamps and knew where to find some small isles of solid ground. We decided to reach these isles and stay there throughout the oblava. I was still concerned about Musio; he wasn't at the end of the column and I still couldn't find him. There was no certainty that I would ever meet up with him again.

We moved out through the woods, parallel to the swamps, trying to reach the point closest to the isles. Two of the men went ahead to scout. A while later we heard a commotion and saw the scouts running back. They told us that they had spotted Germans on a path nearby. We dispersed and lay down and set up our defenses around our only machine gun. I heard German voices and many wagons about two hundred yards from me. But they passed without noticing us and when all was clear we went on. We understood, judging by the tracks on the ground, that a rather small group of Germans had been leading herds of cows and loaded carts. Our first impulse was to run after them and to attack them, but reason prevailed. The sounds of our attack would have alerted the other Germans in the forest. We could not afford that.

It was getting dark when we waded into the swamps. There were narrow strips of solid ground, and fallen tree trunks in the water served as bridges between the dry spots. In parts the swamps were waist-deep. One of the men, with a rope tied to his body, would cross to the next dry spot, and tie the rope to a tree. The rest of us would follow, holding on to the rope. Some parts of the swamp had solid ground under the water, but many parts were extremely treacherous. The bog was muddy and could slowly suck one in unless he was dragged out by the others. There were so many trees that the swamp looked like a forest, and finding our way in the dark made it that much more dangerous.

We moved all night, but covered very little ground. In the morning it was easier. The sun was high in the sky when we finally reached the isle we were heading for.

There we met partisans from our and other otriads, and suddenly there was Markh! He was unshaven and, with a scarf wrapped like a turban round his head, almost unrecognizable. I was delighted to see him. Unfortunately, he had no information about my brother's whereabouts.

I was so tired that nothing could keep me awake. I fell asleep where I dropped. After a short rest we began to reorganize and all the men with rifles were placed as sentries facing the direction from which we had come, which was the only approach to our isle. By then I realized how hungry I was. It had been two days since I last ate anything. At least we had water to drink. I was soaking wet and cold, but we were afraid to light a fire so drying our clothes was impossible. We heard shooting all the time and knew the Germans were still nearby.

The next day, hearing some suspicious rustling noise, we jumped up, instantly alert, and found ourselves face to face with a stray cow. What a find—a heaven-sent gift! We killed it but we still didn't dare light a fire, so we cut up the raw flesh and tried to eat it. It was like rubber. I couldn't chew through it. Even tiny pieces were difficult to swallow, but I did my best until I was no longer hungry.

Markh told me there was a Jewish family living in hiding on the other side of the isle. We went there and, following the feeble cries of an infant, we found an elderly man sitting in a squalid hut, holding the baby. He told us that his daughter had given birth two weeks ago, and after delivering the baby she disappeared and he had not seen her since. The baby was probably the contribution of one of the Soviet partisans she used to meet when she went food hunting. The old man had no food for the baby or for himself and was desperate. We gave him some of our raw meat, which was the only thing we had. It was of no use to the baby.

We left, upset and helpless, with the sound of the baby's cries following us. The baby died a few days later.

We were on that isle for five days. All of the meat from the cow had been consumed. The shots in the distance had subsided, so we decided to go out of the swamps and into the villages, to find out what was happening and to get some food.

I went with three others on this foray. We made sure to cross the worst part of the swamp in daylight, and continued on our way in the dark. We found a deserted hutor and took the few potatoes that were there. We then went on. Very cautiously we made our way to a cluster of hutors and again found no one there. Going through the woods we heard voices and hid. We crawled cautiously toward the voices and found families of Belorussian peasants sitting round a campfire. When they saw that we were armed partisans they were relieved. They told us that they had run away into the woods with some of their livestock when they heard the Germans approaching their village and had been hiding since then.

They told us that a huge force of German soldiers, with the help of Lithuanian and Latvian units under German command, had surrounded a hundred and fifty miles of the forest and, forming human chains, had combed the woods in all directions. This wasn't a hunt just for Jews. They were rounding up anyone they could catch. All the young men captured in the villages were led away, and probably sent to labor camps. All the food and livestock were confiscated. Some of the villages were then left intact, while others were burnt and all the inhabitants killed. They didn't know whether the Germans had left their village.

With this information we returned to our isle. We hoped that, satisfied with this rampage and the havoc they had caused, the Germans were gone. The first thing we did was light a fire, and Markh began to bake some potatoes. It was our first hot food in a week. I kept worrying about Musio, speculating about where he could be, and with all my heart I hoped I would find him. Just to be sure that the Germans were gone, we stayed for three more days before we headed back to the base of our otriad near the lake of Narocz, where we had camped until Volodka divided us up.

On the way we passed through two burnt villages. Even along narrow paths within the forest we found the distinctive tracks of German boots. There were discarded newspapers, chocolate wrappings and other signs of German presence all around. Small German aircraft occasionally circled overhead. We met groups of partisans, each with their own tales of survival from the oblava.

Back at our base we found total chaos, and very few people from our own otriad. Our zemlianka had been demolished by German explosives. Everything, including our "sauna," was in ruins. Everyone was inquiring about friends. Many of the missing people were known to be dead, but nobody knew anything about Musio. My morale was hitting bottom. We dug up the food we had hidden before our hasty departure. On the third day, toward evening, as I was sitting by the fire, someone shouted to me, "Hey, you, your brother is coming."

I rushed to the path and saw him dragging his legs, helping himself along with a stick. His hat was gone. We embraced and kissed, greatly relieved to be together again. By the fire, I gave him some food and then we told each other of our experiences. He spoke first.

Volodka had indeed sent him with a group of people, while I was on sentry duty, to a certain spot in the swamp, and told them to wait there. When nobody arrived, they understood that they had been sent there under false pretenses and decided to go on their own deeper into the swamps. Our friend Papa Posner and his daughter Hannale were in that group. After two days they heard the Germans very close—shots and the barking of dogs. Everybody dispersed through the woods and deeper into the swamps. The Germans gave chase and there was a hail of bullets from all different directions. Musio saw a German a few steps away and began to run. The German ran after him. For some reason he seemed to want to capture him alive. But Musio was so quick that the German fell behind. He kept shooting but Musio kept dodging behind the trees. He ran until he heard no more sounds and then he hid in the bushes.

When all was quiet, the group came together. Musio's legs refused to carry him again, and he could barely move.

After a few days of quiet, some of the people began to head back toward the base. But the Posners and a few others stayed on until Musio could walk. They shared their food with him. After several more days, with Posner dragging him, they began to move toward the base. Incidents like these were a real test of friendship. Musio gradually felt better, and by the time they arrived he could walk on his own, but he was very weak.

Many partisans and Jews had been killed during the oblava, but the exact number was not known. Every day people came straggling in, and many bodies were discovered in the forest. Some people were never found or heard of again.

There was a makeshift hospital by our base. Before the camp was evacuated, all the wounded and sick had been moved out, deeper into the forest, covered and camouflaged, and left there. When we returned we found them dead, all except one. Miraculously a Jewish youth named Avram, who had typhoid fever, survived. Hearing the Germans coming, he had gotten up and in a semiconscious state went into the swamps. His fever was raging. A week later he came back to the base, white as a ghost, but his fever had broken. With no medication, he had been cured.

We partisans began to resettle in our bases and to get back into the routine of the otriads. Volodka hadn't returned yet, but his messengers came to find out what was happening and they told us their stories. Apparently several hours after our ways parted, they stumbled on a German patrol and, in the exchange of fire, some of them were killed. The rest ran into the swamps and stayed on an isle similar to ours, not too far from us. The great Volodka, who knew the way and was so eager to get rid of us, fared worse than we did. He survived, but lost many men.

Two Jewish partisans from the Chopayevsky otriad were rumored to have betrayed fellow partisans when they were caught and tortured by the Germans. It was said they had revealed the hiding place of seven other partisans. Several days after we heard this, a man named Joel, one of the two accused, snuck into our base. His face and hair were burnt beyond recognition. His flesh was raw. Joel described the torture he had been put through by the Germans, who tried in vain to extract information about fellow partisans. First they both were beaten, then burned, bit by bit. When they lost consciousness, they were revived and the whole procedure resumed. But they revealed nothing. Then the Germans took them by car to the edge of the woods, threw them out and, aiming their rifles at them, began to shoot. They intended to leave their disfigured bodies as an example of what would happen to partisans when they were caught.

The other partisan was killed by the first volley. But Joel was not hit, and with a burst of strength jumped up and ran among the trees. His experience further convinced us of something that we had known all along. It was worse to be caught alive than to be killed.

But Colonel Markov didn't believe Joel's account, and Joel was arrested and brought to headquarters for interrogation. Later it was proven that Joel did not betray anyone and that it was the Germans' dogs that had discovered the seven partisans, who were also caught alive and were never heard of again. Joel was released but the story of the supposed betrayal would not die down. Some partisans still kept shouting slurs at us, saying that Jews could not be trusted.

We also found out that Glazman and the seventeen Jewish partisans, who had gone toward the Rudnitzkaya puszcza to join the Lithuanian otriad, had been surrounded by the Germans while resting in a small forest clearing. Most of them were taken alive and nobody knew what happened to them. One girl came back and told us the story. She had survived by hiding under a bush.

It was later discovered that some of the policemen who had previously worked for the Germans and later joined the partisans were spies. When the Germans entered the woods during the oblava, the spies led them to the bases of the partisans. Until then, Markov had naively believed that these spies had become partisans because of their switch in loyalties, and had accepted them trustingly.

After a week Volodka returned to the woods with his men, but not to our base. He sent a messenger to say that those with arms were to join him immediately at his new base. We went there, and both Musio and I were accepted. Much as we hated Volodka and his anti-Semitism, it was safer to be in an organized otriad than on our own. His newly formed otriad was not far from the Hatzke area. We were regrouped into three platoons, Jews and non-Jews together. There were fifteen Jewish partisans with arms and fifteen without. The name of the newly formed otriad was Kalinsky.

Volodka himself left. Rumors were that he had been demoted and would be court-martialed for his actions before and during the oblava. But much later, after the liberation of Belorussia, during the triumphal parade of the partisans in Minsk, Volodka was seen occupying a seat of honor on the reviewing stand.

The chief of staff became our new commander, the commissar remained in his previous position, and Bomka stayed on as head of the razviedka. We set up living quarters in hutors in the woods, each platoon in a separate one.

We were told that our otriad was to move far away to the county of Glubok in order to sabotage the German communication lines and railroads. The commissar lined up the entire unit and again singled out those without weapons. Musio, whose sawed-off rifle had never come back from repair, was included in that unarmed group. They were told to stay in the area and dig ditches across the main roads, and to cut the telephone posts and lines. They would reunite with us after we returned from the completion of our missions within a few months. We were to move out within half an hour.

I didn't trust the commissar and did not believe a word of his promises. I felt that if I parted from Musio, I might never see him again. We conferred for a few moments. He felt the same way about it as I did.

After the partisans were dismissed from the line-up, I went to the commissar to tell him that I would not leave without my brother. I requested that Musio come with us and promised to acquire arms for him. I explained that we two were the sole survivors of our large family and did not intend to be separated. The angry commissar replied that he made no exceptions. He refused to take anyone without arms, and if I wished to be with my brother, I could stay behind with him, but I must then turn in my rifle. I asked to be transferred to another group that we knew would accept us both with one rifle. His answer was negative. He would not let me go anywhere with my weapon.

I was faced with a terrible dilemma. I could not conceive of leaving Musio, but I couldn't leave my weapon either. I asked Musio for advice, but he refused to influence my decision. He knew the value of a weapon in the partisans—it could be the decisive factor between the dignity of a fighter and the status of a hunted animal.

Within fifteen minutes we were to start our march. I decided not to leave Musio, and to keep my weapon as well. Among the sentries surrounding the group was a friend of mine. We confided in him, and together agreed on a plan. If he were to be asked about my whereabouts, he would point in a direction that I had supposedly gone and say I had promised to return immediately.

Holding on to my weapon, Musio and I quickly entered the surrounding woods and ran for about a mile, until we found a hole in the ground which served as an adequate camouflage for us. From afar we heard our unit moving out. When all was quiet we came out of hiding and went to the previous base of the Komsomolski otriad, where some of the Jews without weapons stayed. We spent a few days there.

14

THE PARTISANS GAIN POWER

Mid-October–December 1943

We found out that a new Jewish partisan unit within Markov's brigade was being formed in the village of Luz. The commander was Shurka Bogen, the artist who had been a platoon leader of our Miest otriad. We heard that he would accept both armed and unarmed Jews. We went there and were received into the unit.

The village of Luz, which was surrounded by woods, was totally demolished by the Germans, and only two houses remained intact. Our special unit based itself in these two buildings.

Our first priority was to acquire weapons for all those who didn't have any. We were also to guard the tiny airport which had been built by the partisans for small aircraft and served as their only contact with the Soviet partisan command in Moscow. In addition, we were supposed to gather information on the German positions around the nearby villages and to pass it on to Markov's brigade headquarters, which was about five miles away.

We always had horses on hand to be used for transporting our acquisitions from the edge of the forest.

Not having to hear anti-Semitic speeches and barbs, not having to fear an attack from my fellow partisans, I felt safer and more comfortable.

Some evenings we didn't have to go out on any missions. We sat around the bonfire, singing beautiful sentimental Russian songs and dreaming of freedom at the end of the war and of our future.

The song that most touched me was called "Let's Light a Cigarette." I loved the words and the music. And I didn't even smoke.
The most meaningful verse said, "When Hitler will no longer be in
existence, and in glorious victory we will return home, I shall remember my unit, and you my friend, for giving me a cigarette. Let's
light up."

Acquiring weapons was a very complex operation and we used
the exact devious psychological strategies which we had learned earlier from Suvorov, with our own variations. Sometimes we would
spend many days tracking down a farmer who supposedly had
arms, just to end up acquiring one gun. Usually they didn't resist
too much, so we never really hurt or killed anyone in these operations.

I was emotionally prepared to kill Nazis and their collaborators
in cold blood, but I detested these missions. I hated to see people
suffer, emotionally or physically. Some were innocent folk who had
not done anything bad but were victims of circumstance and the
war. I could identify with their terror and misery.

Yacub, whom we last saw before the oblava, found us.
Throughout the oblava he was hiding in the hutor of one of his contacts very close to the German garrison in Vileika. Because it was
permanently under German control, they didn't look for partisans
there. After the oblava he continued his important work in Markov's
razviedka. He was an imposing figure, arriving on his horse, with
his submachine gun strapped to his back, and grenades attached to
his belt.

While in hiding he found out the name and location of a peasant near Vileika whose barn had been used to kill and burn a group
of Jews. The peasant personally participated in the murder of these
people and in looting their belongings.

Yacub came up with the idea of taking action against the peasant, whose house stood about a mile from the German gendarme
station. Four of us joined him on that mission. After two days of
preparation we arrived at night, on horseback, and stopped within
walking distance of the house. We crawled up to the house. Then
one of us knocked on the window and said in German, "This is the
German police. Please open." Since the peasant collaborated with

the German authorities, he didn't hesitate to open the door.

Instead of Germans he saw five armed men not in uniform, and looked into five rifle barrels aiming at him. He immediately understood, and didn't utter a word.

We ordered him outside but one of us stayed in the house with his family. Silently, we led him to a closed pit used for storing potatoes. It was empty. We took him into the hole and two of us began to beat him up, all the while reminding him of how he helped kill and loot the Jews. At first he cried and begged for mercy but then he became silent. While all this was taking place, I could visualize the Jews being burned at this very place, the parents, the brothers and sisters, the children who were brutally murdered here, and I beat him without pity. When he fainted we stopped.

The partisan in the house brought his wife to her husband's side. We told her why we did it, and left them there. Quickly and quietly we left the village.

Our official missions usually were to gather information regarding the German positions and strength in the area. For that we needed to be in touch with our liaisons located around the German garrisons. We would take horses with carts, driven by their peasant owners, and go from village to village. We would promise to reward our liaisons generously for important information, and for their loyalty. Occasionally, we would give them cows and pigs, which of course we would get from other farmers. The liaisons were just as poor as the rest of the villagers, and appreciated the reciprocity of our relationship. In any affluent village near the German garrison, we managed to get such luxuries as sausages, bread, butter, boots, clothes, pigs, cows. Taking these opportunities to acquire food, we would sometimes get carried away by greed, and would lose track of our priorities.

One night we loaded six carts. We presented one cart and the livestock to our liaison. Then, with each of us sitting atop a loaded cart, holding the reins with one hand and a rifle with the other, we headed back toward our base. I was in the first cart, wearing a newly acquired sheepskin coat. After almost a week on the road, I dreamed of sleeping in a bed. The squeak of the wheels and the neighing of horses were the only sounds accompanying us.

The Germans by now had become aware of our partisan tactics

and practices and often set up ambushes outside the villages which were on the routes used by the partisans. The penetrating cold, the long sleepless hours and the passivity of sitting all made it extremely difficult to stay alert.

Seeing a village from afar, I was jolted awake. We stopped at a solitary house about half a mile before the village. The peasant gave us some vodka. I became pleasantly warm, and the desire to lie down and sleep overwhelmed me. I was appalled at the idea of going out again into the cold. The peasant told us that the previous evening had been quiet and no Germans were seen. But caution prevailed. I had to give up my dream of sleep and go out again to continue our journey.

I sat hazily at the edge of the cart, my legs dangling, holding on to the rifle lying across my lap.

At the outskirts of the village there was a small wooden bridge surrounded by trees. As soon as the horses' hoofs echoed on the bridge, I heard a voice shouting in Russian, "Stop! Who is there?" I thought that this was the outpost of another group of partisans in the village. The driver of my cart stopped the horses. Cautiously I answered, "Our own." Then came a question in pure Russian, "Who are our own?" I calmly said, "Partisans."

Immediately a volley of machine guns and rifles deafened me. Rockets lit up the night like daylight.

I found myself in a ditch by the road, without knowing how I got there. Bullets whistled over my head and the horses began to run away in a panic, pulling the wagons every which way. People were shouting. Doubled up, I ran as fast as I could in the ditch, away from the village. I tripped a number of times, but kept on running without wasting a moment's time to look back. I bypassed the hut where we had stopped. After about a mile I saw a small forest. I crawled out of the ditch toward it, and only in the safety of the forest did I allow myself to stop and evaluate the situation. The machine gun and rifle fire were still continuing. More rockets were lighting up the sky. This must have been a large group of enemies.

I sat down under a tree. I heard twigs snapping under someone's feet, heading toward me. I aimed my rifle and whispered, "Who is there?"

The usual answer, "Our own," came in a friend's familiar voice.

He then joined me. Another friend, from the last cart in our group, was reunited with us in a similar fashion. We had no idea what had happened to the remaining men.

The shots gradually ceased, the rockets stopped lighting the sky, and it was mercifully dark again. After some minutes, the missing men came crawling toward us. One of them was slightly wounded. We were either extremely lucky, or God was on our side, or it was hard to hit targets at night. Perhaps all three elements worked together in our favor. Discussing what to do next, one of the men suggested that it was possible that our attackers were partisans who had mistakenly fired upon us, and it was a pity to leave such good supplies behind.

Carefully, in single file, we returned to the ditch and crawled back to the village to try to retrieve our supplies. After we passed the hutor where we had originally stopped, machine gun fire opened on us again. We had been detected. By then we knew for certain that these were enemies. We returned the fire very briefly in their direction, to impress upon them that we too were armed. We hoped that they would not follow us. We ran back to the safety of the woods, but had to leave our supplies behind. It took us two days to walk back to our base.

We needed to be extremely cautious in such situations because sometimes Russians working with the Germans posed as partisans in order to lure us out. Also, some partisans would occasionally wear the uniforms they removed from Germans, and in the dark it wasn't always possible to identify each other fully. In some cases partisans would become suspicious and shoot before they recognized the other party. Sometimes groups of partisans ended up fighting each other, thinking they were fighting the enemy. So unless the two parties recognized each other, questions were tossed back and forth, specifying names of partisan groups, until there was no doubt of their identities.

We arrived at our base by daylight and reported the ambush to Shurka. Musio was very concerned for our safety because our return had been delayed by two days, and he was relieved to see us back safe. Later we found out that the ambush which we had survived had been laid by Germans and policemen.

Exhausted, I removed my boots and coat, lay down on the bunk and instantly fell asleep, completely oblivious to the lice taking their regular stroll all over me. When I woke, I tried to get rid of them, at least temporarily, using the primitive version of the "steambath" which we had built at the base.

In my effort to keep reasonably clean, I would exchange my scruffy clothes with the peasants when I "visited" them, though theirs were not in the best of shape either. But they were better than mine.

In between missions, I spent a lot of time sleeping and sometimes helping in the kitchen. On our missions we sometimes couldn't sleep or get anything to eat for days, so like camels, we learned to store sleep and food in advance.

On one mission that took us to the Kotlowskaya puszcza, we met groups of Jewish families who had dug out zemlianki to live in and subsisted by begging for food from neighboring villagers. Some of the families were unable to get food and were starving. In one zemlianka we met up with Rivka Gvint and her mother, our friends from Kurzcnicc. We offered them bread and other food which they at first refused to accept. But we insisted and left it with them, before we continued on our mission.

The Germans had two important garrisons, strategically located at crossroads which we needed to use on our missions—one in Uzle and the other in Svoboda. Each one included about a hundred Germans and fifty local policemen loyal to them. The Germans rarely left their garrisons and the protection of the bunkers and watchtowers. They moved only in large convoys. They depended upon the help of the policemen to get information on our locations and movement, and often called for reinforcements from the big garrison in the town of Miadziol in order to set up ambushes for us.

In addition to Markov's there were now several brigades in the forests. The commanders of all the brigades finally decided to oust the Germans from these two posts and take control of the entire region. Markov's brigade, of which our Jewish unit was a part, was given the responsibility of attacking the Svoboda garrison. Another brigade was given the task of taking Uzle.

We set out before sunset and arrived at our destination in the complete darkness of a cloudy and moonless night. We surrounded the village and each platoon was given a specific sector to attack.

The Germans, dug into their bunkers, shot at us with machine guns, mortars and light artillery, while we had only rifles, grenades, submachine guns, and just a few machine guns. It took us most of the night to flush the Germans out of their bunkers, and it cost us several casualties, killed and wounded. Though our equipment was less sophisticated, we outnumbered them and cleared the area of enemy forces. By morning, most of the Germans and the policemen were killed. Others escaped or surrendered.

The village was ours. We burned all the bunkers, blew up the watchtowers with grenades, and destroyed all the buildings, leveling them to the ground so that the Germans would not be able to come back and use them. This was our first major confrontation on such a large scale, and we returned to our base exhilarated. The mission at Uzle was also successful. The entire area was now firmly in partisan hands. The closest German garrison was about thirty miles away.

Several days later a large force of Germans came back to Svoboda and stayed for a day. They left that night, without leaving any troops behind. They made no effort to regain their control of the area.

The partisans issued new orders in the two towns, and organized the production and distribution of food—mainly bread. They controlled the amount of flour given to bakeries and rationed the bread. They levied taxes on the farmers.

Later, the Germans tried a number of times to recapture Uzle and Svoboda, but did not succeed. They finally sent the Luftwaffe, and the planes completely destroyed both towns and the surrounding villages. The villagers were either killed or managed to escape to safer places. The partisans had to move their bases from the villages back into the woods.

We now had to go further in order to ambush German troops moving between their garrisons. And more Lithuanian militia arrived to help the Germans fight the partisans. The police were not much of a military threat, but through their families and friends, they gathered information about the partisans' movements, strength and locations. They were also familiar with the partisan routes and led the Germans in their ambushes.

We started a campaign against the local police and their families and friends. We went into their villages, burnt their houses, and warned them against cooperating with the Germans. We shot some whom we considered traitors, and after that most of them fled to the German garrisons.

We then concentrated for the second time on the larger German garrison in Miadziol, and set ambushes on the roads leading to it, cutting off their food and other supplies. When German reinforcement arrived to restore the roads, we would retreat into the forest, and as soon as they left, we would return to continue our job. More of the local policemen switched sides and joined us, but the partisans were now more wary. Special units were established in each brigade, consisting of NKVD (later known as the KGB) men, whose duty it was to weed out traitors and spies. They also interrogated each newcomer wanting to join the partisans. They were ruthless, and any suspect, after a night of grueling interrogation, was either accepted or shot.

Standing guard one night at our base, I saw a figure in the dark. I pounced on him, and ordered him to put his hands up. He looked scared and aroused my suspicion. What reason did he have to be so deep in the woods, away from any road or village? I took him to headquarters and handed him over to the commissar. Then I returned to my post. When my shift was over and I returned to the base, I found out that the man had been shot.

Later I had a discussion with one of the NKVD men about this incident. He was called "Little Volodka." When I asked how he could be so certain that someone was really a traitor, he said, "I don't have to be sure. If the suspicion is sound, it is better to kill him."

Sometimes such instantaneous life and death decisions were influenced by alcohol, which was a major part—and one of the basic needs—of partisan life. A lot of time and energy was expended acquiring locally-made vodka. Whenever it was available, there was no limit to the quantities that were consumed. It was a serious problem, causing many deaths among the partisans. In a drunken stupor, their reflexes were slow and their judgment impaired. They were often unaware of simple dangers and made rash decisions.

Once, four drunken partisans set out for a village, took a cart and horses, and in broad daylight drove along a main road between

Miadziol and Glubok. Fifty policemen coming from Miadziol met them face to face. They opened fire, killed two of the partisans and captured the other two, whom they took with them back toward Miadziol. Some of the policemen rode on carts, and some on bicycles. The captured men were tied up in one of the carts.

By chance, about six miles from the point where the partisans had been captured, fifty other partisans were set up to ambush Germans on the same road. I was among them.

Lying on both sides of the road we saw the approaching policemen and heard them talking and joking. When they were just in front of us, we opened fire from both sides. The attack was intense. Some of them shot back, but most of them tried to escape. In the end, there were fourteen policemen dead, including the chief of Miadziol police. To our great surprise, we found the two partisans lying drunk, tied up in one of the carts!

Before leaving the spot, we put a mine under the body of the dead chief of police. We heard that when a German unit came by and tried to pick up the body, the mine exploded, killing and wounding several Germans. From then on, they were very cautious about removing bodies and objects, and used the local peasants for that job.

At the end of November 1943, eleven members of our group, including a man named Berke, left on a mission around Swenzciani, one of the largest towns with a German garrison, to find out the positions and the strength of the German forces.

It took four days to reach Swenzciani. Four of the partisans hid in a deserted bathhouse in the woods. The other seven went to a peasant whom they knew, who lived in a hutor right near the garrison. They went to him to gather information and to hide during the day. He welcomed them warmly, fed them, and told them that all was quiet in the vicinity. He promised to get all the information they needed while they rested. The partisans wanted to have one of their own stand guard, but the peasant said it wasn't a good idea. Seeing a stranger standing outside might arouse the suspicions of other villagers. He himself would watch out for any signs of danger. The partisans went to rest, but decided that one of them would stand by the window at all times.

At about 2 P.M., the guard at the window suddenly shouted,

"The Germans are coming!" Instantly the partisans jumped up and out of the windows, trying to reach the woods, about half a mile away.

The Germans, who had by then almost surrounded the hutor, opened fire with machine guns and rifles. Though the escaping partisans had only a few guns, they managed to fire back at the attackers. But one by one the partisans were hit. One of the wounded men managed to reach the edge of the forest and fell. He then took his revolver and shot himself.

Berke kept running. When he was very close to the forest, he felt a wave of heat overcome him, and realized that he was hit. But he continued to run, and he didn't stop running until he was deep inside the forest. His pants were all covered with blood. Half of his penis had been blown off, and the bullet had gone through the flesh of his thigh. Unable to walk any further, he crawled until he came upon a hutor. The peasant, who was friendly toward the partisans, took him in, cleaned and bandaged his wound, and took him in his sled to a village which was under the control of the partisans.

I was on my way from our base to partisan headquarters with two other men when we chanced upon the peasant, who had something covered with fur lying on his sled. We recognized "Black Berke," as he was nicknamed, deathly white. We carefully transferred him onto our cart, thanked the peasant profusely, and gave him a pair of boots in appreciation. We brought Berke to a field "hospital." On the way he told us what had transpired.

Berke suffered terribly, especially when he urinated. It took months for his wound to heal but he then returned to action.

The four partisans who had hidden in the bathhouse found out about the events at the hutor when they came out in the dark. Checking to see that there were no Germans around, they went to the hutor where the seven had been. The peasant and his family were gone. They found the mutilated bodies of their six comrades, their arms and legs broken. One of them found his brother among the dead. The four men dug a pit, buried their comrades and then returned to our base.

It was decided that this act of treason merited retaliation. Four men returned to the hutor, caught the peasant and administered a beating, after which he admitted that the Germans had threatened to kill him for having contact with the partisans, so he had to prove his loyalty to the Germans. He was executed by the partisans and his house was burnt down.

A few days after this incident, our unit, with another entire otriad from Markov's brigade, was in a village between the towns of Miadziol and Glubok. Our goal was an ambush.

We arrived in daylight. Suddenly we heard a shout, "Germans are coming!" A scout on horseback riding into the village was saying that he had spotted several trucks full of Germans and police coming from Miadziol. He estimated there were some two hundred of them.

Our commander decided to engage them in battle. We were also about two hundred strong. He sent a commissar with two platoons to go around the village and approach the Germans from behind. One platoon remained in the village, spread out between the houses. The rest of us hid behind two embankments on either side of the road. When the first German truck approached, we opened fire from both sides simultaneously, and hit many policemen. The Germans and policemen from the other trucks jumped out and returned heavy fire, using machine guns. We didn't want a confrontation with them in an open area, so we retreated into the village, to draw them in. They followed us between the houses, and at that time we were joined by the other partisans and started a fierce counterattack.

The policemen were the first to retreat. The Germans also began to flee toward their trucks, at first gradually and then in a panic when they realized the extent of our force. As soon as they reached their trucks, they were attacked by the two platoons at their back. The confusion was unbelievable. Still, some of the trucks managed to escape. In the end, we counted seventy enemy dead, fourteen captured. Two of our partisans were killed and two wounded. After a brief interrogation, the captured men were executed. We returned to the woods.

One mission took us to a village near the town of Svirno, where a German garrison was stationed. Ten of us arrived on foot at night at the village and entered one of the huts. We didn't know whether the people in the village were loyal to the Germans or not. To our surprise, the peasant brought out several bottles of vodka in order to please us. By the time we were through with the meal, our mood was really high. We decided to play up their good will toward us. We gathered the young people from the village and told them the latest news of the war, how we were winning against the Germans, and that the Red Army would soon be back. One of the partisans had an accordion which he carried with him at all times. It was not an uncommon thing for a Russian partisan or soldier to do, and it frequently helped boost the morale of the entire unit. He began to sing and taught the youngsters some partisan songs until it was time to go. We hitched up the horses and with our guides went toward the next village, which was miles away from the German garrison.

We were warned by the guides of the frequent ambushes laid along the road by the Germans. But warmed by the vodka and lulled into a false sense of security, we were beyond fear and logic. We told the driver-guides to continue on.

Lying on a pile of hay in the back of a cart, half drunk, I was loudly singing all my favorite songs, while the convoy of carts made its way along a side road. I caught glimpses of stars through the swaying branches of the trees. It was peaceful and idyllic.

Suddenly I heard three shots. I found myself standing behind a tree, with my rifle cocked, alert and completely sobered. We waited for about a quarter of an hour. There was not a sound, and no more shots. We thought maybe the shots had come from a partisan group, so we decided to continue on our way on foot, cautiously and silently. About half a mile away from the village, we left the horses and drivers in the woods and, spreading out in a line, carefully made our way through the fields. Near the village we heard voices and the sound of movement—a very unusual occurrence for this time of night. I thought of turning back—perhaps this was a German ambush—but didn't want to be the first to suggest it, as it might be construed as cowardice. We proceeded even more cautiously.

Still out in the open field, we began to crawl toward the first houses. When we were about two hundred feet away, a huge volley of fire greeted us. I began to crawl back toward the woods as fast as I could. Judging by the random direction of the shots, I gathered that the Germans didn't really know where we were.

We all met up back in the woods. Nobody had been hit. Our

mood improved, and from our position of safety we briefly returned fire, to ensure that they knew that we were armed. We hoped they would not chase us. We found our carts, but the peasants had fled. Only one peasant was lying on the ground covered with his coat. We told him to come with us, but he kept saying, "I'm not getting up. They are shooting." But when he saw us get back on the cart and start to move away, he jumped up and got on.

Later we found out that about a hundred Germans and their Lithuanian allies had set up an ambush on the main road to the villages. Luckily we managed to surprise them by coming along a side road.

Though there was camaraderie and cooperation between the various partisan units, there was also a degree of rivalry. On one point, however, there didn't seem to be any disagreement, and that was the attitude toward Jews. From the time policemen and other German loyalists switched sides and joined the partisans, incidents of anti-Semitic behavior even toward fellow partisans increased markedly.

It happened once that four partisans of the Lithuanian partisan unit were returning from a mission. One of the men was Jewish. During breakfast in one of the villages friendly to us, vodka was served, and in a short while tongues began to wag. The talk turned to Jews. Enthusiastic Jew-bashing became the tone. The Jewish partisan expressed his resentment of the conversation. One of the other partisans, who had just returned from a successful mission with him, picked up his gun and killed the Jew, and then tried to escape and join the Germans. He was caught however, and was tried and executed.

Another incident took place in one of Markov's otriads. In one zemlianka the only Jewish partisan was a girl. At night a shot rang out and the Jewish girl was found dead. The partisan who was arrested claimed it was an accident and went unpunished.

In the Soviet Union there was no official anti-Semitism but, in fact, it was rooted so deeply in everyday life that it sometimes outweighed the Soviet hatred of the Germans. So here we were, fighting against a common enemy—the Germans, whose aim it was to totally annihilate the Jewish people and to take over the Soviet Union—side by side with fellow fighters whose own hatred of Jews was notorious. In this demoralizing situation I told myself again and again that I was fighting as a Jew—with them, but not as one of them. I dreamed of having my own country, of fighting for it, and even dying for it. That was what kept up my morale.

At the end of the summer of 1943, the Polish unit within our Soviet partisan brigade was disbanded and incorporated into the Soviet units. At about the same time, the exiled Polish government in England formed an independent Polish partisan command called AK (National Army). As a result, most of the Poles deserted from the Soviet units and joined the AK.

Though the AK was formed mainly to fight the Germans, these Polish partisans directed their fight against the Soviet partisans as well. A large number of Poles who had previously been policemen working with the Germans now found it convenient to join the AK partisans because the tide of the war was changing.

The AK were intensely anti-Semitic and did not accept Jews in their ranks. In fact, rumors reached us that the AK was systematically searching out Jews hiding in the villages and forests in their areas of operation. We didn't know the fate of those Jews who were discovered until two Jews arrived in our part of the woods, one from around Svenciany and the other from around Oszmiany, and told us their stories. One of them had been hiding in a zemlianka in the woods with his family when they were found by the AK, who opened fire on them. He managed to escape, alone. The rest of his family was killed. The second man was hiding with his family in a peasant's hutor. The AK partisans found out about it, caught the Jews and killed them. He escaped. The peasant's hutor was burned down for concealing the Jews.

Groups of Soviet partisans, to which our brigade belonged, often passed through the woods around Svenciany and Oszmiany on their way to missions. They were constantly attacked by the AK group located there.

Once, five partisans from our brigade were out on a mission which passed through AK-controlled area. They were caught alive. One of the partisans was a Jewish girl. We later found out from our liaison that they were all murdered. The girl was dealt with especially cruelly.

Brigade Commander Markov decided to rid the area of the AK

menace. Our entire brigade was moved to the region close to the AK bases. We surrounded and attacked them. After three days of fighting, the entire area was free of the AK. Many of them were killed, many were taken prisoner, and the rest ran away to the areas close to Vilna, where another AK brigade was located.

15

THE JEWISH SUPPORT GROUP

January–February 1944

In the beginning of January, Markov called our commander, Shurka Bogen, to appear before him at the headquarters. While he was there, we heard from one of the partisans coming from the headquarters that there was a rumor that our special Jewish unit would be disbanded, and we would be disarmed. Shurka would get another position at headquarters. A group headed by the commissar would be coming to our base to take away our weapons. Musio and I decided not to wait, but to escape with our rifle. We ran through the woods to the zemlianka where Rivka Gvint, her mother, and other Jews were living. We buried our rifle in a hole near the zemlianka, and we stayed with them. After a few days we heard that the special Jewish unit was indeed disbanded; some of the partisans were transferred to other otriads, and many had their weapons confiscated. All those without arms were told to fend for themselves. Shurka was given the job of coordinating the writing of the history of Markov's brigade and doing the illustrations.

Musio and I waited a few days more and then dug out our rifle, cleaned it, and went to the Proizvodstvennaya gruppa, a Jewish industrial group consisting of men and women who were skilled craftsmen—shoemakers, tailors, candlemakers, leather tanners, and the like. There was also a baker and a sausage maker. It was a special otriad that was to provide the other partisan otriads with the food and clothing they needed. It was located in the woods, with all the workshops in underground zemlianka. The commander of the otriad was Barkan, an older man in his forties, who had a rifle. The starshina (sergeant major), Boruch Kudowitsky, who we knew from the Zazierie forest, was in charge of production, and kitchen, storage, and supplies. The craftsmen worked for all the partisans in the woods, who supplied whatever raw materials were needed for their products. But as far as providing for our own needs, our unit had to be self-sufficient. We were gladly accepted into the group because of my rifle. Of the fifty people, about twenty were young women. Ten of the men had rifles, and they were responsible for protecting and providing for the support unit. Musio and I joined the armed men. We found Markh there and were overjoyed at being reunited again. Our ways had parted after the oblava, when he had joined the Manochin brigade. We had not been in touch except once, when we chanced to meet on a mission.

When the Proizvodstvennaya gruppa was formed, Markh transferred there. We also met most of our close friends from the Zazierie forest there. In addition to the Kudowitsky brothers, we found Kviatek, Hannale Posner and her father, and Bonchak.

Deep in the woods, several large zemlianki housed us all. Along two walls were bunks, where we slept side by side. An iron stove stood in the middle and heated the entire zemlianka. The cooking area was outside. Over an open fire hung cauldrons for cooking potatoes and other food. Three times a day meals were prepared and distributed army fashion.

Every member worked according to his skills. The daily work load was planned and allocated by the headquarters of Markov's brigade. My main job was to go on zagatovka. I spent most of my time on the roads. It was becoming more and more difficult to get food and supplies near us, so we had to go further and further afield, to villages close to German garrisons.

Most of all I enjoyed the evenings when I didn't have to go out. Gathered around an open fire, or in the candlelit zemlianka, we would sing Jewish and Russian songs. It was intimate and warm, like a family. Posner and Hannale, and another member of the group, Burgin, sang beautifully and led the sing-along. Yacub stayed on at the razviedka in Markov's brigade headquarters. But he visited us frequently and we began to see a romance flowering between him and Hannale.

There was a group of Zionists with whom my brother, Markh, and I formed a deep friendship. We would gather around the stove to sing Hebrew songs and discuss our plans for a future in Palestine. With us were Yuditka, a tall, young, intelligent, good-looking girl, who had been an active member of the Zionist organization in Vilna, and Yehuda, a young man of Musio's age, educated and eloquent, with strong opinions which he vehemently expressed.

When it was freezing and snow covered the ground, we used horse drawn sleds to go on our missions. It was safer, quicker, and silent, and far more pleasant than going by cart. In one night we could manage to cover over a hundred kilometers and enter a number of villages. The winter nights were now long—it was dark at five o'clock, and dawn began at seven in the morning. Sometimes we had to stay away for several days at a time in order to obtain a sizable supply of food. On these occasions, we would spend the days in the hutors of peasants we knew. We kept all the food and livestock in the sleds in the peasants' yards.

It was a particularly bitter winter. I suffered greatly from the cold, despite my fur coat and hat. I wrapped my feet in layers of rags and stuffed straw into my boots. But the cold penetrated anyway. It caught my breath and froze my eyelashes. In order to keep my eyes open I was constantly tearing my lashes apart. I wore heavy gloves, and when I took them off I had to make sure that my bare hands would not come in contact with the metal of my rifle, or else my skin would stick to the metal and be ripped off.

The worst time was when we left the woods and came out into the open areas, where the wind blew and cut into any exposed skin. Coming into a hut at dawn, I was so frozen that my hands were too stiff to pick up the potato pancakes that the peasants prepared for us. I had to wait for my hands and mouth to thaw out a bit.

When I returned to our base from a zagatovka, I hurried to our zemlianka. It was quite warm, and as soon as I walked in, I would remove my boots and coat and go to sleep. Everybody slept in their clothes. When I was awakened at dusk to go back out, I felt I had just gone to sleep and had barely begun to warm up.

One of the major ways to cope with the cold was by drinking

vodka, which we got from the peasants in any way possible. We used threats, bartered, and pleaded to get Samogon—home-made vodka. It smelled awful, but after drinking half a quart, it didn't bother me, and I was warmer and happier. But it also made me sleepy.

On one occasion, we were on our way back from a long mission. I had not slept for several nights. It was already dawn when we had entered the woods where our base was located. I was sitting high on top of bags of flour on the sled, my rifle across my knees, while the peasant drove. The rising sun was beginning to warm me, as did the vodka inside of me. I must have fallen asleep. I slid off the sled, but even that didn't wake me. I stretched out in the soft snow and dreamt that I was in a large, comfortable bed.

The driver wasn't aware that I was no longer there, and since this was the last sled in the group, nobody else saw me fall out either. Several miles later, the driver suddenly realized that he had lost his passenger. Luckily, he was a loyal peasant and returned to look for me. Finding me sound asleep, he began to rub my face with snow. I woke up with a start, and couldn't understand where I was. Instinctively I looked for my rifle. It was firmly held between my knees, the strap wound around my arm.

I was extremely grateful and thanked the peasant, as I could easily have frozen to death. This had happened to several partisans.

I got used to taking food and clothing from the peasants, and gradually became somewhat callous and insensitive to their cries and pleas at least to leave them their livestock. I knew that they had more ways to survive than we did. But we always left them the basic needs—one horse and one cow.

Markh stayed with Musio and me in the zemlianka. We shared everything. Tobacco was very hard to come by, and since neither Musio nor I smoked, any tobacco that we managed to get we gave to Markh. The smokers suffered greatly from the shortage of tobacco, and when they got any they would roll it in newspaper to form a long cigarette, then take a few puffs and pass it around. One cigarette would be shared by as many as ten smokers. Heavy smokers would even dry horse dung and smoke that. I was so shocked to see the effects of cigarette dependency I decided never to become addicted to it. To this day I don't smoke.

Not far from our base there was a zemlianka of Jewish families that no otriad of partisans was willing to accept, and not being craftsmen, they could not even join the Proizvodstvennaya gruppa. We helped these families as much as we could, and brought them potatoes or peas, and sometimes bread. They were grateful beyond words.

There were young girls at our camp, both among the Jewish families and in the partisan units, and even in these difficult times romances flourished. The girls were mostly attracted to older partisans though, because they were able to provide security and help for them and their families. Several couples were formed from these relationships, and most of them got married after the war and raised families. Yacub married Hannale, Posner's daughter. Shimon married his high school sweetheart Riva, who ran away with him from Kurzeniec and stayed with him throughout the war. Palevsky, one of the men from the Vilna ghetto, who lost his wife and child in the ghetto, married Hayale, a beautiful girl who worked as a nurse. I had several brief romantic interludes, but nothing serious. Neither Markh, Musio, nor I formed any long-term relationships, but we did develop friendships among the girls that last to this day.

The lice continued to be a constant source of discomfort. One peasant gave me some smelly ointment to cure the sores, and that eased the pain for a while. I must have smelled pretty bad, but no one complained.

In February 1944 the Soviet partisan headquarters decided that all the men without weapons would be sent eastward to cross the frontlines onto the Soviet side. There they were to receive arms and either join the Soviet army or return to the partisans to continue fighting. The frontlines in Belorussia at that time were stable and relatively quiet, and it was possible, though very dangerous and difficult, to pass through the German lines to the Soviet side. Markh and Musio were among those who were ordered to leave for the east. I intervened again, and it was agreed my brother would stay, but Markh had to go.

The last evening before his departure we were very sad and depressed at having to part from Markh again. The only way to deaden our grief was to get drunk. The three of us took a liter of vodka that I had saved for special occasions and went out into the cold starry night. A full moon shone on the snow. It was beautiful. We took turns drinking until the vodka was all gone. Warmed and relaxed, we began to daydream about how we would meet in Palestine after the war, and how we would keep the memory of this night with us. We sang beautiful Hebrew songs together, and, somewhat calmed, we went back into the zemlianka. The other men who were supposed to leave the following day were also drunk. As soon as we entered the warmth of the zemlianka, my head began to spin, but I could still stand. Markh got some more vodka and continued to drink inside until he began to feel bad. He went outside and passed out in the snow. I went out after him, and with Mirka, a nice girl who had a crush on him, dragged him in and put him on his bunk. We removed his boots and covered him up. Musio was lying on the bunk, asleep. I sat down on the bunk where Hayale and Yuditka were lying and began to talk. I told them about my parents and how much I still missed them, especially my mother. I shared my emotions, my closeness with Musio and Markh, and the fear of being separated from them. I spilt my heart out until I fell asleep.

At dawn Musio and I accompanied Markh to the brigade headquarters, which was his point of departure, and said our last goodbyes.

Several days later—to our great joy—Markh came back. Two groups had left, heading toward the east, he said. He was in the second group. The Germans had most probably become aware of the groups leaving the woods and were waiting for them. The first group was attacked and almost all the people were killed. When the news reached the brigade headquarters, the second group was ordered to return to base. There were no more attempts to send people to the east.

The weather was becoming milder; the sun was warmer, and the cold was not as bitter. Rumors circulated that the Germans were planning another oblava against the partisan bases. New German reinforcements arrived with tanks and artillery. We began to dig ditches and bunkers for defense. We were tense, and all the discussions centered upon ways to defend ourselves, and how to avoid situations that had occurred during the previous roundup in the fall of 1943.

At about that time, a specgruppa consisting of two otriads, named Gvardia and Nikolaev's, came into our forest. They were not a part of any existing brigade in the area. The units consisted of paratroopers who were dropped by the Soviet army, equipped with the most up-to-date arms, including heavy machine guns and anti-tank guns.

One day, the commander in charge of the specgruppa—a Major Sergey—came to us with his radio operator, Lena, a Russian girl who told us she was Jewish. They had come to see if our group could do some work for them, and whether there were any Polish-speaking partisans who could help them communicate with the Polish villagers when they moved deeper into Poland. Musio, Markh, and I volunteered. As Sergey was not familiar with our part of the forest, I led them back to their base. On the way I became friendly with them. When I realized that this group, coming from the Soviet side of the front, was not as anti-Semitic as the partisans of Bielorussia, I really wanted to join them. Before I left them, I finalized with Major Sergey that the next morning the three of us would report to him. I also asked whether we could bring another Polish-speaking partisan with us. He agreed and we brought Yehuda. The next morning, we saluted the major and asked to be accepted. He told us to report to Captain Voronov, the commander of the Gvardia otriad, who would accept us and issue us new arms.

The four of us appeared at Captain Voronov's zemlianka. He had already heard all about us from the major, but he began to question us again about our experiences and familiarity with the roads, our knowledge of Polish, and why we wanted to join them. We said that we wished to be part of a unit more actively fighting the Nazis in order to avenge the murder of our parents and fellow Jews. We stressed that we had already been in a fighting unit and were experienced in partisan warfare. We were accepted and told that we would be issued new arms when we returned on the following morning.

We returned to the Proizvodstvennaya and I turned in my rifle to Barkan, the commander. This inanimate object had become so much a part of my life that it was like leaving a trusted ally. With the words, "We'll meet again after the war in Eretz Israel," we left our friends.

16

THE GVARDIA MISSION BEGINS

March–June 10, 1944

When we arrived at Gvardia, we were issued new submachine guns and short carbines with plenty of ammunition. Most of the men in the Gvardia and Nikolaev's otriads were trained in partisan fighting, and had been parachuted behind the German lines. In addition to the two otriads, Major Sergey also commanded a group of foreigners, which consisted of two Germans, Hans and Willy, five Spaniards, three Frenchmen, two Poles, and two other Germans. They were all communists who worked with the Soviets against the Germans. Our radio communications system was run by a hand-operated generator, and two radio operators, including Lena, had to carry that equipment.

The entire specgruppa consisted of over 150 partisans, well-armed and in good shape.

Eighty of them belonged to Gvardia. In addition to the Soviet paratroopers, there were men like us, who were accepted on personal merit. The unit had the best equipment that I had ever seen. There were six heavy machine guns and two anti-tank weapons, sixty small machine guns, many carbines, grenades and different types of mines, and dynamite. The commissar was First Lieutenant Bikov, and the chief of staff was First Lieutenant Babienkov.

Voronov mentioned that he needed a tailor. I offered to bring one, and went back to my old base to bring Bonchak, with Yuditka as his assistant. Bonchak had been a tailor before the war, and Yuditka was his girlfriend, as well as a very close friend of ours. We were now a total of six Jews in the Gvardia—Markh, Musio, Yehuda, Bonchak, Yuditka, and I.

The main purpose of Gvardia was to create havoc behind the German lines. We were to blow up trains, which were their main source of supplies, set up ambushes against units moving along the roads, and gather and pass information to the Soviet military headquarters in Moscow. Exactly what I wanted to do! When we joined the group, Gvardia was preparing for a long journey, the destination of which was still unknown to us. They were waiting for the return of a group of scouts which had set out before we joined the unit. Meanwhile, my job was to guide groups to the villages around the forest to replenish our supplies. Rumors of a forthcoming oblava were growing because it was noticed that even more reinforcements were pouring into the German garrisons in the area every day.

For the first time since coming to the woods, I became ill. I had an abscess in my throat, and a raging fever. Lying on my bunk, I was unable to move or eat. Mark and Musio fed me hot milk in the hope of bursting the abscess. I couldn't swallow or talk, and even drinking milk was painful. I had difficulty breathing and felt that the swelling in my throat was choking me. A medic came to see me, but could do nothing. There was no medication available.

On the seventh day of my illness, an alarm was sounded and we were informed that the oblava was about to begin the next morning. I was lying there delirious. At about midnight Markh rushed into our recently completed zemlianka with the information that the entire specgruppa was preparing to leave at any moment, and that they could not take the sick people along. Those who could walk should come and those who couldn't would have to stay behind. Musio pressed, coaxed, and finally persuaded me to make all the effort to go with them. With their help I got dressed, put on my fur coat, strapped my carbine across my back, and, supported by them, I walked out of the zemlianka. My head swam, my knees buckled, but I knew that I had to go. It was a matter of life and death.

The partisans lined up, and I somehow took my place among them. It was pitch dark. The only sound I heard was the rustle of trees and the whispered orders of the commanders.

The first order was to go to a Lieutenant Flaksin, who was distributing additional ammunition. I got my 250 rounds of ammunition and two hand grenades, which I stored in my backpack. I put nothing more in there. Other partisans put in some personal items, like clothes. About half an hour later we departed from the base.

In total silence we reached the road and in groups of three continued toward an unknown destination. This was the life of the partisans. Before we could settle in anywhere we had to be on the move again. There was no sense of permanence. Maybe because of my raging fever, my heightened sensitivity, I was even more aware of the insecurity I felt when I was away from the base. As long as there was a base and a zemlianka to return to, it somehow gave a false sense of safety—a semblance of home. But now we were leaving for an indefinite period, to an unknown place.

Covered in sweat, somehow I managed to drag myself along, supported on either side by Markh and Musio. Luckily, a short while later we met a group of scouts coming from the direction of the German garrisons. They gave us the latest information, which was that the rumor about the forthcoming roundup had been a false alarm. The commanders decided to return to camp. They told us that if an oblava were to occur, the plan was to break through the surrounding enemy ring and to move westward, deeper into German-occupied Poland.

By the time we returned to our camp I was utterly spent. Musio removed my boots and coat and I dropped into a deep asleep. When I awoke, my fever was gone and there was less pressure in my throat. I could actually talk. To my surprise, the abscess had burst without my feeling it, probably while we were marching. The effort of the trek must have caused it. The crisis of my illness was over. From then on my recovery was speedy. Three days later, still weak, I was able to get up. I gradually regained my appetite and my strength.

The expectation of an imminent roundup constantly hovered over us. The commanders decided to move the units westward to the Rudnitzkaya puszcza, a huge forest near Vilna, hundreds of miles away, which would take at least two or three weeks to reach.

Twenty partisans led by the chief of staff, Babinkov, were the first to leave, to scout the way. They were also supposed to select a site and start setting up a new camp in the puszcza. Markh, who knew the Rudnitzkaya puszcza from when he had led a group of Jews from the Vilna ghetto, was chosen to guide Babinkov's group. They had radio contact with us. Several days after they left, the rest of the partisans prepared for the long march ahead.

Each of us received even more arms and ammunition, which meant more to carry on our backs. I was still quite weak but managed it. I was becoming increasingly bothered by a persistent internal pain in the lower right side of my body. I tried to ignore it and wait for it to go away, but the pain intensified. Gradually, I noticed a bulge beginning to form under the scar tissue of an appendectomy I had had when I was a child. When I put pressure on the bulge, and pushed it back into my pelvic area, the pain subsided somewhat. So I found a long piece of cloth and bound it around my abdomen as tightly as I could. I wore it all the time, but under my baggy clothes nothing showed, so nobody was aware of it. I was afraid that if anyone found out about my condition, I would be ousted from Gvardia.

I was given a twenty-pound mine for blowing up trains and dynamite sticks which looked like soap bars. All that, plus the bullets, grenades, and some clothes that I had put into my backpack, added up to over fifty pounds. My boots were torn so I was given "valenki," Russian army boots, made of felt with leather soles. They were warm but very heavy when wet.

We left the base in the morning moving toward the town of Vilya, accompanied by wagons which carted the food and ammunition that we were unable to carry on our backs. Dragging along under my heavy load, my heart was heavy too. I was thinking that since we were heading west, it was unlikely that we would be coming back to the Kotlovskaya puszcza again. I was leaving behind most of my closest friends. We had gone through so much together, starting with our first partisan action burning the factory in Kurzeniec. Yacub remained in Markov's razviedka. Papa Pozner and Hannale, Hayale, Leibel and Boruch Kudovitzky, and Kviatek stayed with the Jewish Proizvodstvennaya gruppa. Shimon and Riva were somewhere in another of Markov's otriads. Shurka was still in Markov's headquarters. Zalman, our friend from Kurzeniec,

whom we met sporadically, was also in the vicinity of the Kotlovskaya puszcza in some other brigade. Rivka Gvint and her
mother stayed with other Jewish families in a zemlianka not far from
the Proizvodstvennaya gruppa. I hoped they would all survive, but
who knew whether we would ever meet again? At least the six of
us would still be together.

We had to traverse about two hundred miles through hostile
population, mainly Poles and Lithuanians, and cross the Vilya River
and two railroad lines in order to reach the Rudnidzkaya puszcza.
The bases of the AK partisan units were also situated in the woods
in the area.

We had to move by night and set up temporary bases within the
woods by day. Every few days we would stay over for an extra night
so that several of the men could go into adjacent villages for food.

The first two days of our trek were uneventful. We covered over
twenty miles a night, and rested during the day. It was extremely
difficult to go in the dark along the forest paths, stumbling over tree
roots and not seeing the obstacles. My valenki were soggy. I tried
to remove them and go barefoot, but after stubbing my toes, I
quickly put the boots on again.

By the dawn of the third day we were about two miles away
from the River Vilya. We stopped in the forest, where the commander said we would stay for a few days to rest before we crossed
the river into territory which was heavily guarded by the Germans.
It was a relief to sleep and eat unhurriedly, and to relax. Our only
duty was standing guard two hours per day. I regained my strength
fully.

After two days, we began to reorganize. We discarded all excess weight that we could not carry across the river. We gave some
of the wagons and food to the villagers. The extra ammunition was
taken off the wagons and buried in the forest. At five o'clock that
evening we began to move toward the river.

At the banks of the Vilya we met the Manochin brigade, which
was supposed to join us in the crossing. One of their groups had
crossed over on the previous night and set up a defensive position
on the other side. The river was about five hundred feet wide. There
were no bridges there, but we found an old shallow crossing which
the villagers had made by laying stones on the river bed. We removed

our pants and boots, and, carrying our loads on our heads, waded up to our chests in the icy water.

I moved as quickly as I could so as not to freeze. But the stones on the bottom of the river cut into the soles of my bare feet like knives. Halfway across the river, the pain was becoming unbearable. I wanted to put on my boots, but there was no way I could do so. Biting my lips I advanced, standing on one foot every once in a while to give the other foot a rest. By the time I reached the other side, my lips were bleeding. We put on our wet clothes and began to advance immediately, together with the Manochin brigade. Two platoons of Gvardia, under the command of Commissar Bikov, were ordered to protect the area until the last men had crossed, so we stayed behind.

While we were there, we detected two people hiding behind some bushes. When they realized we were neither Germans nor AK partisans, they came out. I struck up a conversation with them. They told us they had been among a group of forty Jews hiding in the Vilya forest in a zemlianka they had built. They were attacked by AK partisans and were the only two survivors. In constant fear of being discovered by the AK or handed over to the Germans by the peasants, they begged to be included in our group. We appealed to Captain Voronov, the kindest of the commanders, but to no avail. He said it was impossible for him to accept them. They left and we never saw them again.

As soon as the last men crossed the river, we quickly set out. We still had fifteen miles to cover, then to cross the railroad tracks that night, otherwise we were in danger of being caught in daylight in heavily guarded enemy territory.

Silently, we followed the trails in the woods. About a mile before the tracks we stopped for a brief rest. The scouts went on to probe the area. All of the men were as exhausted as I was. I fell on the ground to rest without even removing the load on my shoulders. I was still tired when the whispered order came to move on, with our guns ready.

Leaving the woods, we came out into the open fields. Almost running, we headed toward the railroad crossing. Breathless, I pushed on.

Our scouts silently attacked and strangled two guards on duty at the crossing, took control of their booth and frantically motioned to us to hurry. We began to run. There was a German bunker about a thousand feet from the crossing. We planned to move so silently and quickly that by the time the Germans were aware of our presence we would be on the other side of the tracks.

Suddenly there were shots coming from the bunker. We had been spotted. I was about a hundred and fifty feet from the crossing. We all hit the ground and lay motionless while the shooting continued. When all was still again, Commissar Bikov ordered, "Run forward and return fire." We got up, and running, opened fire on the German bunker.

I shot blindly in the right direction. Our guns and machine guns fired such a loud volley of shots, I couldn't hear whether there were any coming from the Germans. I reached the crossing still shooting, and proceeded across. After covering about fifteen hundred feet on the other side, we arrived at the edge of a forest and stopped shooting.

We heard a train coming from afar and were ordered to spread out, lie down and be ready to defend ourselves in case the train stopped and the soldiers on board tried to attack us. The train passed by without stopping.

At roll call we discovered that five men were missing. We never knew where we lost them. There was no time for searches or burials. We had a destination to reach, and could not afford any deviation from our plans.

At about three in the morning we entered the woods. We proceeded quickly and silently, resting for five minutes every few miles. My backpack was getting heavier by the hour, and it was increasingly difficult to get up after our five-minute rest. I was worried about my abdominal bulge, which kept bothering me more and more. I untied the cloth around my body and found that it was increasing in size, and the skin stretched so tight that it felt as though it would tear and my intestines would spill out. I kept tightening the cloth frequently, hoping that it would keep my abdomen from erupting. And my feet were so chaffed that I had to remove my boots and add them to the weight on my back. I continued barefoot.

Dawn was breaking when we came out of the woods and into the open fields of a village near Oczmiany, which was held by the

AK. Manochin's brigade and our specgruppa converged in that area and we spread out. This was the first time that a Soviet partisan force of such magnitude had moved into AK territory.

I saw the village from afar. Our commissar came galloping up on horseback and told us that it was essential to take this village from the AK. We were to lie down and await further orders. I was exhausted and hungry, and gratefully lay down to rest. My legs felt each of the miles we had walked.

To the right of the village was a small woodland where one of the Manochin otriads had settled in. Just as I was dozing off, I heard shots coming from that direction. Immediately alert, I sat up with my rifle at the ready. But all was quiet. I saw Commissar Bikov on his horse galloping toward us. When he was near, he gave the order for all of us to head toward the village.

The shots from the woods increased. When we were near the village, Bikov ordered us to spread out and set up defense positions on the outskirts of the village, facing the woods where the Manochin group had established itself. Lying in the grass, I propped my rifle on a large stone. To my left were the two Spaniards. One of them stood up and looked through his binoculars. Suddenly we heard machine gun and rifle shots, coming from the woods. We saw men from the Manochin otriad racing toward us. We asked them who was attacking. Nobody knew. They were told to set up a line of defense behind us. We were expecting the unknown enemy to come at us from any direction at any moment. But no one appeared.

From behind my rock, I was tense and ready. But gradually my eyes began to close. I was angry at myself for being unable to stay awake in the midst of all the excitement, but I wished for nothing more than to be able to fall asleep. It all began to seem surreal—like a dream. Forcing my eyes open, I saw Aloshka on my right, loading his machine gun. On my left, one of the Spaniards was passing along an order for all of us to get up and head for the village. I dragged myself up and followed.

Bikov gathered us around him and explained the situation. The AK had launched a surprise attack on one unit of the Manochin otriad inside the woods. The unit began to retreat. Another unit of the Manochin otriad came to their rescue and stopped the attack.

Our mission was to go around the village and to reach the AK from behind. Bikov led us. We crossed a swamp and after about half an hour, judging by the sounds coming from the woods, we felt that we were behind the AK forces, but still far away. We spread out and very cautiously crept closer, crossed another little woods and another field, and finally saw the enemy, with their backs to us, firing at the Manochin group. Bikov ordered, "Fire!"

I shot at anything that was moving. The AK partisans began to flee in panic, in all directions. They hadn't expected to be attacked from behind. We tried to shoot them down or to capture them. Within minutes it was all over. Most of the AK, however, managed to escape into the swamps. We counted only six killed and five captured. Some of the captured AK wore German uniforms. The only things that distinguished them from the German army were their armbands that said WP, which was a symbol for the Polish forces, and their caps which displayed a crowned eagle, a Polish emblem. Four of the Manochin otriad were killed. Two of them had been eating inside a hutor, against orders, when they were attacked by the AK forces. It was hard to obey orders when one's stomach ached with hunger, but disobedience sometimes ended up in loss of life.

We stayed in the village because we were all too exhausted to move on. Our men took turns standing guard. Musio and I, with several other men, went into one of the houses and asked to be fed and given a place to sleep. We all lay down in our clothes, three to a bed. We told the owner of the house to wake us at six o'clock in the evening. Despite the tension that the day had brought—two skirmishes, crossing the river and the tracks, and the fight—I fell into a deep and quiet sleep. My body was totally unprepared to get up at six o'clock. We planned to be out of the village by seven.

Before we left, we buried our dead men in the village. They were eulogized in a patriotic speech by the commissar of the Manochin brigade. Their bodies were lowered into the graves while a guard of honor shot into the air. This was the first time I had witnessed a military funeral and I was impressed. I wondered whether I would at some point also be honored in the same way. The AK dead were handed over to the villagers for burial.

When we assembled for departure, one of the local men came up to me and asked whether we were the Red Army. He had never seen such a large gathering of partisans.

We moved quickly across some fields, stopping briefly only to rest. We arrived at the large woods near Oczmiany before dawn. Several miles within the forest we set up camp. My only duty during the next twenty-four hours was to stand guard for four hours. We still had a supply of food and ate two meals a day—boiled potatoes and a bit of meat. Nobody left the forest so that the presence of the partisans would go undetected.

After two days we ran out of provisions and began to get hungry. We were told that the only reason we stayed put was because our specgruppa was waiting for the commander of the Manochin brigade to make up his mind whether his brigade would continue with us to Rudnitzkaya puszcza or go their own way. After the second day, a small group was sent out to bring back food. That night I stayed behind, but Musio went with them. I asked him to try to get me a pair of boots, as my valenki had completely fallen apart and I had to walk barefoot.

The prevailing mood in the camp was bleak and all sorts of rumors circulated. One was that there was a German oblava in the woods around Naroch, which we had just left. Another one was that we were still in the camp not because of Manochin's indecision but because we were surrounded by a large force of Germans.

On the morning of the third day we received some good news. Over the radio, Lena heard that on the previous day the Western Front, also called the Second Front, had been opened in France. Allied troops, largely American and British, had successfully landed in Normandy on June 6 and were advancing into France.

This was what the entire Soviet army and the partisans had been impatiently waiting to hear. There had been previous unconfirmed rumors of the invasion of Europe, which had later been denied. But this was apparently true. The end of war seemed more of a reality. The Red Army would now be able to speed up their advance. By having to contend with the Western Front, the Germans would be forced to move some of their forces out of the Eastern Front. My spirits soared. Maybe the nightmare would soon be over. Maybe I would survive.

At around four o'clock, Musio returned with the group that had been out getting food. I greeted him excitedly with the good news. Luckily they had not seen any Germans, and brought back several pigs. Musio also managed to get me a pair of boots. I was delighted.

Our mood was quickly dampened when, within an hour after their arrival, we were given an order to move on. There was no time to cook the pigs. We each got a chunk of raw pork, tasteless and tough. I was hungry and started to chew the disgusting fatty meat. Musio also brought me a piece of bread and my hunger was gradually satisfied. The leftovers went into my backpack.

When we were about to move on, the commander of the Manochin brigade came on his horse to bid us goodbye. He had decided not to go with our specgruppa. After he left, Captain Voronov gave a short speech.

"A very difficult trek awaits us. All around us are German forces and Lithuanian and Ukrainian units under their command, as well as Polish AK, all of whom are eager to destroy us. We will take no carts with us and will take only what we can carry. Each of us will carry as much as he can, but no one is allowed to leave behind any weapons, ammunition, grenades or mines. Discipline will be at its highest. All orders must be obeyed instantly and precisely. Any disobedience will be punished by death. We shall move across open fields, each one in his unit. We will wait for nobody. Stragglers will be left behind."

I was totally deflated by his speech. Going again. Dragging ourselves on again.

At dusk we set out. The scouts led the way, followed by the commanders, Captain Voronov and Commissar Bikov from the Gvardia, and Captain Nikolaev of Nikolaev's otriad. Then came the otriads, in single file. The rear guard consisted of fifteen men.

We straggled through fields, swamps, and woods. The night was dark. My feet kept slipping into ditches, tripping over obstacles, and my backpack became heavier and heavier, pushing me to the ground. The straps dug into my shoulders and my arms were numb. I tried to carry my backpack in my hands and it seemed to pull my arms out of their sockets. Even my precious submachine gun and ammunition became objects of resentment.

We could not stop under any circumstance, even to relieve our bladders. Anyone unable to stay with the group was left to his fate. Some inner force kept me going. My eyes kept closing. I tripped and fell several times. But I got up and ran to catch up with the others.

I tried desperately to stay alert. My brain kept telling me, "Just a little bit more. It will soon be time to rest. If the others can do it, so can I. If not, I will perish."

After every hour of walking, we had five minutes of rest. I hit the ground, without removing my backpack. With a sigh of bliss, I would rest my head on it and my eyes would close of their own accord. All too soon came the soft whispered order to get up. It took a lot of willpower to lift myself onto my knees and then up, under my heavy load.

We bypassed all the villages and hutors on our way, and met nobody. Evidently no one was aware of our presence. By dawn we reached a small forest. Inside, as deep as we could go, we settled in for the day.

Each commander started counting his people. We found that five men were missing, including our cook Luchin. No one saw or knew what happened to them. We never saw them again. I was proud of myself and of Musio for surviving this night. Compared to the strong, hefty Russian fighters, we were puny and underfed.

I removed my boots and promptly fell asleep. At 2 P.M. I was awakened to take my turn at guard. I was starving and aching all over. I took out the piece of raw pork I had been issued, cut it into three parts, and began to chew on one of the pieces. It satisfied me for the time being.

Toward evening I heard movement. I lay down silently and saw a cart with one farmer on it. I decided to capture him. When he got off the cart, I leapt out from behind a tree and yelled in Polish to him to raise his arms. He began to tremble with fear. I asked him what he was doing there and he answered that he came to chop firewood for his farm. He was a Pole in his twenties. I took him to the commander and returned to my post. I was soon relieved by another partisan. When I came back to the base, the farmer was being interrogated by one of our partisans, who was also a Pole. Since I had also spoken Polish when I captured the young farmer, he was sure that we were all AK and began to tell us everything that was happening in the area.

We found out that there were two AK brigades in the vicinity, and that they were very well armed with equipment they received from the Lithuanians, in return for promises that they would fight the Soviet partisans. Our captured farmer was also acting as a courier for the AK since he could not leave his farm to join them. He told of plans by the farmers to fight the Soviet partisans if they arrived, using rakes and spades and any available tools as weapons. If the Soviet army arrived, the farmers were to leave for the woods and form partisan groups to fight the Soviets, whom they perceived as enemies.

Captain Nikolaev, hearing all this, stood up and in pure Russian told him that we were Soviet partisans, and whacked him with a stick. He said, "You wanted to fight us with sticks, well, here is your opportunity."

The poor farmer turned white and almost fainted. He began to plead for his life, promising to do anything we ordered and to cooperate with us fully. Nikolaev placed him under guard and we prepared to move on.

When dusk set, we departed. On the way I heard a shot and then saw one of our Spaniards running to catch up with us. I never saw the captured farmer again.

We quickly crossed fields, avoiding any roads. I was hungry again and took out my second piece of raw meat, which I ate on the go. I resolved to keep the last piece for an emergency, and not to think of food or hunger.

When I found myself lagging behind the group, I envisioned the cook Luchin's situation. Since he couldn't keep up he was never seen again. He was probably rotting away somewhere. Or else, even worse, captured and tortured by the Germans. These images prompted me to keep pace with the group. I tried to be among the first in the column, so that if I had to stop for a moment, I still would not be left behind. In the pitch dark we went through the woods, holding on to each other so as not to get lost.

Toward dawn we found ourselves at the edge of a forest. The plan had been to stop there for the day, but since the commanders saw how sparse it was, they decided to try before morning to reach another forest which we saw on the horizon. We began to run toward it, hoping it would be larger and more dense.

When we arrived, we found that forest even thinner than the previous one. There was no possibility of hiding there. We were about three miles from a large German garrison. By then it was fully light. We were all nervous and tense. Staying in these surroundings for a day would be disastrous. The commanders took out their maps and saw that the closest large forest and swamps were about five miles away. While the agitated commanders were conferring, we all stood around waiting. Tired as we were, we didn't even sit down. To my right, I could see a village at a distance stirring awake. People were coming out of their houses and chimneys were beginning to smoke.

At last the commanders reached a decision. They explained that it was suicidal to stay where we were. We would be visible to all, and it would be impossible to defend ourselves from attackers. The village we could see was on the main road to Oczmiany, and a few miles beyond the village were swamps and dense forests, which surrounded the town. The plan was to take the shortest and quickest route to a particular swamp in the forest, which would mean going through the village. We would rest in the swamps, and then continue through the forest to the other side of Oczmiany. In case of a German attack, it would be easier to defend ourselves there than in our present surroundings.

We headed quickly toward the village, trying to appear confident, arrogant, and vicious. The farmers coming out of their houses looked at us curiously, wondering who we were. To confuse them, Willy, one of our two Germans, began shouting in German to them to go back into their homes.

We marched through the village and into the fields again. Half an hour later we reached the nearest wooded marshes.

17

INTO THE SWAMPS

June 1944

I felt somewhat more secure in the marshes, but the deeper we moved into the swamps the more difficult it became to walk. My legs began to sink more and more into the soil. I was amazed at the way the women held up throughout the trek. I sympathized with Yuditka. She was brave and had joined us on previous missions as well. But now her legs were covered with sores, and I admired her for the added effort she had to make to keep pace with us. Lena, too, had a hard time, helping to carry the radio equipment. Their resilience and spirit reminded me of my mother, who never complained no matter how difficult the situation.

Captain Voronov finally had to get off his horse and unload bags of German money, which was distributed among us all. Each of us received 20,000 German marks. All this money had been brought by Gvardia from Moscow. We then threw off all excess loads, such as clothes and fur coats, and only took our weapons and ammunition. Every pound of weight made a difference in the swamps.

After several miles we stopped, set up camp and put guards all around. It was wonderful to rest, though the ground was wet. I was hungry and I received a small piece of bread from Willy, who had acquired it in a village and was now dividing it among us. Musio and I, Yuditka, Bonchak, and Yehuda all sat down together. We each took out whatever meat we had and shared it. We consumed our entire supply. The tiny meal just whetted my appetite and my hunger persisted. I went to sleep.

At noon I was awakened to take my shift at guard. At 2 o'clock I was replaced. Just as I returned and lay down to rest, we heard a shot. We all jumped up, ready for action. The shots increased and we heard them getting closer and closer. We could now hear the bullets whistling by us. Each of us hid behind a bush or tree but we couldn't see anything. Captain Voronov was not far from me. Captain Nikolaev stood up and gave a command to retreat deeper into the swamps, where the woods were denser. The bushes obstructed our view, but we now sensed that the shots were coming from the direction of the village and were drawing nearer. Apparently they could not see us either, for the shots were haphazard. We refrained from shooting back at them so as not to reveal our location.

We began to move, crouching, quickly and silently, deeper into the swamps, away from the shots. The bullets were crisscrossing all over the place. Suddenly a new volley of shots came from alongside us. Captain Nikolaev, who was leading us, changed direction, and we all followed, running. I feared that we had been surrounded.

In our haste it was difficult to find the logs and firm ground necessary to move safely in the treacherous bog. Some of the men began to sink, but others dragged them out to safety. We reached a long, wide ditch full of stagnant water with a dry-looking open field beyond it. I removed my boots and pants, and like everyone else, plunged into the ditch. I was almost up to my armpits in water, carrying my submachine gun, ammunition and clothes overhead. On the other side of the ditch, I put on my clothes and lay down. Nikolaev sent two scouts ahead to see what was beyond the field. Ten minutes later they came running back, shouting frantically that about a hundred Germans were advancing toward us. Nikolaev ordered us to retreat immediately, across the ditch again and back into the swamp. There was no time to remove my clothes before I jumped back into the ditch. We went back in the swamps and tried to camouflage ourselves. I crawled under a bush and lay down on the wet soil. I was soaked through. I lifted my legs and saw the water pour out of my boots. We stayed there motionless for about an hour. The Germans were still not sure of our whereabouts and after a while the shooting stopped and all became quiet. We then got up and tried to move slowly and cautiously in another direction within the swamp.

All my energy was draining out of me and my stomach began to ache from hunger. Every so often someone would sink in the swamp and we would all drag him out. We would step from stone to stone, or onto a log in search of something solid underfoot. If we slipped, the mud would drag us in. It was impossible to get out on one's own. The only way to reach safety was to hold on to something firm and wait to be dragged out by the others.

Commissar Bikov was the last in line and organized help groups. He proved himself to be a real hero, trying to save his men rather than worrying only about himself. Despite all our efforts, several men disappeared into the bog and were lost.

It was getting dark. We were afraid that we would all sink into the swamp. Captain Nikolaev saw how exhausted we were and, as soon as we found more solid ground, he ordered us to stop for the night. I was reaching the end of my strength. I filled my cap with muddy water, drank some and poured the rest over me. I lay down and began to lap up the water, like a dog. The only thing I could do to revive myself was to fill my empty stomach with muddy water. Soaking wet, I lay down and fell asleep immediately. I dreamt that I was on a soft bed, floating on billowing cushions.

We were rudely awakened to reality at dawn and were on the go again, trying to cross the swamps. We wanted to emerge on the other side of Oczmiany, in the hope that no enemies were waiting there for us. The hunger pangs in my stomach came and went, and became a familiar part of my being. I became weak, frequently dizzy, and lethargic. Some inner force, some survival instinct must have kept me going. Woozy, I stumbled along, tears streaming uncontrollably down my face. I kept thinking, "This is enough, I can't go on." But at the same instant another voice seemed to say, "Keep going." This inner battle continued for hours. The swamp was endless. The hopelessness of the situation and the senselessness of this suffering struggled against the innate drive to survive.

The swamps were becoming more difficult. More and more frequently people were sinking. I had fallen in at least twenty times and had been dragged out. Musio was by my side and we encour-

aged each other with our words and our glances. My head was
spinning and my eyes kept closing. I turned around and saw that
we were the last in line. I imagined that behind us, stuck in the mud,
were the still bodies of our mates. I clung to a tree, stood on the
roots, and moved precariously to the next tree, trying not to slip
into the mud. My legs were heavy, and my grip was slackening. I
cursed my backpack. It weighed a ton and was upsetting my balance, but I couldn't throw it away. Musio slipped, and I helped him
to get out. We moved on, slowly. Standing on a root, I tried to advance. Suddenly one leg slipped. I tried to grab on to something but
failed. My leg began to sink, pulled in by the muck. I tugged and
tugged, but couldn't pull it out. My second leg slipped, and I felt
myself sinking. With all my might I tried to pull myself out, holding on to the roots. It wasn't helping. My legs were being sucked
in. The more I tried to move them, the deeper they sank. I was now
up to my hips in gook. Any movement only made my situation
worse. I bent my body forward, sprawled out on the mud and
didn't sink anymore. My weary body was grateful for the rest.
Even my backpack was not causing any discomfort. I closed my eyes
and gave in to a sense of peace. As if through a fog I heard Musio's
voice saying, "Selim, wake up, wake up. Or else we will be left
here."

I thought, "What? To get up again, to struggle? What for? Is it
worth it?"

My right hand was still holding on to my loaded weapon. I
touched the trigger. All it would take to put an end to this suffering was to aim at myself. I opened my eyes and saw Musio standing over me, holding on to the tree.

I said, "What for, Musio? We won't survive this anyway. I have
no more strength. It's so peaceful here." I began to draw my submachine gun toward me. Musio understood what I was doing. He
bent over and quickly yanked the weapon out of my hand. He said,
"Selimku, we shall survive. We must be stronger than they are. It is
our duty to avenge the death of our parents and our people. We can-
not perish of our own accord while we still have the chance to survive. We are obligated to tell the world what happened here. We
will one day be sitting on the shores of Tel Aviv, under its blue skies,
and will recall this moment."

No one paid any attention to us, for by now it seemed that each one was preoccupied with his own survival.

I suddenly realized that if I stayed behind, Musio would not make it either. Who would be there to help him if he was stuck? Musio, holding on firmly to the tree, stretched out his rifle butt to me. I grabbed it and with his help inched my way out of the mud.

On firm ground again, we continued to struggle on. After a short distance, the scenario repeated itself in reverse. Musio slipped and was sinking into the mud, and did not have the strength or the will to get out. It was now my turn to try to convince him and remind him of what he had told me just fifteen minutes earlier. Philosophically I added, "Of course it is easier to give in to death. But that's not the way. We need each other. We can't leave each other." I then proceeded to pull him out. He was considerably taller than me, and in my weakened state I found it extremely difficult.

Suddenly, out of nowhere, Commissar Bikov appeared. He saw our plight and cautiously came up to help me drag Musio out. As he bent over, his spectacles fell into the swamp. When Musio was safely on the ground again, all three of us, on our hands and knees, holding on to the roots, groped around in the dark with our hands to retrieve his precious glasses. We found them. The realization that Musio and I were not entirely alone and that there was someone willing to help us gave us the emotional strength we needed to follow him. By the evening we arrived at the end of the marsh. We were told that the whole trek had taken about four days. I had lost count.

We stopped in a small, dry forest and lay down to rest, without removing our backpacks, in case of an emergency. Captain Nikolaev then took over command of both units because Captain Voronov had succumbed to his fear, and was incapable of leading under such stress. He was basically an army-trained officer who was out of his league in a partisan environment, and had lost his cool. It frightened me to see someone I had utter faith in reduced to such indecisiveness that he had to turn over his command to Captain Nikolaev.

Nikolaev was younger and more decisive. He sent out scouts to explore the area. It was getting dark when they returned with the information that there was a village with a military force in it not too far away. They could see that these were not Germans, but were either Lithuanians or other auxiliary forces used by the Germans to fight the partisans.

We were ordered to prepare to stay overnight at this spot, but to be alert and to double the regular number of guards. The commanders began to count those missing. Seventeen men had been lost to the swamps.

18

PLAYING THE ENEMY

Still June 1944

The commanders sat down apart from us to discuss the situation and the findings of the scouts. From where I was lying I couldn't hear what they were saying. I tried to force myself to stay awake. I heard them call to the "foreigners" of the specgruppa—the Spaniards, the Germans, and the French. They sat together working out a plan of action. I was very curious, but after a while I dozed off. When I opened my eyes I was astounded. I saw that the foreigners, who were always dressed in gray and brown overalls, had removed their outer garments and were in full German uniform. From their backpacks they took out German field hats, ranks, medals, pistols, and bayonets, and put them on. How had they managed to carry all this with them through the swamps without any of us being aware of it? With all the trimmings, they looked like authentic German troops. Willy had the rank of a lieutenant, Hans and Otto were sergeants, and the others were corporals and privates first class. All of them had German Schmeiser machine guns and big Parabellum revolvers. Even the French and the Spaniards were fluent in German. Before our eyes a transformation had occurred. Within minutes about a dozen partisans had become German soldiers.

They cleaned themselves up, polished their boots, and went to the village, casually chatting in German. "Lieutenant" Willy led the group.

I lay fighting sleep, waiting to see what would happen. After about an hour we heard shots from the direction of the village. Something must have happened. We all jumped up and were ready for action. Then it became quiet again.

Some two hours later our "Germans" came back, unharmed. They told us that in the village they had found a group of Lithuanian soldiers who were working for the Germans. Willy told their commander, who was the only one who spoke German, that they were sent to inspect the units surrounding the partisans hiding in the swamps. The Lithuanian commander called all his units for a parade inspection. Willy took the rifles from several of the soldiers to inspect their readiness. To be more convincing, he tested them by shooting them into the air. Those were the shots we had heard. After the inspection, the Lithuanian commander invited our men to eat at one of the houses. During the conversation at the table, it turned out that the entire swamp was surrounded by Germans and by units under German command. The units consisted of Lithuanians, Belorussians, Latvians, and Vlasovtsy (Russian soldiers under General Vlasov, who joined forces with the Germans and were used mostly to fight the partisans). Each unit was patrolling a specific area, and was ordered to shoot any partisans on sight.

After the meal, Willy expressed his satisfaction with the Lithuanian unit and encouraged them to stay alert, as there was a definite possibility that the partisans would try to escape from the swamps through this village. He said he was now on his way to inspect the next unit.

Willy left with his men, marching along the road. It was getting dark. When they were confident that they were far enough to be unobserved, they changed their course and came back to us. They felt that all had gone well and that they had not aroused any suspicions.

Captain Nikolaev gathered us around him and softly told us that he knew we were nearing the end of our strength, but we were in an extremely dangerous situation and needed to make another tremendous effort in order to survive. According to the information that he received from Willy, there was no other option but to break through the chain of Germans and their allies surrounding the area. As soon as we moved out, each of us should be at the height of his alertness, and under no circumstance were we to open fire unless a command was given. If we succeeded in breaking out, ahead lay another dangerous area of about sixty miles before we would arrive at the next railroad track, beyond which the Rudnitzkaya puszcza began. There, our forward unit was awaiting us. We each had to stay with our unit. Discipline was essential to our survival.

We assembled and began to move out of the woods into open fields. It was still dark. We saw ahead of us a number of hutors where, according to Willy, the enemy was waiting. We spread out in a chain and headed cautiously toward the hutors. I was on the right side of the line, right next to Hans, who was again dressed in brown overalls. Suddenly, to our left, a machine gun sounded. We hit the ground, and listened to bullets flying overhead. Nobody returned fire. The machine gun became silent and after a while we moved forward, crouching. Every so often we lay down flat again to listen for sounds.

When we were near the first hutor, someone shouted, "Who is there?" I fell to the ground and began to crawl away from the voice. Again we heard the question, but nobody answered. Some rifle shots exploded from the direction of the voice. When it was quiet again, we got up and began to run as silently as possible toward the hutors. It was totally dark. The machine gun came alive again, and we hit the ground again, and continued to crawl forward. I felt that they had heard us but hadn't seen us.

We reached the hutor, passed it, and were out in some open fields again. We began to run, under heavier fire that was now directed toward the hutors.

We reached a road and ran along it in the direction away from the swamps. I don't know where I got the energy to run, but there seemed to be no limit to my instinct for survival. Also, this was far easier than the ordeal of trudging through the swamps. Back in something resembling civilization, and possibly closer to food, I felt more hopeful.

We walked on quickly, in total silence, almost until dawn. There were no trees on the horizon, only a village straight ahead. We knew that the Germans and their followers were waiting for us all around, and that as soon as day broke we would be spotted, and they would come in full force to attack us. There was nowhere to hide, so we could easily be surrounded and killed. There were only about a hundred and twenty of us, with scant ammunition—most of it had been lost in the swamps.

We stopped on a roadside, and our commanders began to consult. Then they called us all together and told us of their ploy. We would appear to be a Vlasov unit which had been used largely to fight the partisans. The Vlasov units were usually under the command of German officers. We would pretend that we had defeated the partisans in the swamps and were now taking our captives back to the German garrison. Since some of the real Vlasov units still wore their Russian uniforms without the red star, it was possible to make ourselves appear as such a unit by removing all our Soviet insignia.

Our "foreigners" again removed their overalls and were back in all the German trimmings. They became the "German commanders" of our unit. I was with the partisans who wore what looked like Russian army uniforms. We lined up in fours on the road and were divided into groups each led by a German sergeant.

The rest of the men and women, who were really bedraggled, were herded together as the prisoners, surrounded by guards. Musio, Yuditka, Bonchak, Yehuda, Lena, and even Captain Nikolaev, who was huddled into a heavy coat, were among the prisoners. Willy commanded the entire operation. Hans was walking alongside with maps, shouting commands in German. Marching openly along the main road, we entered the village. I tried to appear as straight and strong as possible. The "prisoners" were dragging their feet, stooped over. They didn't have to act very much.

Inside the village, Hans's orders became harsher and louder, and our other "Germans" repeated his commands to halt. We weren't perfect, and were cursed out by Hans in his best German. We saw the faces of the villagers appearing in the windows. Hans divided us into groups of ten. Our first mission was to eat. He took each group separately, with a "Vlasov" soldier as translator, into a different house, and ordered the peasants to feed the group which had fought so bravely defending the villagers from the murderous partisans. The "guards of the prisoners" went in and obtained food for the "captives," who were all grouped in a yard. Those peasants who were not quick enough in their actions were cursed, scolded, and even hit by our Germans to enforce obedience. We sat at tables and the women brought in the food. I didn't say a word, as my poor Russian would arouse suspicion. But my colleagues got into conversations with the peasants, cursing the partisans and bragging of their own heroic deeds. The villagers told us how bad and murderous the partisans were.

We fell upon the food, mostly potatoes, milk, and butter, which disappeared instantly. The women kept supplying us with more. Lieutenant Willy came into the house with a translator, and we all jumped to attention. One of us gave a report in Russian, which was translated into German. Willy asked us whether we were being well fed, and after hearing some grumbling, shouted at the peasants to give us good food as we were all hungry after fighting the partisans day and night. During our conversations with the peasants we found out where the nearest units of the Germans and their loyalists were. They were about three miles away. About half an hour later we heard the command to reassemble on the road. Again, in the same formation, we hit the road toward the town of Oczmiany.

When we were sure we were out of enemy sight, we got off the main road and, crossing fields, took shortcuts toward the railroad tracks. According to our estimate, we had another forty miles to go. But now, well fed and somewhat rested, it was easier and we progressed quickly. At the head and alongside the group were the scouts. In several instances they indicated that there was something suspicious ahead and we all lay down in defensive positions. But nothing happened. Our ploy had succeeded; we had outwitted them. The Germans were not aware that we had slipped out of the woods and were escaping through their loyal villages.

At dusk, we arrived in the woods about five miles from the tracks. We were happy and bolstered by our success. After a brief rest, when it was totally dark, a few of us went to nearby hutors in search of food. Our plan was to cross the tracks at midnight.

I found a tree stump covered with moss, which I used as a pillow and fell asleep immediately. At midnight we began to head toward the railroad tracks.

About a mile before the tracks, we stopped. Captain Voronov had meanwhile regained his self-control and returned to command our unit. He asked softly for ten volunteers. I came forward with nine men, and we were given the order to find a place where the crossing would be safest for the entire group.

We set off, rifles ready for action, in single file. When we were out of the woods we saw hutors between us and the tracks. Quietly we reached the first hutor and walked around it to see if all was safe. A dog began to bark at us. The leader of our group of volunteers shot the animal with a silencer-equipped rifle. Another man went inside the house and led out a frightened peasant. We took him with us to show us the best way to the tracks. He walked ahead and we followed, holding a rifle to his back in case of any wrong moves, all the while reminding him that he must bring us to a spot where there were no German bunkers.

He bypassed the other hutors and led us to within two hundred yards of the track, which was visible even at night. An unpleasant surprise awaited us. The entire area on both sides of the tracks was cleared of any obstructions. Trees, even wheat, had been cut down. There was nothing to hide behind. We lay down to observe the track. Our leader, together with the farmer, went back to bring up the rest of the partisans. During the entire hour that we waited there, only one German patrol passed on foot.

When everyone had arrived, ten more volunteers were chosen. The twenty of us were to run to the tracks, spread out and take defensive positions facing all four directions, on the lookout for enemy movement. We were to fight if we were attacked, while the rest of the group crossed. We would then become the rear guard.

We crawled toward the tracks, silently and quickly. I began to climb the embankment, helping my partner carry the heavy machine gun and ammunition which we were to set up on the other side of the tracks. Crouching, we ran to the left, with our load. Two other men joined us. We lay down, positioning ourselves. I saw that everyone was ready. A hand signal was given, and the units began running to the tracks and toward the woods on the other side. I tried to open my eyes wide to be able to see in the pitch dark. I put my ear to the track to hear any oncoming trains. All was quiet. When the last of the unit crossed, we got up. I stumbled, rolled down the slope, picked myself up and ran across the open field, instinctively looking over my shoulder for danger. I reached the woods and joined my unit. We continued walking quickly through the forest for the rest of the night.

At dawn we arrived at a village which was in the area of the Rudnitzkaya puszcza. It was deserted. We found some raw potatoes, which we cooked on the spot and ate. Lena made radio contact with our vanguard unit, which had left ten days before us, and gave them our location. By evening several of them came and led us to a base camp which they had prepared for us deep in the puszcza. Major Serge received us with a speech praising our bravery and ingenuity. Musio and I were reunited with Markh. Our joy was immense at finding that we were all together again, alive and unhurt.

After a well-deserved and restful sleep, we ate the meal that Markh had prepared for us, the first in a long while. He had saved a leg of lamb for us, and we relished the delicacy.

Both Musio's and my legs were swollen and hurting. We spent the next few days resting, and gradually regained our strength.

As our food supply was depleting, several men went out on a zagatovka, but returned empty-handed. In the village they had come across some AK partisans and a fight had ensued. One of our partisans was killed and one was wounded.

The following night another group set out, and Musio was with them. They also fell into an AK ambush, managed to escape with no casualties, but again returned empty-handed. On the third night, a group finally managed to acquire some food to replenish our supplies.

After several days we moved on to another location, set up camp, and built crude huts. We found several camps of Soviet partisan units in that vicinity. Among them was the Barba unit, which consisted of Jewish partisans who had fled the Vilna ghetto under the command of Abba Kovner. Markh knew most of the people from the time he had spent in the ghetto, and we went with him to visit them whenever we could. We sat there for a few hours, exchanging stories. They were well organized but very limited in arms. An added source of danger were the AK units, which frequently engaged them in shoot-outs, and, by ambushing them, tried to cut off their supply of food.

Our unit had so far been free of anti-Semitism, but Sergeant Major Petka, someone we had never really dealt with, began to instill bias and hatred. We complained to Major Sergey, the head of the specgruppa. He, with the help of the Spaniards, put a stop to Petka's actions. We never knew how they achieved it, but the atmosphere in Gvardia became amicable again. We had a few days to rest up before our next mission.

19

BORIA'S STORY

The Gvardia and Nikolaev's otriads usually set up their temporary camps separately but adjacent to each other, and each otriad went on its own zagatovka. One night several men from Captain Niko- laev's unit, who had gone to replenish their supply of food, brought a Russian Jew back with them. They found him hiding in the vil- lage. He was somewhat disoriented, and smelled of rotting human flesh. The stench was terrible. He washed himself and was given clean clothes, and the smell gradually became more tolerable.

When we heard about him, we went to Nikolaev's otriad to look for him. We found him lying by the fire, and he told us of his experiences. His name was Boria. After graduating engineer- ing school in Moscow, he joined the Soviet army and in the mid- dle of 1943 was captured and imprisoned by the Germans. In De- cember of 1943, SS officers came and selected a hundred Soviet prisoners of war who were Jewish and brought them to the Ponari forest.

This forest was not far from Vilna, and before the war was an elegant resort. The Nazis had surrounded the entire area with lay- ers upon layers of barbed wire, and no one was allowed to enter. Whoever went in was never seen again. The SS and the Einsatz- gruppen would round up groups of Jews from the Vilna ghetto and the towns around it. They were told that they were being taken to work in Kovno, the capital of Lithuania, but they wound up by the thousands in Ponari.

The Nazis lined up the people along huge ditches, each one capable of holding five thousand people. Shot down by machine guns, the people fell into the ditches, piled up one upon another—young and old, men, women, and children—mostly Jews. Certain people were selected to handle the dead and to arrange them in orderly piles in the ditches, like sardines, to enable them to contain a maximum number of bodies. When the ditches were full, they were covered with earth and new ditches were dug. Then the diggers were included in the next batch of victims. Some of the people were not killed by the machine guns but merely wounded. They fell in among the dead and later died of suffocation. One woman, who was only lightly wounded, managed to dig herself out and escape back to the Vilna ghetto. She told of the incomprehensible horrors that took place in Ponari, but nobody wanted to believe her. However, as more witnesses succeeded in running away, the reality of the atrocities began to sink in. Ponari was simply a slaughterhouse for human beings. Among them were non-Jews, like the three thousand priests who were shot and buried in their garb.

When the Soviet army began to advance westward, the Nazis did not want to leave any trace of their atrocities, and they tried to erase the evidence. They brought in groups of Soviet prisoners of war—mostly Jews—to Ponari. Boria was among them, together with his father, who was also a Soviet prisoner. They were forced to open the mass graves, remove the bodies, and burn them.

Upon their arrival, Boria and the other prisoners had to dig pits twenty feet deep, into which they were lowered by ladder. There they lived after work, in shacks which they built in the pits. Each person was shackled around the ankles so they could walk but not run. The ladder was pulled up and guards stood around the pits from dusk to dawn.

Boria's job was to pull out each neatly placed body, carry it some five hundred yards and stack it between layers of wood. The smell was horrendous. Some of the bodies disintegrated, and the limbs had to be gathered separately and put on the pile. SS guards supervised the work. A guard counted the "figures," 3,500 per pile, stacked like a pyramid. Then the pyramid was doused with flammable fluid and ignited. It took a week for each pyramid to burn out. A special machine was then used to grind the remains of the bones, and one third of the ground mass was mixed with two thirds soil and the mixture was used to refill the open ditches. The ground was then leveled out and planted with the natural vegetation of the terrain. After a couple of months it was indistinguishable from the rest of the surrounding area.

The prisoners were guarded by a special unit of the SS, who beat them severely in order to spur them to work harder, to fulfill the norm of five hundred "figures" per day. When the prisoners were out of the pit, even during working hours, their legs were shackled, which made it difficult to move. At first the stench of the rotting bodies was unbearable, but eventually the prisoners got used even to that. They felt themselves drawn down to the level of animals. The commander, Schuian, a sadist, was heavily perfumed to be able to tolerate the smell, and always strutted around wearing white gloves.

One day, while he was supervising the work, the body of a woman holding her two babies in her arms was removed. Schuian was so charmed with the sight that he ordered the bodies laid aside and photographed for him.

After work, he would gather the prisoners before him and ask them whether they were happy, and of course everybody had to shout "yes!" He would then order them to sing cheerful songs. Once Schuian asked who wasn't feeling well. Several people raised their hands and were told that they would be taken to the hospital. The next day they were found among the dead. Schuian once asked who of the men had a higher education. Three men raised their hands. He told them this work was not appropriate for them and he would find them better work. The following day they too were found among the newly killed.

Every day more freshly killed bodies were brought in. These were not tossed into the pits but were burned straight away. Some pits were filled with naked women and children, some with men, some mixed, some partially or completely dressed.

Secrecy was of the utmost importance. Even the SS guards were not allowed to leave the area, and lived in nearby compounds.

Boria's group of a hundred prisoners dwindled down to below

eighty, and they knew that as soon as the job was done they would all be killed. They looked for a way of escape. Boria and another engineer came up with the idea of digging a tunnel from their pit. At night they dug, at first using their bare hands and later some pieces of metal which they stole and threw down into their pit. The beginning of the tunnel was level with the bottom of the pit, and then gradually slanted up. They worked all night, every night, in shifts. They pressed the scooped-out soil along the walls and bottom of the pit, so that the Nazis, who never entered the pit, would be unable to detect anything from above.

Twice the tunnel collapsed, so they stole some pieces of wood to reinforce the next one. They also stole a key to their shackles. It took three months of intensive digging to complete the project: the tunnel was wide enough for one person to crawl through at a time.

One dark, rainy night they decided to escape. They drew lots for their order in crawling out because they knew that the chances of survival were greatest for the first in line. Because Boria was the leader of the project, he was given number two without having to draw a lot. His father drew number 50.

At about midnight Boria kissed his father goodbye and started to crawl. Together with the other engineer in the group, who was number one, he cleared out the last obstacle at the top of the tunnel and they were out, crawling away from the camp. When he first looked back he saw that about twenty men were crawling behind him. Suddenly the glare of searchlights lit the area. Rifle and machine gun shots rang out. Boria thought that it was all over. In desperation he jumped up and began to run. After a while he fell into a ditch and stayed there till the shots subsided. The sides of the ditch were steep, and as he tried to claw his way out, he fell back a number of times before he finally managed to climb out. He walked as silently as he could until he reached a barbed wire enclosure. He dug and crawled under the barbed-wire, his clothes were torn, his body scratched. Then he continued to run until dawn. He found himself in a small forest, where he lay down and camouflaged himself.

Later in the morning he heard shots close by and understood that the SS, looking for the escaped prisoners, had reached the forest where he was. One of the guards passed so close to him that he crushed Boria's hand with his boot, but the branches and leaves made a perfect camouflage. Boria lay there motionless until dark, and then ran until he reached a village. He knocked on the window of the first house, and asked the peasant where the nearest partisans were located, but nobody wanted to tell him or help him. He went to another village and there he met the Nikolaev partisans who brought him to our base. We later heard that only eight of the prisoners had succeeded in the escape. The rest were captured and killed.

Boria ended his story saying he didn't run away in order to stay alive. With his own hands he burned about fifty thousand bodies. He could not return to normal life. "There is no one left in my family. I am staying alive just to be a living witness to the unbelievable atrocities done to human beings by the Nazis. The world must open their eyes to what the Nazis are."

Boria stayed on with Nikolaev's otriad. He had attacks of flashbacks and would start screaming that everybody around him was dead, and he would try to run away. It was hard to calm him down. Gradually these episodes became less frequent. His stench also became less noxious over the days, or perhaps the people around him simply got used to it.

The last time I saw Boria was when the Nikolaev otriad was pulling out of their base. He was still too weak to walk, so they put him on a horse and strapped his slouched body carefully so that he would not fall off. Another partisan was leading the horse. I never heard of him again.

20

DISRUPTING THE GERMAN
WAR MACHINE

July–August 1944

We began to get good news from the Eastern Front through our field radio. The Soviet army had broken through the German defense lines around Vitebsk and Orsza in Belorussia, and were advancing in our direction.

We got orders from partisan headquarters in Moscow to blow up trains and tracks so as to disrupt the flow of German soldiers and supplies to the front. We were divided into groups of six and assigned specific areas. Markh's group and mine were to work in coordination in the same area. Musio's went on a different mission in a different direction. Each group's goal was to blow up two trains. We were laden with two big mines specially prepared to destroy trains, dynamite, a heavy machine gun, and personal weapons.

The railroad we were heading for was the line between Vilna and Lida, and was about sixty miles away. Sergeant Usiakov headed my group, and Lieutenant Flaksin led Markh's group. We moved uneventfully, non-stop, for two days and nights through forests to reach another big forest, where we set up a temporary camp. This was still some fifteen miles away from our target. After resting through the day, we went out at night to familiarize ourselves with the terrain.

We found out from the local peasants that there were many Lithuanian garrisons led by German officers set up within several miles of each other in order to guard the railroads. One of the peasants was willing to cooperate with us and promised to gather information regarding the train movements and schedules, as well as the garrison positions and their patrols.

Meanwhile, after collecting food from the villagers, we lost our way back to the temporary base, and spent the whole night wandering around. At dawn we finally found our camp.

For two days we ate, rested, and awaited information from our contact. When we started planning the details of the operation, we realized that our base was still too far away from the targets. We decided to leave the non-essential equipment and food in this camp, with one partisan to guard it. Just as we were about to leave, Lieutenant Flaksin complained of unbearable stomach pain and said he was too ill to go on the mission with us, so he stayed behind with the guard.

We went to our contact's hutor, and received all the information that he had collected. He provided two Belorussians to lead us, and on their advice, we headed for a cornfield about two miles from the railroad. The corn was high enough to hide in.

The plan was to come close to the tracks early in the night, observe the movement of the enemy patrols, and lay the mines that same night. There were two sets of tracks and each group was responsible for blowing up one set. But the road was difficult to travel on, and it was already late when we hid in the cornfield near a village. Our two groups separated and lay down about a mile apart. One of the guides went to the village, where he had a friend, to find out the latest news. He came back and told us that the Germans had set up an ambush in the area we needed to go through in order to reach the tracks. He refused to continue that night, so we decided to change our plans and stay put for another day.

When it became dark on the second day, all was quiet and we continued to move toward the tracks. There were enemy bunkers strewn all along the way, and their patrols moved constantly. Also, the areas which were closer and more accessible to the tracks were cleared of obstacles and planted with mines. After a brief discussion with our guides, we decided to approach the tracks from an open field close to one of the bunkers. It seemed to be the place from which an approach would be least expected.

We set off again, cautiously crouching, our weapons ready, careful not to make a noise. We stopped on a small hill, hidden by a few trees, and looked around. There was an open field sloping down to the tracks. Lying down, motionless, we began to observe the surroundings and plan our move. Our guides refused to go further, and we agreed that they should await our return at that spot.

Planes flew overhead constantly. From afar we could see fire and we heard echoes of distant bomb explosions, probably around Vilna. We watched patrols passing and timed them. Trains rarely moved at night, but the patrols guarded the tracks anyway.

I was excited, in anticipation of blowing up German trains. It would again fulfill my personal vow of revenge and be yet another contribution in the fight against the enemy.

The second group was about a third of a mile away from us. At exactly 1 A.M. Sergeant Usiakov signaled and we began to move toward the tracks. Crawling confidently behind him, I could clearly see the tracks down the hill. When we reached the bottom we saw that the tracks were on an embankment, which we had to climb.

We reached the tracks. Usiakov and his helper began to prepare to lay the mines, while I continued to crawl along the tracks, away from them, for another thirty yards. My job was to protect the two men while they were laying the mines. Someone else was protecting them from the other side of the tracks. We were supposed to fight off any approaching enemy, and thus enable the rest of our group to retreat. I saw Markh and another partisan dragging a heavy machine gun, which they set up at the bottom of the embankment to protect both groups from another direction.

With my automatic rifle cocked, I looked ahead along the tracks. Glancing back, I saw the two men digging frantically under the tracks. My fear dissipated and I keenly observed what was happening around me. Occasionally I placed my ear on the tracks to check for the vibration of an oncoming train.

At one point, it seemed to me that I could hear something. I tensed. I put my ear to the track, and sure enough, I heard something but didn't know what. I waited for a minute and put my ear to the track again. Now I was certain. The vibration was stronger; a train was definitely approaching. I lifted myself a bit and gave the prearranged hand signal. But the two men continued laying the mine. I wasn't sure they had seen my signal, and by now I could clearly hear the train. I signaled again and again, but they were still working. Each second dragged on eternally for me. By now I was sure the men heard the train too. I saw the outline of the locomotive. The men went on working. Desperate, I surveyed the situation. Ahead of us, open fields. The night wasn't very dark. The train was about five hundred yards in front of me. If the mine exploded under the train, I would be blown up with it. Or else, if the guards on board saw me fleeing, I would be a very easy target for them.

The train began to slow down; the locomotive was now about two hundred yards from me. I looked back and saw Usiakov and the second guy jump off the tracks and run away into the open fields. They were not carrying the mine. Relieved that I could leave my post, I also jumped off the tracks and rolled down the embankment. I picked myself up and ran as fast as I could. I was trying to run back up the hill to hide behind it, but the ground was soft and my feet sank into the dirt at every step. I still had to cover about a hundred yards to the top of the hill, so I dragged myself along. I was short of breath, and my knees buckled. Ahead of me I caught a glimpse of Markh, desperately running, bent under a load of ammunition from the machine gun. Behind me I saw the train approaching the point where the mine had been placed. There was another fifty yards to the top of the hill, but my body gave up. I hugged the ground, covered my head with my arms and waited for the big explosion. Nothing happened.

I heard the train slowing down. I lifted my head a bit and saw the locomotive standing just about where the mine was supposed to be. Then it slowly moved on, past the danger point, and began to pick up speed. Still nothing happened. Later, we assumed that the driver of the locomotive had seen some shadows or movement which aroused his suspicion and caused him to slow down and move cautiously. When he saw that all was quiet, he had continued on his way.

I got up and ran back to the top of the hill, where I met the rest of my group. It turned out that the mines had been laid under the tracks, but at the last minute the detonator was removed because the men saw that there was no time for us to take cover. If the train had blown up we all would have been killed.

As soon as it was safe, we returned to the track to finish the job. We reconnected the detonator and replaced the whitewashed pebbles as they were before, so that the patrols would not detect that anything had been tampered with. The detonator had been set under the rail of one of the tracks, and was now adjusted so that the weight of people or even an empty car would not set it off. It needed the weight of a locomotive or a heavily loaded boxcar to explode it. We planned it this way, because the Germans often pushed an empty train car ahead of the locomotive, so that if it exploded, the locomotive and the train were not damaged, and the tracks could be quickly repaired.

As soon as we finished, both groups retreated, satisfied that the first part of our mission was accomplished.

We decided to go up a hill one or two miles beyond the village, from where we could watch the tracks. Our guides were very nervous and tried to tell us how dangerous it was to stay until dawn, because we might be seen by the villagers. But we decided to wait and see whether the mines would explode.

It was about six o'clock, and in the early morning light we saw a train approaching. From the distance we were uncertain just where the mines were. Someone said he thought the train had passed the spot already, but an instant later there was a tremendous blast and the locomotive took off into the air and fell into the ditch, dragging along a string of cars, which piled on top of each other. From a distance they looked like toys. There was something surreal about the whole scene.

We hugged each other in excitement. About half an hour later another explosion tore the air. We couldn't actually see a train coming from the opposite direction, but we assumed that the second group's mines exploded another train.

We left the spot as quickly as we could and went deeper into the woods. There we lay down to rest. We didn't want to return to our temporary base because we wanted to know the extent of the damage we had caused, and were too impatient to wait until the next night.

Just before dusk, two of our men set off toward the hutors to reconnoiter. Shortly after that we heard shots. We spread out in the forest and waited. An hour or so later our men returned and told us what had happened.

When they arrived at our contact's hutor it was still light. They came upon three Germans on bicycles, carrying some confiscated chickens and eggs. The Germans jumped off their bikes and opened fire. They returned fire and the Germans fled. No one was hit.

We went to our contact and received his report stating that a train from Vilna was blown up at 6 A.M., and the locomotive with thirty cars was destroyed. The train was carrying ammunition and military equipment. At 6:30 A.M. another train, coming from Lida, exploded and another locomotive with thirty-five cars full of military equipment was also destroyed. Many soldiers on the trains were killed and wounded—the exact numbers were unknown.

We headed back to our temporary base, proud and excited. Lieutenant Flaksin, whose stomach pain had miraculously subsided, was awaiting us. He heard our stories and lavished us with praise. Later he read out to us the report he was preparing for headquarters. In it he described our heroism, under his command and under the command of Sergeant Usiakov. Of course he neglected to mention that he had remained at the base.

On fallen trees that were used as tables, we found a spread of food and many liters of vodka. While we were on our mission, Flaksin and the guard had gone to a village to acquire the goodies.

We picked up the glasses of vodka to toast the success of our mission. Thinking this was ordinary vodka I gulped down the whole glass. I began to gasp for air and passed out. When I regained consciousness, I was lying on the ground and my friends were pouring water on me. Gradually I recovered. Everybody was laughing at me. I found out that what I had drunk was not vodka, but pure alcohol spirits, 190 proof. The alcohol burns all the oxygen in the throat, so each gulp has to be followed immediately with water before breathing. I learned the hard way.

We all stuffed ourselves, got totally drunk, and slept through a whole day and night. Then we went to replenish our supplies before going on the next mission. We collected food, clothing, boots, leather, and vodka.

We waited for a night that was cloudy and dark, and then set out in a different direction. Lieutenant Flaksin, true to form, was sick again and didn't join us. We quickly reached a hutor on the outskirts of the village of Mosti, and there our contact told us that there had been Germans in the village. They had taken away several people for questioning, and had doubled the number of guards around the railroad tracks.

We decided to place our mines in a spot about half a mile from the train station, where we thought no one would expect us. Each group would place their mine on a different track, not far from each other. This would cover trains coming from both directions.

With the help of a guide supplied by our contact, we went through fields close to the station. We lay down and observed the terrain. From afar we heard airplanes still bombing—Vilna on one side and Lida on the other. Flares lit the skies. We were so close to the station that we could hear people talking, doors slamming, and patrols passing. We lay there until way past midnight, until there was not a sound anywhere.

We then crawled up to the tracks. This time I was one of the two men whose job it was to lay the mine. I strapped my weapon on my back so that my hands were free to carry the mine to the tracks. I put down the mine and carefully started collecting the pebbles, which were painted white, and set them aside. The mine had to be placed under the inner track, midway between two railroad ties, so that the blown-up train would be thrown out into the ditch. With our bayonets we dug a hole under the track, collecting the dirt into rain capes which were spread alongside. I checked to see whether the hole was deep enough for the dynamite. No, I needed to dig more. I dug and dug, covered in sweat. Again I checked, and this time the size was right. I carefully placed the mine in the pit, and pushed the detonator into the hole on top. Then I screwed on a special mechanism for blowing up trains—a fine steel shaft with a flat adjustable head, which I placed directly under the rail.

Next came the most critical part. I adjusted the head to almost touch the rail, but left enough space to run a match under it. In that way only a heavy weight like the locomotive would bend the rail enough to press the shaft, which would detonate the bomb. Very, very carefully we began to cover the mine and to fill in the hole with the dirt which we had dug out, leaving the shaft above ground. It was visible only if one bent to look under the rail. I constantly re-minded myself not to accidentally hit the plunger. When the ground was level, the final detail was to replace the white stones. Everything looked untouched.

Dragging away the soil that remained in the cape, we began the crawl back to where our heavy machine gun was positioned, and met up with both groups.

Our guide signaled to us that there was danger. I lay down with my weapon ready, but heard nothing. After about ten minutes I crawled to the guide and asked him what he had seen. He said it seemed to him that a patrol was coming. We waited another ten minutes and then quickly and quietly left.

We were back at the village of Mosti by daybreak, but we couldn't resist seeing a train exploding again. We went back up the hill and watched and waited.

It was a beautiful summer morning. The sun was just out. I looked down at the station, trying to figure out just where I had placed the mine. I saw a train leaving the station. It looked so small, like a matchbox. It gathered speed and approached the danger point. I held my breath. Another ten yards, another five. Will it explode? At that instant I saw a pillar of flame rising into the sky, and the train was thrown into the air, writhing like a tortured snake before it fell into the ditch. And then I heard the boom. It blasted the win-dows in the village. Then all I could see of the train was smoke and fire.

Later, we found out that the train was full of German soldiers. Thirty cars were destroyed, several hundred Germans were killed and hundreds more wounded. Another train from Vilna, coming to evacuate the wounded and bring reinforcements, was also blown up by the mine laid down on the other side.

I needed to see the destruction and the havoc that I personally helped create. Seeing the wreckage I felt that, in the only way I could, I was fulfilling my aim to fight the German war machine and take revenge.

Quickly we returned to our temporary camp. To our surprise, we found Musio and another partisan there, with an order from Major Sergey to return quickly to our base in Rudnitzkaya puszcza.

The Soviet army had already taken Vileika, and was moving toward Vilna.

Our specgruppa was ordered by the partisan headquarters to move westward, deeper within Poland behind the German lines, to continue to destroy their communication and transportation lines, and to create panic and havoc by attacking the retreating Germans.

Fourteen of us set out immediately for the Rudnitzkaya puszcza. We marched along a path in the woods in single file for hours. I was near the end of the line, and as time went by, the line stretched longer and longer. I couldn't see the people leading the way, and although I tried to move faster, I was too tired. One of the partisans, a Russian who always carried a guitar strapped on his back, took his instrument, hung his carbine on his back, and began to strum and sing Russian marches. I enjoyed the music immensely, and noticed that gradually I was marching in tune. So were all the other men, and the line tightened, while everyone joined in the singing. We pulled ourselves straight and the way became less difficult.

When we returned to our main base, Captain Voronov gathered us together and made a speech thanking us for performing our mission successfully. He had recommended that partisan headquarters award us medals of honor for this mission.

By now, we were informed, the Soviet army was close to Vilna and within a week or so would oust the Germans from there. We would be leaving the Rudnitzkaya puszcza the following day.

We six Jewish partisans gathered in our zemlianka. We had become a close-knit group within a group, and consulted each other on all major decisions. Now, a discussion arose as to whether we should continue with the Gvardia or join the Jewish otriad formed by Abba Kovner, which would be the first group to enter Vilna when the Soviet army took over the area. Yuditka, Bonchak, and Yehuda were for joining the Jewish otriad, while Musio, Markh, and I were reluctant to agree with them. We thought that this would mean the end of our fight against the Nazis before the war was over, and felt that at this stage we would be abandoning our mission. The argument continued throughout the night. Finally, we decided to part ways. The next morning the three of them left Gvardia, and joined Abba Kovner.

Days later the Red Army entered Vilna, and with them was Abba Kovner's otriad. There the Jewish otriad was dismantled.

Markh, Musio, and I continued westward with Gvardia, ahead of the advancing Red Army. Along the roads we laid daily ambushes for the retreating Germans, who tried to escape rather than fight. We managed to create panic, kill and wound as many Germans as we could from a distance, then disengage from the confrontation and disappear into the woods. This caused a minimum of casualties to our own forces. We also continued to blow up trains full of retreating soldiers. As we were in territory where no partisans had previously attacked, the Germans had not prepared the usual kind of defense—patrols, bunkers, and the cleared-out areas that had surrounded the tracks. On these missions, there was no direct face-to-face confrontation with the enemy.

For four weeks we ambushed, attacked, stood guard, and were on the go non-stop. Utterly exhausted we reached the Nyemen River, across from which was the beginning of the Byelovetskaya puszcza—our destination.

That night I was sent with Commissar Bikov's patrol to canvass the bank of the river, while the otriads remained some miles behind. We reached a hutor near the river, and I spoke Polish to the farmer so he would have no clue of our identity. According to him, the German army had put up a temporary bridge several miles to the north, and were using it to retreat across the river. We moved stealthily to the bank. The river was wide but we saw no currents or turbulence. At a distance we made out the temporary bridge, which was well lit. There was very light westward movement along the bridge. We observed it for an hour, then returned to our otriad.

The following night, near the same hutor, we found several boats which had somehow appeared. Throughout the night, the entire otriad silently crossed the river and entered the Byelovetskaya puszcza. We headed toward a high wooded hill and reached the top at midday. Looking down we saw the river, and movement along the bridge.

Shortly after I lay down and fell asleep, I was awakened by explosions and cannon blasts. I ran to the ridge of the hill and saw shells exploding around the bridge. The bombardment continued, and we assumed that this was Soviet artillery. When a few hours later mortar fire was added, we realized that the Red Army was indeed near. The shelling lasted all night and stopped at dawn. Through our binoculars we saw the damaged bridge and no movement. There were no more German soldiers around. By noon military units arrived, but we could not distinguish whether they were German or Soviet. They began to build a floating bridge alongside the destroyed one, and it was finished within two hours. Units began to cross and came in our direction, toward the bottom of our hill. Even looking through the binoculars we still couldn't identify the units, until suddenly someone shouted, "These are ours, the Red Army! Hurrah!"

Spontaneously, our entire otriad began to run down the hill toward the approaching unit. I was among the first to reach the road, and saw a horsecart coming toward us. Several Soviet soldiers were sitting on top with a heavy machine gun, and a few more soldiers walked alongside. This was my first glimpse of the victoriously returning Red Army. We embraced them, shouted our welcome, laughed and told them that we were Soviet partisans.

Meanwhile, more troops arrived and we mingled among them. Captain Voronov spoke to their leader, then ordered us to gather our things and to move toward the floating bridge. By the time we reached the bridge, a large number of Soviet soldiers had already gathered there. The bridge could only accommodate one-way traffic, and the flow westward was so heavy that we had to wait a long time to be able to cross eastward. We spent the time talking with the soldiers and officers, who were very interested in how warfare was carried out by partisans. We discussed the tides of war, and found out that the Nazi empire had suffered great setbacks on all the fronts. The Americans and British were already established in France and were pushing the Germans out. In the Middle East the German army had been defeated by the British. On all the Soviet fronts the Germans were retreating under the attack of the Red Army. I still couldn't comprehend that for us the partisan war was over, and that we had survived!

After about two hours we crossed the bridge, and a Soviet officer pointed out the way to the military headquarters of the Red

Army of that zone, where we were supposed to report. After two miles we found a camp of tents on a hill overlooking the river.

Our commanders, Sergey, Voronov, and Nikolaev, told us to wait outside while they went into the tents to see the officer in charge. When they came out an hour later, they were accompanied by an impressive Soviet officer. What a difference from the way I remembered the appearances of high-ranking Soviet officers in 1941. Instead of having their rank on the tip of their collar, their ranks were now impressively established on gold-embroidered epaulets. Ornate epaulets were once considered a symbol of imperialism and scorned by the communists. But not any longer. I asked one of our paratroopers what the rank was. He said this was a brigade general. Previously, officers in charge of brigades, divisions or armies were all called commanders. The title "general" was also considered an imperialist term.

The general gathered us around him and made a speech, thanking us in the name of the Soviet army for our heroic struggle against the Nazi occupiers. He said our missions contributed to the success of the Soviet army. But, he added, the war wasn't over yet, and we would only be able to rest on our laurels after the enemy was totally vanquished. Meantime, all the ex-Soviet military personnel were to report to a base about thirty miles away, where they would be regrouped and incorporated into the Soviet army. All the rest of us were to report to one of the tents, to receive travel permits to Minsk, where we would appear at the general headquarters of the Belorussian partisans. There we would join other Belorussian partisan units for a victory march. Then, with a shout of cheer, which we echoed, "Hail to our Fatherland, hail to Stalin, Hurrah!" the general ended his speech. First the Fatherland and then Stalin? That was something new! I remembered that in 1941 every speech was ended with a hail first to Stalin and then to the Fatherland. These were significant changes in the ideological approach of the Soviets.

Those fifteen of us, including Markh, Musio and me, who had joined Gvardia as civilians, were now supposed to go to Minsk. We embraced and said goodbye to the specgruppa, to the "foreign" contingency and the paratroopers from the Soviet Union, with whom we had shared so many experiences. It was a sad yet exhilarating time. Our commanders patted us warmly on the shoulders. I gave a special embrace to Commissar Bikov, who had saved my life in the swamps. Four abreast, they marched off while we waved to them.

We were told to surrender all our military equipment, except rifles, submachine guns and ammunition.

As I bent down to pick up something, my head began to swim, and I realized how weak and undernourished I was. I had been under too much stress to notice it before. I sat down. For the first time in years, in broad daylight, without the pressure of immediate danger and missions, I was relaxed and had the opportunity to really look at Musio and Markh. They were gaunt and scruffy, in ill-fitting peasant clothing and torn boots, clutching their rifles. Their heads were bare, exposing Musio's messy hair and Markh's bald pate. But their eyes were bright and alert.

I told Markh and Musio that I wanted to rest, the bulge in my belly was bothering me. I opened my pants, removed the cloth, and showed it to them. I could feel the interior rip in my abdomen. It was a good six inches long. They were appalled and said that as soon as we arrived in Minsk, they would take me to a hospital.

Meanwhile, most of our group of fifteen disappeared, probably to go home. After a short while the three of us headed for the tent where we were supposed to report.

Several officers were sitting at the table. Musio, who knew Russian best, was our spokesman. He turned to the colonel and briefly told him our story, then asked for travel permits for us to Minsk. The colonel wrote a letter permitting us to travel by any means of transportation. A major sitting next to him told us to be careful. He warned us that there were still armed groups of Germans and their supporters left behind the front, roaming in the woods and they sometimes attacked Soviet units. Also, the Red Army had orders to shoot anybody who bore arms and had no proper Soviet identification. We should have our letter of authorization on hand all the time. He then asked us to accompany him out of the tent.

We sat down with him on the precipice of the hill, overlooking the bridge. He told us he was Jewish—his name was Major Epstein—and that he was a member of the Anti-Fascist Committee. This was the first time he had ever met Jewish partisans and he wanted to hear our story. He knew Yiddish, and Markh began to tell him. What he didn't fully understand, Musio translated into Russian. We sat there for over three hours. At times he cried. When we finished, he embraced us and told us, "You have gone through enough. Don't join the army. Don't tempt fate. You must stay alive to bear witness to what has happened to our people." He suggested going to the railroad station, which meant going for about fifteen miles along roads in the woods. He explained that we had two choices. We could leave our weapons behind and thus avoid a misunderstanding with Soviet units, who, before asking for identification, could start shooting at civilians bearing arms. But then, if we were unarmed, we would have no means of defense if we met German bandit units or their supporters. Of course, we chose to keep our arms. He showed us the way to the railway station, where we could take a train to Minsk. We were very hungry, since we hadn't eaten in a long time. Major Epstein brought us some food, which satisfied only the first pangs of hunger, and not for long. We embraced warmly and set off, hoping to reach the station before dark.

Markov, commander of the partisan brigade, which included the Jewish otriad, was awarded the highest medal by the Soviet government for his heroism in 1945.

Partisans capturing moments of pleasure and music between missions, 1943. Hannale in the middle, and her father, Papa Posner, fourth from the left in the back row, were part of the entertainment group that was enthusiastically received by the fighting units. They sang of fighting, of victory over the Nazis, of love and yearning for home and their dear ones.

A group of partisans, 1943. No less important than their machine guns to this group of partisans was their accordion, which helped to sustain morale and the spirit to fight under even the most difficult conditions.

A partisan laying explosives beneath railroad tracks.

Вражеский эшелон, пущенный
под откос партизанами Брест
ской области.

An enemy train after the explosion.

RIGHT: One of the many signs posted by Germans along the roads:
"Danger—Partisans.   Single vehicles must stop!   Through traffic only for 8 vehicles or more.   Arms at the ready." [signed] *"The Commanding General"*

Партызаны — небяспечнасць !
якія папярэджванні ставілі гітле-
аўцы на подступах да раёнаў скан-
янтравання партызан.

"артизаны — опасно»!
кие предупреждения устанавли-
ли гитлеровцы на подступах к рано-

BELOW: Ordinary-looking heroes, peasants who were informants for the partisans, were awarded medals for their bravery by the Soviet government after the war.

Yacub Shafran, Selim's closest friend, a reconnaisance scout, 1943. He was known among the partisans for his bravery and ingenuity.

21

BECOMING A RED ARMY SOLDIER

End of August 1944

On the way to the train station that hot August day, Musio, Markh, and I met three of our compatriots from Gvardia. They too were heading our way, so they joined us. It was getting dark when we arrived.

At the station a group of Soviet soldiers, seeing six armed men in civilian clothing, aimed their rifles at us and demanded to know our identity. We showed them our paper signed by the general, and explained that we were Soviet partisans. They embraced us and told us that since they too were waiting for the train to Minsk, we should join them. They were interested to hear our partisan experiences, and shared their meager supply of food with us.

There was no sign of the train, and nobody knew when it would arrive, so we lay down on the platform to rest. I instantly fell asleep.

Commotion woke me up. It was already dawn, and I saw the soldiers running and shouting. Instinctively, I grabbed my weapon and ran in the same direction.

Beyond the platform, under a tree, I saw a group of soldiers holding and frisking a man in German uniform. When I came closer I saw his clothes were in disarray. A sergeant had taken command of the situation and was interrogating the soldier, who didn't understand what was said. I came forward and offered to translate. The sergeant was shouting, "You are a Nazi SS! You were left behind in order to blow up the train!"

When I translated, the German began to whine and plead. He took out a picture of his family and showed it to me. There were his wife and children, and his parents—a regular family picture. He said that he belonged to the Wehrmacht (army) and not to the SS, and had become separated from his unit. He begged for mercy. For some reason, seeing the man face to face, pleading for his life, touched me. Killing trains full of faceless soldiers didn't affect me as much—I was disrupting the German war machine. Here, I was witnessing a lone man surrounded by his enemies, a plight I could identify with. The sergeant yelled that it was known that Nazi and SS all claimed the same when they were caught.

I said I was not sure that the German was lying, and suggested handing him over to a prison camp, where he would be properly interrogated. The sergeant was furious with me. He said there were no camps there and it was dangerous to drag him along with us. Also, he was sure that the man was a Nazi SS, because it was common practice to leave Nazis behind the frontlines to sabotage. "We shall execute him," he decided.

When I tried to express my doubt again, he turned to me and said cynically, "You Jew, knowing what the Nazis have done to your people and your family, why are you still hesitating to shoot him?"

"If I knew for a fact that this man is a Nazi SS, I would have no mercy for him," I replied. "But maybe he is just a soldier, a human being like us, just fighting on the wrong side."

The sergeant motioned to the German to get up and run toward some distant bushes. The German rose, not fully understanding. "Run," I said to him. At first he started to walk away, and when he saw that nothing happened he began to run. The sergeant took his rifle, aimed at him, and shouted, "Everybody fire!" We all fired. The German collapsed. Some of the soldiers ran toward him. I turned around and walked away. I had never shot a defenseless person in cold blood. It turned my stomach.

A freight train eventually arrived. Musio, Markh, and I got into an enclosed boxcar and sat down on the floor by the open door.

The slow-moving train stopped frequently at little stations along the way. At one of these we saw apple trees in the distance. We jumped off and rushed to pick the fruit, collecting as much as we could in our pockets and wrapped in our rain capes before the train moved out. For two days, all the way to Minsk, the capital of Belorussia, we ate apples.

When we arrived in Minsk it was already dark, and on the platform an unpleasant surprise awaited us. The entire station was surrounded by Soviet soldiers, who checked everybody getting off the train.

Musio explained to the officer in charge that we were Soviet partisans who had been sent to the headquarters of the Belorussian partisans in Minsk to participate in a victory parade. We showed him our passes from the general. The officer scoffed at us and said, "The parade is over. Now all the partisans are being drafted into the army, and you are coming with us to a military camp."

We were frisked, our weapons were taken away from us, and we were loaded on to an open truck. There were several hundred people crammed into a number of trucks.

At the military camp we were directed to some huts. Before we entered, a truck arrived, carrying loaves of dark bread. Soldiers sitting atop began to throw the bread down to us and we all began to shove and grab for it. Crushed in the crowd, I somehow managed to catch one loaf.

I found Musio and Markh, and the three of us settled into one of the huts. We went to sleep on the bare floor.

With the first light of morning, we all had to assemble in the yard for roll call, and officers checked everyone's identity papers. Musio took out our paper and showed it to the officer, who read it and said that we were now going to be taken into the Red Army. We asked for some time off to go to the partisan headquarters to get the medals which were promised to us, and to rest up after the years spent in the woods fighting the Nazis. We were undernourished and exhausted. The officer said coldly, "The war isn't over yet. You'll get your medals and rest after the war." He took down our names and told us that soon we would be sent to the frontline. We were dismissed.

We had not expected such a letdown. Instead of some kind of consideration for us as partisans, we were received with scorn, treated not as fighters but as future cannon fodder.

Every day more young men were brought in, some in uniform.

We found out that soldiers who were in the area without the proper authorization were grabbed off the streets.

We stayed in this camp for several days, and then all of us, a few thousand people, were put on a long freight train and sent on our way to the frontline, which was now near Kovno, the capital of Lithuania.

We were packed in a stuffy boxcar, in simmering heat, with no water and very little food. Nobody had bothered to take care of these basic necessities. Occasionally we got some hot water with something floating in it, considered to be soup. The train stopped frequently, for long stretches of time. At every stop, thousands of people jumped off, rushed to nearby fields and frantically dug for potatoes, then lit fires to cook the potatoes in any way they could, using a variety of utensils stolen from the villages. Markh was the most resourceful of us, and became like the head of our family. He was agile, and was somehow always among the first to acquire food.

At one of the stops, Musio and Markh got off, dug up some potatoes with their bare hands, filled a pot with water and started cooking over a fire, while I was on the train. Suddenly the train began to move slowly. I yelled to them to drop everything and come quickly. Markh grabbed the pot and began to run, water splashing all over him. I looked around and saw hundreds of people, all carrying utensils with their precious potatoes, running to catch the train. I leaned forward, took the pot by the handle out of Markh's hand, and helped them both aboard. The half-raw potatoes were going to be cooked at the next stop. This scene repeated itself, with slight variations, at each stop.

The instant the train stopped at a larger station, local villagers were there waiting, offering food and vodka in exchange for anything the soldiers could give. The soldiers knew that at the front they would be issued uniforms, so they traded in their clothes and shoes, and many of them remained just short of naked. We traded our coats and warm clothing for food, and stayed in our shirts and pants.

No one was keeping track of the names of the people on the train, and it would have been very easy to defect, to just stay off the train at the next stop. We were tired of fighting, but on the other hand, the war wasn't over yet—the Nazis hadn't been fully defeated, and we could still do more. These thoughts troubled us, and we mulled them over again and again.

We arrived in Vileika, the county seat near Kurzeniec, where so many atrocities had taken place. This was the station we had reached as a family in 1941, trying to catch a train into the Soviet Union, away from the advancing German army.

We were told that this was a long stopover for the train, so Markh offered to go into one of the more affluent Polish homes to ask for food. About a quarter of an hour after his departure, to our surprise, the train began to move. We looked around for him, called him, but he was nowhere around. The train left. Musio suggested that perhaps Markh had decided to remain in Vileika. I was furious at him for even mentioning such a possibility. I couldn't believe that he would do such a thing without talking it over with us. We were sad and frustrated at the idea that we might not see our "brother" again.

The next stop was at Vilna, which we reached several hours later. We knew that Yuditka, Bonchak, and Yehuda had come there, and thought that perhaps we could find a way of contacting them. But we decided to sit around and wait, in case Markh showed up. A few hours later we couldn't believe our eyes when we saw a "drezina"—a hand-driven cart used by repairmen working on the tracks—coming toward the train, carrying a Soviet soldier with Markh next to him! We ran to him, delighted at being together again. He had bribed the soldier in the cart to catch up with us.

We kept toying with the idea of remaining in Vilna, but couldn't make up our minds. We left the decision to fate—if we saw someone we knew, we would stay. Otherwise we would continue on our way.

Some draftees were brought to our train in Vilna, and there were some Jews among them. After several more hours the train moved on, and we were on it.

The following day we reached our destination—Kleipeda in Lithuania. We got off the train, and were marched off to a military camp outside the town. There our names were taken down, and we were given identification papers. We were sworn in and thus officially Red Army soldiers! Our heads were shaved, our belongings taken away, and we were issued Soviet uniforms. We got khaki breeches, rubber-soled shoes, and shirts to be worn over the pants, tied with a belt. The uniforms were issued randomly, regardless of size. One short soldier got extra-large clothes—his shirt reached to his knees and his shoes were about three sizes too large. Another one, a bull of a soldier, got a shirt he couldn't squeeze into. It was up to the soldiers themselves to switch clothes and to end up with something more appropriate to their size. My uniform fit reasonably well, and Musio's happened to be right for him.

While we were lined up for inspection, the major shouted, "Who can write well in Russian? Take one step forward." Musio reluctantly stepped forward, at our urging. Three others followed suit. The major asked each one several questions, and then chose Musio to go with him. He was installed in the commander's office as a secretary.

We got no training whatsoever, but every day at roll call an officer would pick out men to be sent to the frontline. A military band played marches, and those selected were issued rifles and ammunition, and hand grenades. Then, standing at attention, they listened to a patriotic speech by a political officer, then marched off to waiting trucks.

Within a few days, some of them began to return, wounded, to the hospital in the camp. From them we learned that the soldiers were taken out of the camp straight into the fighting units, to replace the dead and wounded.

Every day we expected to be chosen, but the same officer always passed us by, maybe because of Musio's position.

Musio had open sores on the lower part of his body, but he was afraid to go to the medical clinic in case we were sent away while he was kept there. If we were separated again, it could quite possibly be for good. But as his sores got worse, we convinced him to go for medical help, and he was immediately sent to the hospital. I too developed sores on my rear end, and a few days later also went to the clinic for help. They sent me to the same hospital, but unfortunately, we were in separate rooms.

In the morning a doctor came in with his staff, checked my behind hurriedly, and prescribed some ointment and medicine. I managed to conceal the bulge in my belly; I was afraid that if he found it, more serious treatment would be necessary, and I would be sent away and separated from Musio and Markh. He did take my temperature and I was found to have high fever.

I was put into a room with six sick and lightly wounded soldiers. Next to me was a vicious, anti-Semitic Ukrainian. When I told him I was a Jew, he took every opportunity to express his most violent hatred of Jews. During the chief doctor's visit, I complained. The doctor, a colonel, told me not to get excited—he would talk to the Ukrainian. But nothing changed. The following day I told the doctor that unless he did something about it, he shouldn't be surprised if I dealt with matters on my own and killed the Ukrainian. He pacified me again, and about an hour later the menace was taken out of the room.

During the ten days we stayed in the hospital, Markh visited us several times. The officer still passed him by every morning. When our sores began to heal, Musio and I were released from the hospital on the same day.

We returned to the camp in the evening and we found some sort of celebration going on. There were camp fires, music, soldiers performing Cossack dances, and vodka. We immediately went looking for Markh and found him singing at one of the camp fires. It was a joy to be all together again. He told us that that morning he had succeeded in getting a transfer to the newly formed Polish army under Soviet command. He said we should try to do the same immediately.

The next morning he pointed out the major who was in charge of transfers. After the parade, we waited outside the barracks for an opportunity to approach him. After about an hour, he came out and went to the outhouse. When he was going back, we ran after him, saluted him smartly and explained that we were Polish citizens and wanted to join the newly formed Polish army. He stopped, looked at us silently for a moment, then beckoned to us to follow him. Standing at attention while he sat at his desk looking through some papers, we waited until he turned to us. Then we explained that we were Jews born in Warsaw, and had been Soviet partisans fighting the Germans. He told us to sit down, questioned us further, took down our names and said he would transfer us. He said people like us, loyal Soviet partisans, were needed in the Polish army, and we would hear from him. We saluted and left.

Markh was waiting outside to hear the outcome of our meeting with the major. Musio and Markh were optimistic, but I was rather skeptical.

That night we were called out of our barracks, and an officer waiting for us told us that the following morning we were being transferred to the newly formed Polish army.

In the morning, we were taken to a new camp on the outskirts of Kovno, which had just recently been retaken by the Soviets. The camp consisted of crudely constructed wooden barracks, with outhouses built of planks. Crouched in one of the outhouses I suddenly noticed Hebrew letters scrawled on the planks. I tried to read the writing. There were names and sentences in Yiddish saying "I am going to my death." "If you find this, notify my family." "Let the world know." "Shma Israel" ("Hear, O Israel," a Jewish prayer). Shocked, I ran to Musio and Markh, and brought them to see.

We began to ask questions about what had happened here. We were told that on this site there had been a small Nazi camp where many Jews from Kovno had been tortured and murdered.

Every day new men were brought in. After a few days there were several hundred of us. At roll call, we were given a pep talk in Polish by a commissar (political officer), saying that we were now a part of the Polish army and would fight the Germans alongside the glorious Red Army. We were ordered to march proudly four abreast through the streets of Kovno to the railroad station, where we were going to board the train to Vilna.

Around me I saw a group of men who hardly looked like a proud army. Some were dressed in Russian uniforms, some in old Polish uniforms, most in shabby civilian clothes. But when we saw the crowds in Kovno watching us, we pulled ourselves up, heads held high, and marched proudly through the streets.

I looked around at the well-dressed men and women in silk stockings and high-heeled shoes, with lipstick and elegant hats. I hadn't seen such people in years. I nudged Musio and said, "Look, we're back in civilization! It looks as though here life is normal despite the war, while our world has been turned upside down." Musio nodded sadly.

We arrived at the station and were herded into a train going to Vilna.

22

THE POLISH ARMY

September 1944–February 1945

Back in Vilna, we were ushered into a schoolyard, which was allocated to serve as the camp of the Second Infantry Battalion of the
Polish army. It was in September of 1944, five years from the beginning of the war, that I became a Polish soldier.

Most of the soldiers had previously been in the ruthless AK, and
were patriotic nationalists who had fought against the Soviet soldiers and partisans, as well as the Nazis. There were very few from
the Soviet side, and just a handful of Jews.

At roll call on the first day, I saw Lieutenant Michko for the first
time. He was the commanding officer of the company, and was a
tall and handsome figure, elegant in his immaculate uniform and
highly polished boots. His uniform was very similar to the pre-war
Polish uniforms. Next to him stood Sergeant-Major Gotzky, short,
bowlegged, bullish, and stocky. He was the only pre-war professional military man there. The other soldiers given the rank of
sergeant were promoted based on their military experience during
the war.

Michko asked who of us knew how to write well in Polish. Both
Markh and Musio, with several others, stepped forward. Markh was
chosen to join the battalion staff, and Musio was given the position
of administrative aide to Lieutenant Michko. I was assigned to
Michko's company.

We were all issued rifles and Polish uniforms, which consisted of olive green pants and tunics, caps and shoes—very different from our previous Soviet uniforms, which we had to turn in.

Settled in the rooms of the schoolhouse, life fell into a routine. The day started at 6 A.M. with roll call. Then inspection, where we were checked for lice and cleanliness. We had to remove our undershirts, turn them inside out, and, standing half naked, stretch them out on our arms. Michko and Gotzky tapped each shirt with the small sticks they always carried. Sometimes even our pants were inspected for lice. If lice or dirt were found, Michko would give an order to have the offending soldier cleaned. Gotzky would pick two soldiers to take the offender to a nearby stream, and, with a stiff floor brush, scrub him clean. No screams of pain would ease the punishment.

Next came the inspection of our mess tins, which had to be immaculate. A dirty tin would be thrown out behind the fence, so that that morning the owner of the tin had nothing to put his breakfast in. He had to crawl under the fence, find his mess tin, and clean it thoroughly for the next meal.

After inspection we lined up for breakfast—a piece of black bread and watery soup. The menu never varied for all three meals of the day.

At seven o'clock there was arms inspection. A soldier whose rifle was not very clean was punished by extra after-training duties such as cleaning the latrines and sinks or doing kitchen work.

Then we marched off to the outskirts of town for ten hours of intensive training, with half an hour's break for lunch. We were taught how to march, parade, and salute, and learned how to use our weapons while under fire, as well as bayoneting and fighting in trenches. Michko was a very demanding officer; discipline was stringent and punishment severe. There were days when the exercises of attack under fire were carried out in muddy and difficult conditions. A soldier who lagged had to repeat the exercises over and over again. We would be exhausted, but Michko demanded that the march back to base through the town be impressive for the local Polish population, who proudly cheered us on.

Back in the base, we had half an hour to clean up for the parade before supper. Our arms and uniforms were inspected again.

Whoever didn't pass inspection was sent to extra work instead of supper. After the evening meal we had two hours of free time before the bugle sounded for bedtime.

The bulge in my belly was causing me a lot of pain. Before the exercises I tightened the cloth around my waist as much as I could, hoping that it would help me. Once, when the pain was quite unbearable, I lined up for sick parade. Our doctor was not really a doctor. He was a "felcher"—a medic, qualified only as an assistant to a doctor. When I came before him, he was standing in the room by a table laden with medical equipment. As I was beginning to approach him, expecting to be examined, he stretched out his arm, and said, "Don't come any closer."

He asked me what my complaint was. I pointed to my belly and said that I had severe pain, and would like him to take a look. He said it wasn't necessary; I should take the medicine which he would give me and everything would be fine. He gave me some medicine and called in the next patient. When I found out that it was Epsom salts for constipation, I knew that it wouldn't solve my problem, and didn't take it. I later heard that he always kept the soldiers at arm's length. If the complaint was from the waist up, he gave an aspirin. If the pain was below the waist, he gave the only laxative he had—Epsom salts.

Musio, with his high school diploma, was the most educated man in the company and became the chief aide to both Michko and Gotzky, handling the administration of the company. He was given the rank of sergeant. Markh did well in the administration of the battalion, and also became invaluable to the captain in charge. He was given the rank of master sergeant. I was eventually promoted to the rank of corporal and put in charge of a group of ten men. Michko behaved very decently toward us, and none of the previous AK soldiers dared vent any anti-Semitic feelings—because of our positions, and because it could be construed as counter-revolutionary.

The intensive training went on for six weeks. Our Sundays were generally free of training, but the morning inspection went on as usual. Afterward we were given passes to go to town for several hours.

Markh, Musio, and I used the time to meet other Jewish survivors in Vilna. Markh contacted Abba Kovner, previously the head of the Jewish otriad in the Rudnidzkaya puszcza, and Nissan Reznik, whom we knew from the Jewish Miest otriad. These two men had become the top organizers of the Zionist movement in Vilna. We heard that Yuditka and Bonchak had left Vilna and settled in Bialistok. We had no contact with the rest of the people we knew in the woods, and heard that many of them had stayed in small towns scattered throughout the area. Markh found out that within a week our battalion would be moving out to the Bialistok area, so we got Yuditka's address.

Our battalion went by train from Vilna to Bialistok, and in the camp on the outskirts of town we met other battalions from various parts of the country.

We were reorganized into an infantry regiment, headed by a Russian colonel of Polish descent, who spoke only Russian. Michko was promoted to the rank of captain, and put in command of our battalion. The previous battalion commander now became a major and moved to the regimental headquarters. Markh was now deputy chief of the chancellery of the regiment, and was given the rank of non-commissioned officer. Musio continued as Michko's chief assistant, and was promoted accordingly. I was promoted to sergeant and took Musio's position in the company, under a new lieutenant.

We were told that we would soon be moving toward the frontline—we were waiting for the arrival of the Second Polish Army, which had been formed in the Soviet Union. Then we would become a part of the Second Army, and all go to the front together. Our thoughts and discussions centered on guessing whether we would be sent to the northern or central front, and our chances of survival. By that time, the northern frontline had stabilized on the borders of Prussia, and the central front was along the Visla River, with Warsaw still in German hands.

All training was discontinued and discipline slackened. We used our free time to visit our friends in Bialistok. We found Yuditka and Bonchak living in a shack, which became the meeting place of all those Jews trying to locate their relatives and friends. There were endless discussions—political, military, Zionist, philosophical—and dreams of the future. Yuditka tried to convince us to stay in Bialistok and not continue with the army. She said that we had been putting our lives on the line for such a long time, and had struggled

so hard. Since so few of the European Jews had survived, thus dec-
imating world Jewry, our duty now was to survive, not to endan-
ger our lives any longer.

It was very simple, in the existing chaotic setup, to disappear
from the army and blend into civilian life. Yuditka's arguments
were valid and tempting; again we were faced with this difficult decision, not because of our loyalty to the army, but because we felt
we should not abandon our fight against the Nazis.

One evening we found two young Jewish newcomers sleeping
in Yuditka's house. They were both from Warsaw, and had run
away to the Soviet side with their families. They had later been deported by the Soviets to Siberia, where they spent several years before escaping and making their way to Bialistok. During the course
of conversation one of them mentioned being in Komi, Siberia. I
asked him if he had by chance met my aunt Rujia and her family.
He looked closely at us, jumped up and shouted, "You are Musio
and Selim! I am your second cousin Natek, and Rujia's husband was
my uncle! We were there together all the time!" I could hardly recognize him, but Musio did. He was only slightly older than Musio,
but was stooped over, and in his shabby outfit, with a gaunt face
and prominent nose, he looked almost middle-aged. He told us that
Rujia's family had been sent to a labor camp in Siberia, where her
husband had died of malnutrition. Aunt Rujia and her young son
were okay, and had been released from the camp. He gave us their
address.

We sent a letter to Rujia, telling her of our parents' fate and
asked whether she knew anything about the rest of the family.

In the Bialistok synagogue Markh met a Jewish Russian soldier
from Jaroslav, Markh's birthplace. Before being taken into the army,
he had also been sent to Siberia, where he had met Markh's parents. He said Markh's mother and older brother were there and were
alive! Markh's fiancée was also with them, but she married someone else because she had heard that Markh had been killed. Markh
was still in love with her, and it devastated him.

In the beginning of November 1944, the Second Polish Army
finally arrived from the Soviet Union and we were united with them.
Together we headed west toward the frontline, along the Visla
River, where the Soviet advance had been halted. The front had been

static there for a while, with the Soviets occupying one side of the river and the Germans the other.

We were now an infantry regiment in the Second Polish Army, not in name only but in the real sense of the word—we marched on foot everywhere, while Michko and the other commanders rode horseback. Each company had a few horse-drawn carts piled with paperwork and ammunition; they were also used by those who were ill and unable to walk. In addition to my other duties, I was responsible for the company office and walked behind the cart which carried the files and ledgers, so when I got tired I snuck onto the cart for a little while.

We would march all day, and in the evening stop by the roadside. The kitchen cart would pull up to each company and we would all line up for our ration of watery soup and black bread. In the morning, before setting off again, we would get the same meal.

We moved for several days along the main road leading to Warsaw, then took side roads until we reached a large forest in the heart of Poland, where we set up a temporary camp. We were told that we would be staying there for a while, so we chopped down trees and built crude huts to live in. Each company had a separate base.

Orders came from the Second Polish Army headquarters to expand our regiment from eight hundred to three thousand men. In order to comply with the order, we were told to draft all able-bodied men in the area from the age of eighteen. A special recruiting base was established, and units were formed to go to the surrounding towns and villages. According to lists acquired at the town or village halls, the soldiers went from house to house to search for the men, and brought them to the camp. Another group of soldiers had to guard them, to prevent them from attempting to escape. Their heads were shaved, they were ordered to shower, and then they waited to be conscripted. One after the other, each battalion came to take recruits according to an assigned quota.

In our battalion, Sergeant-Major Gotzky was put in charge of the mission. He chose Musio and me, and another twenty corporals and sergeants, to organize the registration and absorption of the men who were brought in. We witnessed his special skills in organization and improvisation: he divided the men into four groups and each group was to become part of a different company. I was in charge of registering all those who were chosen for our company. They came in one at a time and handed me identification documents, if they had any. I wrote down all the pertinent information from the documents, and if they had none, I wrote what they told me. Then I grilled them about their activities during the German occupation, and whether they had cooperated with the Germans. They were frightened, and I needed to use my intuitive skills to draw out the information, to calm them down, to play on their national patriotism—to explain that they were now going to be Polish, not Soviet, soldiers fighting the German forces who were occupying their land.

After I was through questioning them, they had to sign the registration forms. That took them a long time, and it taxed my patience. Many of them couldn't even sign their names, and just stamped their thumbs. The quartermaster then issued them uniforms, underwear, boots, and caps. The whole procedure began in the afternoon and dragged on throughout the night, by the light of kerosene lamps, lasting until dawn. Then they were sworn in and officially soldiers.

After so many hours in the stuffy hut, I went out for a breath of air. It was fully light. When I saw what was going on outside, I began to laugh, which was something I rarely did now. There was the group of about two hundred men, who had been recruited that night, formed into several lines, and Gotzky was inspecting them. Some of the men wore uniforms much too large or too small for them. Gotzky was running from one to the other, trying to help them switch uniforms according to their sizes. I came up to him as he was shouting at one of the soldiers who was standing in his tunic and underwear, barefoot, holding his pants and shoes in his hands. The soldier said he couldn't squeeze into them. Gotzky said that he would get him a larger pair of pants, but there was nothing he could do about the shoes, since there were no more. He insisted that the soldier could force his feet into the shoes, so the soldier sat on the ground, and, with Gotzky's help, tried to do as he was ordered. Gotzky said the problem was that the big toe was too long and he should bend it; if he couldn't, there would be no other choice but to chop it off. The soldier then managed to somehow squeeze into the shoes, and stood up, toes crunched, looking very uncomfortable. It was funny and pathetic at the same time. After a while Gotzky and his sergeants had everybody more or less satisfactorily dressed and standing at attention in straight lines. They then issued them rifles, and the soldiers were marched off for training.

I later asked Gotzky why there were no more shoes and uniforms when, according to my calculation, there should be at least forty sets left over. He said that at night, while we were working, one of the quartermaster sergeants, at his order, had taken all the extra uniforms and shoes to the closest town to be traded in for such essentials as vodka and sausage for "his" men, and that I would get my share too. One accepted privileges when and where one could.

The other battalions likewise conscripted their recruits, and they were all put through intensive training, from dawn to dusk.

I was with the commander of the company, situated in the woods. Musio was with Michko not far from us, in the battalion headquarters, which was also in the woods. Regimental headquarters, where Markh was, was in a small village on the outskirts of the woods, several miles away.

About a week after the recruitment, I was called one evening into the regimental headquarters and told to appear before the chief intelligence and security officer. As soon as I entered the zemlianka, a sergeant led me into a room. At the desk, clear of everything except a kerosene lamp and a revolver, sat an officer in Polish uniform with the rank of captain. By the way he fidgeted with the stiff collar of his uniform, I realized that he was very uncomfortable because he was a Russian, and was used to the softer collars of the Soviet uniforms.

He told me in Russian to sit down, and came straight to the point. He knew that I had been a Soviet partisan, fighting for Stalin and the homeland, so he could speak openly to me. He lectured me about spies, traitors, and counter-revolutionaries, especially among the Poles, who should be carefully watched and distrusted, even though they were in the Polish army fighting alongside the Soviets. He then bent toward me across the table, and, looking me straight in the eyes, said, "By tomorrow you will bring me a list and the files of all the spies and counter-revolutionaries in your company." Looking back at him, I answered that, had I known of anyone like that in my company, I would have immediately taken care of him myself. Leaning even closer to me, he said, "I know that there are such men in your company."

I thought, "What does this man think of me? I am fighting the Nazis, and anybody helping them is my enemy. Would I leave them be, if I knew of any such people?"

I smiled and said, "We are on the same side." Suddenly I felt a whack on my face. The captain grabbed his revolver, shoved his face even closer, and, after swearing at me, said, "Do you want me to make you look so that even your mother won't recognize you? Now get out, and be here tomorrow morning with your list!"

I was stunned and worried, and ran to find Markh. I asked for his help and advice. He told me that the officer was the chief of the NKVD, the dreaded Soviet Secret Police, and even the colonel in command of the regiment was afraid of him. Nobody could help me. Markh advised me to look through the files, to see if I could find someone who seemed in any way suspicious, and not to discuss my meeting with anyone.

I returned to the company headquarters, went straight to the files, and started reading through each one. I worked all night. Although I didn't know these men, I agonized over each name, wondering whether the men really were staunch supporters of the Germans. I wanted to be reasonably sure before handing over their files and thus participating in their fate. By morning I had put together the names of five men who I found had been connected with the Nazis during the occupation.

I took their files, went to the NKVD officer, and explained that these files should be further examined. He came around the table toward me and patted me approvingly on the shoulder. "I see that you are a quick learner. If you have any further suspicions of anybody, come directly to me." I saluted smartly and left, hoping never to see the man again. I never found out what happened to the men on the list after they were taken in for interrogation.

After the period of training, the regiment was supposed to move to the front. Until then, on Sundays Musio, Markh, and I would meet at the regimental headquarters and spend several hours together.

Markh always prepared something to eat and drink. One Sunday we got drunk and went into the village. After years of unrelenting tension, we now felt carefree, omnipotent in our Polish uniforms on Polish soil and unafraid of the local villagers. In our drunken state, we wanted to have some harmless fun. Markh took his revolver and began to shoot at birds, while Musio and I, roaring with laughter, cheered him on. All the villagers immediately disappeared into their homes. Two military police arrested us and locked us in one of the rooms of the headquarters until we sobered up. We were reprimanded, though not too severely, and Markh's revolver was taken away for a few days in a symbolic disciplinary act. Such misbehavior wasn't viewed as particularly serious.

In December the training period was over. We began to march toward Warsaw, spread out according to battalions, stopping overnight in villages along the way. It was bitterly cold, and though we were issued padded military coats, the going was very difficult. Occasionally it snowed.

I was just behind the carts which Gotzky had loaded with the battalion's supplies. Gotzky frequently dug his hand into one of the carts and magically produced vodka, which he had received in exchange for uniforms. He shared it with the sergeants and officers who were marching near him. I was cold and exhausted, and gladly accepted my share, not delving too deeply into Gotzky's methods of acquiring it. This went on for hours, and I had no idea how much alcohol I had consumed.

We finally stopped overnight in a small town and were all assigned homes to stay in. I entered a warm room, with a fire burning in the fireplace, and barely had time to remove my coat and enjoy the warmth before my head began to spin and I passed out. In the morning I found myself in a bed, with a splitting headache, wet from the water that had been splashed in my face to revive me.

On Christmas Eve Captain Michko invited several officers of the battalion to a Christmas dinner at a house in one of the villages. He included Musio and me though he knew we were Jewish. This was the first time that I had ever been to a Christmas celebration, and I found the ritual interesting. The farmhouse was very simple, but the plain wooden table was laden with good food and plenty of vodka. The head of the family led the prayers, then little white holy breads were distributed to everyone. The Polish family was hospitable and proud to have us, the Polish military, in their midst, and I enjoyed feeling welcome there.

It was taking so long for us to reach the front by foot that our commanders decided to try to get there by train. When we arrived at one of the larger towns, which had a railway station, I was sent with several men from my battalion to check out the possibility of requisitioning a train or at least part of it.

While I was at there, a train arrived full of Soviet soldiers and equipment. The soldiers went into town, and several officers and guards remained. A few hours later the soldiers began to return, heavily laden with loot. There was even a piano brought in on a cart, which they began to load onto the train. Once it was in the boxcar, a soldier sat down and began to play.

I was told by the stationmaster that the train was going west, to the front, so I tried to find out if our battalion could get on. I found several officers drinking on the platform, and struck up a conversation with the captain who seemed to be in charge. He told me that they were from the NKVD army, going to the front too, but the train was too full to take us. He asked why I spoke Russian, though I was in Polish uniform. When he heard that I had been a Soviet partisan, he slapped me on the back in camaraderie and invited me to drink with him. He spoke about his experiences as an officer in the secret police, and later in the elite NKVD army. Even though he was drunk, I was struck by his openness in telling me about taking part in the executions of people accused of being counter-revolutionary. Some of them were even friends and co-workers. His blind obedience to Stalin and communism came through clearly. "Here we are, talking and drinking together as friends," he said, "but if my commander told me to kill you, I would not hesitate to do so, without even questioning why." I asked if he would just as easily kill his mother if he was told to, and he replied instantly that he would. Even his mother? A chill went through me—I said goodbye and left.

We did not get onto the train, and continued on foot. A few days later we reached the east bank of the Visla River, just south of Warsaw. This was the frontline; the west bank was in the hands of the German army. Our battalion was allotted a section of the frontline.

Another battalion from our regiment was to our right, and a Soviet army battalion to our left. We stayed in several rows of interconnected trenches along the river, standing guard, eating, and sleeping there. From time to time an exchange of artillery fire between us and the Germans broke the peaceful silence. Mortar shells were showered on us, and, soon after, I saw ours falling on their positions. It was risky to go outside the trenches, as that drew sniper attacks. Every so often we moved back from the front temporarily for a period of rest, and were replaced by another battalion from our regiment.

Once, on rotation to rest, Musio and I met two men, gaunt and shabby, wandering in the area. We recognized them as Jews, and struck up a conversation. They told us that they had been liberated from a death camp. They described the atrocities—the gas chambers with the shower heads that fooled the people into believing that there was water. Thousands of people were gassed daily, then cremated, and their ashes buried. It was an annihilation factory run efficiently by the Nazis for the total extermination of the Jewish people. Shooting, looting, burning, and killing were somehow connected with war, and more comprehensible. But a death factory, planned and organized like a business, using the ideas and ingenuity of professional engineers, doctors, and architects, utilizing the remains of the human body like hair, teeth, fat, and skin for commercial purposes as soap, brushes, and lampshades, was totally beyond my power of comprehension when I later learned the dismal details. Despite all that I personally had experienced and heard, I couldn't believe what these two men were telling us. I knew that they were telling the truth, but I couldn't comprehend that human beings could be capable of doing such things to other human beings. I dreaded to think that maybe some of my relatives or friends had met with such an end. We provided the two Jews with some food and warm clothing, and they left. For nights afterward I had nightmares.

A few days later, we returned to the trenches on the frontline. We resumed our previous routine. Sporadic exchanges of fire between us and the Germans on the other side of the river continued. Out of sight of the snipers, we would occasionally come out of the trenches and enjoy the peace and quiet. The cold was bearable because of our warm padded clothes.

As usual, the issue of supplementing our meager rations of food was always foremost in our thoughts. The Soviets in the neighboring trench were especially ingenious in acquiring additional supplies. One time, I came up on five Soviet soldiers sitting around a fire, cooking chicken in two helmets which hung over the flame. I struck up a conversation with them, trying to find out where they had gotten the chicken. Suddenly the Germans opened fire on us. I ducked into the Soviets' trench, but they continued to sit by the fire, guarding their precious chicken. I called to them, saying that it was dangerous to remain sitting out there. But nobody moved. One of them replied that it was more dangerous to leave the chicken unattended, because it could disappear, whereas the shooting would eventually stop.

After a while our commanders started to prepare us to attack. We underwent political indoctrination, and intense and strenuous training in attack tactics.

In mid-January the long-awaited offensive along the entire Visla front began with a barrage of fire from more than ten thousand pieces of Soviet artillery. It continued for over two days and nights, non-stop. The response from the German artillery was very weak, and subsided to nothing after the first twenty-four hours. Sitting crouched in the trenches, covering our ears, we couldn't even hear ourselves talk; the noise gradually dulled our senses. We expected momentarily to be ordered to move out of the trenches and cross the river.

At last, on the morning of the third day, the Soviet artillery shots stopped. The sudden quiet was unnerving. We got orders to leave the trenches and run toward the river. At the banks there were small boats. We packed into them, and as we started rowing across, I looked around me and saw the river full of boats crossing. The German side was silent.

When we reached the other side, our company was ordered to attack. We immediately spread out and began to run, shooting all the while into the German trenches. There was no resistance. We jumped into row upon row of trenches, and found many dead and wounded bodies. Within several hours the entire German line was in our hands. Our artillery barrage must have been so severe that whoever could move ran away, leaving behind the dead and dying.

We continued advancing on foot within Poland for two weeks, meeting hardly any resistance, until we reached the Oder River, which was the pre-war border between Poland and Germany. We stopped on the bank of the river, and were told to build trenches and defense lines, and to position ourselves and our artillery along the newly formed frontline—very similar to the setup along the Visla. Rumors spread that this was where we would be until a new offensive attack brought us into Germany. Our days settled into routine again.

I decided to use this period of quiet to try to find any survivors of our family. I asked Captain Michko for a pass to go to Warsaw for a week, and explained my reason. To my surprise, he granted me permission without hesitation.

Taking my submachine gun, I hitchhiked to Warsaw. The city was beyond recognition. The Jewish quarter, where almost half a million people had lived, was burnt. The streets and houses were totally destroyed, razed to the ground. Only some burnt skeletons of buildings remained standing. I tried to find Aunt Rujia's home and Uncle Wolf's apartment, where we had stayed during our flight from Raciaz, but it was impossible even to identify the streets and buildings. I asked people in the streets if there was any Jewish committee or organization where I could get information about my relatives, and I was finally directed to a half-ruined house which was a meeting place for Jewish survivors. Everyone coming there signed up and wrote out a list of relatives whom they were seeking. I wrote down the details of my military unit and began to read the lists of names, trying for hours to find someone from my family. I recognized the name of my cousin's husband, Ignazi Bleiberg, who lived in Warsaw under an assumed Polish name, Zawatzky. I took the address and went off to look for him.

I found Ignazi in the garage where he had worked throughout the war. It was easy for him to assume a Polish identity because he was blond with blue eyes, and spoke fluent Polish. He told me he had heard that his wife, her sister and mother, who was my aunt Zivia, were all alive and had been released from labor camps in Siberia. I spent a day with him.

Since the trains were already running, I decided to go to Raciaz, where we had lived before the war. The fifty mile ride took all day. Wondering whether I would find anyone I knew there, I assumed that Plato, who was of German heritage, had most likely fled with the retreating German army, but that the watchman Yan and his family might still be there.

When I arrived at the station in Raciaz it was already dark. I saw lights in the house that had been our home. Nothing had changed. I crossed the street and quietly knocked on the door. A stranger opened, and I asked whether Yan lived there. He pointed to the small house in the yard which Plato and Yan had shared before we left. There was a light in the window, and Yan opened the door to me, but he didn't recognize me. When I told him who I was, he embraced me warmly and invited me in. He was very impressed and surprised to see me in Polish uniform, with a sergeant's rank on my epaulets. He told me that the Germans had taken all the machinery and the wood in the yard and had transported it all by train to Germany. The factory building, too, had been dismantled and sent away. Plato and his family had left on the train with the equipment. All that remained on the grounds was the two houses—the big house where my family lived, and the small one. The big house was now occupied by four families. Yan wanted to know what had happened to the rest of my family, and I told him.

His wife served me some food, and a short while later he led me into an adjoining room with a separate entrance. I locked the door, undressed, and lay down to sleep. My submachine gun was tucked under the blanket next to me, a habit I had acquired in my partisan days. An hour or so later, after I had dozed off, I was awakened by a knock on the door. When I asked who it was, a man answered, "I am Kazik, we used to play together. Do you remember me? I am now a policeman. Please let me in." I opened the door to two men in Polish police uniform holding rifles. I recognized Kazik, and they entered. I got back into bed, and they sat down on chairs. Kazik inquired about my family, then casually mentioned that every stranger coming into town had to sign up at the police station, and that the chief of police had sent them to bring me down. Somewhat surprised, I said yes, I would be at the town hall in the morning and would stop at the police station to see the chief. Kazik insisted that he had his orders to bring me in now. His tone of voice changed; it became more authoritative and abrasive. This upset me and aroused my suspicion, so I put my hands under the cover to make sure that my submachine gun was ready. My instincts told me that something was wrong. There was nothing urgent that the chief of police would want of me in the middle of the night. I told him firmly that as a military man I was not under the jurisdiction of the police, and would not take orders from them. If the chief of police wanted to see me, he could come in the morning. I told them I wanted to sleep and asked them to leave. They stood up abruptly, annoyance clearly written on their faces, and a change in the angle of their rifles as they picked them up felt threatening to me. I suddenly suspected that they wanted to take me out into the night to kill me. I jerked my sub-machine gun from under the blanket, aimed it at them and said, "Get out and don't bother me. Otherwise I will shoot you. And don't you dare come in here again."

They both turned pale, dropped their rifles, raised their arms, and began to shake. "We didn't mean to upset you. Don't shoot! Don't shoot!" They started backing out toward the door. I told them to pick up their rifles and get out, which they did.

Somewhat shaken, I locked the door behind them and switched off the light. Back in bed, with the submachine gun in my hands, I waited to see if they would return. But all was quiet, and I fell asleep.

The next morning I walked to the center of town, along the road I used to take to school so long ago. The last time I was here was when I ran to fetch cigarettes for the Nazis in the beginning of the war, five years ago. So much had happened since then that I felt like a stranger, yet somehow on familiar territory. I felt eyes following me, and each time I looked at a window, I saw curtains being drawn closed.

At the town hall I was very graciously received by the mayor, who expressed his condolences on the loss of my parents, such fine people. He brought me into the office, where he officially transferred to me the ownership of what was left of our houses and land. Later the chief of police came too, and I recognized him. Awkwardly he apologized for the incident of the previous night, saying that it was a misunderstanding, since he didn't know who the stranger was when he sent the two men to bring me to him. Trying to appease me, he said he hadn't expected them to bring me in that night. Then he and the mayor invited me to lunch. I asked whether there were any Jews who came back to Raciaz, and they gave me directions to a house where six men were living.

I went to see them. They were all young, between the ages of twenty and thirty. Two of them were people I had known. They told me of their experiences, and I told them of mine. When I described the incident of the previous night, they were not surprised; they said that I was lucky that I instinctively responded the way I did, because Jews who came back to this area frequently disappeared at night, never to be seen again. These six men lived in constant fear. They barricaded themselves at night in the house, and had axes for self-defense. They asked me to stay with them for as long as I could, as that would give them a measure of security. I agreed, but could only stay with them for two days because my leave was coming to an end, and I had to return to my unit at the front.

Back at the front, I shared my experiences with Musio. Several weeks later I chanced to meet a Jew from the Raciaz area, and he told me that about two weeks after I was there, the six men I had stayed with were taken out of their house at night, and disappeared. They were most likely killed.

23

ENTERING GERMANY

March–August 1945

In March 1945 we heard news that the American and British armies had entered Germany from the west, and were advancing deep into the country. At the same time the commander of the Central Front, Marshal Zukov, led his command into Germany from the east and was heading toward Berlin. Our army, which was south of Zukov's, was still waiting for orders to break into Germany. Our objective would be Dresden. Uplifted, we all eagerly awaited our orders to attack. But it was not until the beginning of April that we were finally told to advance.

With very little resistance we crossed the Oder River and started to move into Germany. We took over picturesque little towns and villages outwardly unaffected by war. There were only women and elderly men around, as all the young and able-bodied men were drafted. There was rampant looting by our advancing armies. The cellars were well stocked with sausage, sweets, canned food, and other delicacies which we hadn't seen in years. To the hungry soldiers these were the most important treasures; there was also a supply of underwear, clothes, boots, and other items to be taken. In the immaculate houses in every small town and village, these were the first things we looked for.

In one small town near Dresden I entered a house with several other soldiers and asked for food. We were quickly given everything we asked for. I looked at all the beautiful furniture. Turning the pieces over, I found that they had been made in Poland and other European countries which the Germans had looted. Two young women and an elderly couple occupied that house. I told them in my broken German that I was a Jew, that the Nazis had made soap out of my people, and that now we would make mincemeat of them. Petrified, they started stammering that they knew nothing of what had been done. Seeing the terror in their eyes, I turned away, saying, "We are not Nazis, we won't behave like they did."

In another house, an imposing mansion on the outskirts of town, we found photographs of the owners dressed in uniforms. One was a Nazi SS officer. There we felt justified in looting everything we wanted, and destroying everything else. Even the down comforters were ripped open with bayonets, and feathers flew all around.

We kept advancing unresisted. One day, there were about twenty of us eating in a solitary farmhouse when I chanced to look out the window. To my amazement, I saw through the open gate a number of armored cars full of German soldiers driving into the yard. "Germans!" I shouted.

While they opened fire on us, we all jumped out the back door and windows, and fled. We returned fire, mild in comparison to theirs, and seeing more of their armored cars and tanks approaching, we retreated eastward as fast as possible. On the way we met more soldiers from our battalion, all having experienced the same thing. For three days the armored cars and tanks chased us, pushing us back. We found out that this was happening all along the front—that two intact tank divisions stationed in Czechoslovakia were attacking from the south, trying to stop our advance into Germany.

We hastily retreated to the Oder line. There we were met by the NKVD forces, who immediately stopped everybody, not letting anyone retreat across the river. They shoved everyone into the trenches regardless of units, Polish and Soviet together, telling us to halt the Germans there. Anyone trying to cross the river would be shot. Two officers who happened to be with us began to argue that their orders were to cross the river and join their own units there. An officer from NKVD interrogated them and then took them aside and shot them in front of us all. There were no more arguments.

Gradually, most of the units from our regiment joined us. We regrouped, and on April 15 we began to attack again. This time we advanced quickly, mopping up the remains of two tank divisions which had lost most of their equipment and men. By the end of April we entered Dresden.

The city was burning from being heavily bombarded by Soviet artillery and Allied air forces. Moving through the city was difficult, due to the fires and the occasional slight, sporadic pockets of resistance. Fortunately, most of the German soldiers surrendered and were taken prisoner. Those who resisted were killed. It took us several days to take full control of the city.

Our regiment was then stationed for a few days in a small town called Prinzdorf, to reorganize. There I met up again with Markh and Musio.

Our battalion was given orders to move on, toward Berlin. Musio and Markh stayed behind, at the headquarters, and our ways parted once more.

We loaded our American-built Studebaker trucks and moved out of the area. It was the beginning of May, and the weather was pleasant, as we advanced slowly and cautiously along the main road. Occasional incidents of resistance held us up for a short while, but we managed to overpower the Germans.

Rumors began to spread that Marshal Zukov's army was already fighting in Berlin. Then we heard that Hitler was dead. Despite the fact that the rumor had yet to be confirmed, our spirits were at an all-time high. We felt the end of the war was near.

On May 7, 1945, I was on one of the trucks going toward Berlin when Soviet soldiers heading the other way stopped us. The soldiers shouted to us, "We have come from Berlin! Hitler is dead! The war is over!" One officer filled us in. "The Germans have surrendered unconditionally. Tonight at midnight the final cease-fire will be in effect and we should not attack any German soldiers unless they attack us. Our orders are to disarm them and take them prisoner."

Our column stopped. We got off the trucks and set up for the night. Exactly at midnight I was lying on the ground when the entire horizon turned into a blare of artillery shots, machine gun fire, and rifles all shooting into the air. We jumped up and added to the celebration with all we had. Cries of joy, in Russian and Polish, echoed through the night air. "The war is over!" There was a spontaneous outburst of song, and the Soviet and Polish anthems.

Overwhelmed with excitement, I couldn't fall asleep all night. I wanted to be with Musio and Markh at this moment. All my war experiences flashed before me. I remembered my mother and father, who weren't there to share this day with me, and terrible sadness filtered into my joy. My mother's last words came to me, "Go, save yourselves, and take revenge." I began to cry. We had fulfilled her last wish—we had fought the Nazis and had survived to tell the world. She would have been proud of us.

The next day we returned to the headquarters in Prinzdorf. Musio and Markh were there. They were relieved to see me, as they had heard nothing of my unit's whereabouts. They had celebrated the end of the war by getting thoroughly drunk, but their joy was dampened by their concern for me. We celebrated again by getting drunk together, and talked for hours about the past and our dreams for the future. Softly we sang the Hebrew song, "The Nation of Israel Lives."

We stayed in Germany for two months, with the rest of the occupation forces. Patrolling the towns and villages in the area, we kept busy confiscating everything which could be considered as belonging to Nazis. Gotzky again proved his ingenuity in amassing horses, provisions, and everything he found of value. Alcohol was now the most desirable item on the list of priorities.

On one of my patrol duties, our truck stopped by a pharmacy because one of the sergeants said he thought there was alcohol there. Three of the men went in, and ten minutes later emerged with a huge round bottle full of yellow liquid. The sergeant said, "Here, we've got alcohol." He began to pour a cup of the liquid for each of us. When I sniffed it, I realized it was perfume, and said so. But nobody cared: there was alcohol in it and that was the main thing, so they all drank it. They smelled of perfume each time they burped. I unobtrusively poured mine out.

In July we set off for a victory march back through Poland. For six weeks we marched to our destination—Poznan. We were drunk the entire time. We started drinking in the evening and woke up in the morning with pounding headaches, which we cured instantly by a drink of vodka on an empty stomach—Gotzky's remedy for counteracting hangovers. Since we had looted and confiscated everything we wanted as long as we were on German soil, we reached the Polish border with a tremendous number of horses and carts piled up with all sorts of things. In Poland we traded part of our loot for food and more vodka.

Before entering any Polish town or village, we would all line up in formations and march to the band. We, the victorious army, were greeted everywhere with cheers, flowers, and kisses. In the evenings we partied, and the Polish women offered themselves freely and willingly to their heroes. For the first time in my life my sex life picked up. I lost my virginity, but it wasn't memorable due to my drunkenness.

We arrived in the large city of Poznan to participate in a grand parade organized by our regiment. All dressed in our cleanest and shiniest uniforms, we paraded proudly through town. The streets were festive with Polish and Soviet flags, crowds cheered us heartily. Dignitaries and high-ranking military officers, both Soviet and Polish, welcomed us from the podium. After the parade we marched to a pre-war military camp, which became our permanent base.

Within two weeks the regiment had become organized, and the three of us began to think of the future. We wanted to be discharged, to leave Poland, and to make our way to Palestine. Musio wrote a letter to our oldest aunt, Ida, who lived in Tel-Aviv, at 9 Shalag Street. Her address was forever etched in my memory because my mother had constantly reminded us to contact her if we survived. Musio wrote what had transpired, and, in a roundabout way, indicated that we hoped to meet her soon. We approached the commander of the base about the possibility of discharge. He reacted with a patriotic speech, saying that people like us were needed in the Polish army. As former Soviet partisans, we had an important part to play in instilling the socialistic ideologies in the newly formed people's army. We had a bright future ahead of us in the military, with the possibility of quick promotions. He didn't want us to be discharged, but to stay in the army for at least a few years longer. We thanked him for his advice, saluted smartly, and left. Back at our barracks we decided it was time to take matters into our own hands.

24

ESCAPING THROUGH EUROPE

September 1945

In the beginning of September, Markh asked the colonel in charge of the regiment for two weeks' leave in order to go to Lodz and Warsaw to look for his mother who, he had heard, had arrived in Poland from Siberia. The colonel agreed, and asked Markh to do him a favor. Since his wife and children had also settled in the vicinity of Lodz, would Markh bring them some gifts on his way? Markh of course agreed. The gift was a cartful of loot. The cart and horse belonged to a farmer, who would drive Markh and the loot to the destination and then return.

We had already agreed that Markh would try to contact the Jewish Aliya Organization, which smuggled Jewish refugees who had survived the Holocaust through Europe and into Palestine. The British Mandate in Palestine forbade the entry of Jews into the land without special permits, which were very limited in number. The only recourse was to enter illegally. If Markh succeeded in his efforts to contact the Aliya he would not return to the base, but would find a way to notify us to leave as well. If it didn't work out, he would be back.

Musio and I waited anxiously to hear from Markh, but for a couple of weeks there was no word from him. Then one evening Musio was called to the gate of the camp by a guard who told him that someone was looking for him. It turned out to be a man sent by a friend of Markh's, Hillel Zaidel, who was the head of the Aliya in Lodz. The messenger wanted us to leave with him the next morning by train to Lodz, but we needed a day or so to make our own arrangements. Musio provided us with the necessary fake passes to Lodz and Krakow, using forms from the battalion office where he worked. We told our compatriots that we had received special leave to meet our closest surviving relatives who were arriving from Russia, and would return within a few days.

We left very early in the morning for the train station in Poznan. On the platform we found thousands of people waiting, some of them in Russian and Polish uniforms. A few hours later a train arrived from the west, heading east to Lodz. It was already packed beyond full; people were standing on the steps, holding onto the railings, and some were even lying on the roofs of the cars. The Polish police and Soviet military police stopped the surging crowd on the platform and said that the soldiers had first priority getting onto the train. Musio and I, along with several other Polish soldiers, pushed our way forward and tried to climb on. Each compartment on that long train had its separate entrance, and all the doors were closed from inside. We desperately needed to get away, before it was discovered at camp that our passes were faked. We looked through the windows to see where there was available space, but the possibility of getting on the train looked hopeless. Finally, I saw a large Soviet sergeant standing inside, in front of the door, obstructing the view of his compartment. I bent down a bit and from under his outstretched arms I saw an almost empty compartment. I called to Musio to come and help me pry open the door. He came rushing with several more Polish soldiers, and we all tried to press down the handle, while the sergeant from within tried to resist our efforts. We managed to overpower him, and the door swung open. The sergeant aimed his submachine gun at us, and letting out a stream of curses at the "Dirty Poles," threatened to shoot anyone who dared to push in. I burst out at him with my entire vocabulary of Russian curses. He looked stunned at this tirade, then turned to me and asked, "Who are you? You speak like one of us!" I told him that I was a Stalinist partisan. He embraced me, and said to the few Soviet soldiers in the compartment, "He is one of ours. We'll let him in." He also let in Musio and two other soldiers, after I told him that these were my brother and my friends. The sergeant then continued his vigil at the door, preventing anyone else from coming in.

During the next few hours, while the train was standing, I observed the cruel antics of this man. An elderly couple standing on the platform with their suitcases asked the sergeant to please let them in. The sergeant agreed, offered to help them with their luggage, and as soon as the suitcases were in our compartment, he slammed the door on them and refused to let them in. The couple started shouting that he had robbed them. A Polish policeman came up and tried to talk to the sergeant, who aimed his machine gun straight at the policeman's head and yelled, "How dare you Poles insult the Soviet army that liberated you from the Nazis, by calling me a thief? You deserve to be shot." The policeman turned and fled, and the couple disappeared too. The sergeant and his friends emptied the suitcases, offering to share the contents with us. We refused. We did, however, accept the vodka, sausages, and bread the sergeant shared with us. He was quite drunk by then.

When the train began to move, there were two young women standing on the outer ledge of the car, between the doors to the separate compartments, holding on to the handrail with one hand and to their meager bundles with the other. The sergeant poked his head out of the window and asked, "Are you cold? Do you want to come in?" The girls nodded. "Are you ready to give?" he asked. Embarrassed, they both turned their heads away. "Okay, stay where you are," he told them. After about half an hour in the slow-moving train, he asked again, "Well, are you ready to give?" One of the girls nodded hesitantly and he let her in. Then the other one nodded too, and was also admitted into the compartment. After everyone had some more vodka, the sergeant disappeared into the toilet for a while with one of the girls, and another Soviet sergeant went into the next one with the other girl. The men looked smug when they all returned. The girls were downcast.

The train spent a long time at each station, we arrived in Lodz in the morning. We found Hillel Zaidel at the address given to us, and met Markh there. The three of us spent the night and then went by train to Krakow the following day. We had an address there, and a letter to a woman who would arrange the next stages of our journey.

At the address in Krakow we met an attractive young woman and two men who were very efficient in organizing the illegal "aliya" to Palestine. They laid out our plans in detail. We had to exchange our Polish uniforms for rather dowdy civilian clothes. This was the final step in ending our military careers. We looked at each other, at these new images of ourselves, almost nostalgically remembering how smart we had looked in uniform. But this was a happy occasion, possibly bringing us closer to our dreams. Our first destination would be Budapest, but in order to get there we would have to cross through Czechoslovakia. We were each put in charge of ten people, including several young women, whom we were going to lead across the border. We were given detailed instructions to follow. We got false Red Cross papers identifying us as Greeks on our way back to Greece after being released from German work camps. We each got a new name and identity. I was born in Dimetica, a small, isolated town near the Turkish border. It would be harder to trace my fake identity in a lesser known, out-of-the-way place. We stayed in Krakow for three days, and met our groups at the train station. All of us had the same type of identification.

For two days and nights we rode in a crowded, rundown train with broken windows. There was no electricity and thus no lights. We crossed the Polish-Czech border without arousing the suspicions of the guards checking our papers. Among the other passengers were groups of Soviet soldiers, some of whom tried to flirt with our girls. We all had to pretend that we didn't know Russian, that we spoke only Greek, with a smattering of German. I heard the soldiers telling the girls that they would like to learn Greek, pointing out objects and asking what they were called. The girls racked their brains for Hebrew words that they had learned from the prayer books, and the soldiers meticulously wrote them down. A window became "torah," a door was "Shabas," and so on. I was worried that the girls would run out of Hebrew words before the soldiers ran out of their interest in Greek, but the girls were very enterprising and didn't arouse any suspicion.

On the second night of our journey, we suddenly became aware of figures wandering around the cars in the pitch dark, grabbing people's belongings off the overhead racks. I heard a scuffle and a woman's scream, then I saw something that looked like a human

shape being thrown out of the broken window. Suddenly a glare
from two torch lights shone on the assailants—two men in Soviet
military uniforms with rifles. A voice calm with authority told them
to put down their rifles and put their hands over their heads, or they
would be shot. Two Soviet officers, whom I had noticed before sitting at the other end of the car, were standing with their revolvers
in one hand and their flashlights in the other. The assailants raised
their hands, and the officers pulled the emergency cord and brought
the train to a stop. They then ordered the assailants to get off the
train, and followed them out. We heard shots. The officers returned
and told us that these bandits were deserters from the Soviet army,
and had been executed. They picked up the discarded rifles and sat
down. Being deserters ourselves, albeit from the Polish army, we
dreaded to think what would happen if we were discovered.

On the third day of our journey we crossed from Czechoslovakia into Hungary and at midday arrived at Budapest. We were expecting someone to meet us at the station, as arranged, and take us
all to a given address—8 Arena Street. After waiting for an hour and
not finding anyone, the leaders of the four groups, Musio, Markh,
Mulka, and I, decided to go into town and find the place ourselves,
then have someone come back for the rest of the people. We had no
local currency and couldn't take the tram, so we walked, asking for
directions every once in a while. On a busy main street we suddenly
saw a number of trucks full of Soviet soldiers with the NKVD insignia on their collars. They closed off the street and started checking the identification papers of everyone there. We had no place to
hide, but felt very confident displaying our Greek papers. To our
surprise, we were not allowed to go on our way, but were told to
wait with the soldiers. For about an hour the inspection continued,
and four other pedestrians were told to wait with us. Then we were
all hauled onto a truck and brought to a military camp, where quite
a number of "undesirable elements" were held. On the way, we
gathered from the conversations around us that the other four people were real Greeks, and we understood that we had been arrested
not because our papers were forged, but because we were thought
to be Greeks.

In the camp, we all lined up and a soldier was to write down
our particulars. He looked Jewish to me, and when I came up to his

table, I said in Yiddish, "We four are not Greeks, we are Jews. Help us to get out of here." He nodded, and answered in halting Yiddish, "Don't worry, everything will be okay." A short while later he got up and left and I never saw him again. Another soldier took over his shift. He didn't help us, but at least he didn't betray our secret.

We were kept in the camp overnight and throughtout the following day. At one point Markh, on his way to the latrine, became aware that someone was following him. A man addressed him in Polish, saying that he knew he was a Polish Jew, and that unless Markh gave him some gold, he would tell on him. Markh promised to give him gold soon, then came and told us of the incident. We had no gold, and knew that if the Pole carried out his threat and reported us, our true identities would be discovered and we would be executed. We had to do something. When the Pole approached him again, Markh told him to be at the latrine after dark, to get the gold. When he arrived, the four of us were waiting for him. We pinned him down and started choking him. Speaking German to him, we threatened to kill him if he said a word about us. We told him we didn't know or care who he was, and that if we didn't have the op portunity to kill him, later our organization would. We didn't give him a clue as to who we were, or the organization we referred to. He swore to be silent.

The next day we and the four real Greeks were transferred to the Hungarian police, who again questioned us, wrote down our particulars, and took us to a temporary jail. We were shoved down a few steps into a large dungeon filled with a sea of faces. It was very hot, and all the people were half naked. In the middle of the cell was a man, lying on the floor, flailing about. My first impression was that he had been tortured, but then I realized that he was in the throes of an epileptic attack. No one paid any attention to him. What really upset me was that nobody seemed to care, or tried to help him. We were surrounded by the prisoners, all Greeks. They tried to talk to us, and we had to fabricate a convincing story. We told them in broken German that we were Greek Jews, and before the war had been sent by our parents to study Hebrew in Palestine. We were on vacation with our parents when the war broke out and we were stranded in Europe. We were deported by the Germans to concentration camps, which we somehow survived. That is why we forgot

Greek. They accepted us warmly. Then they asked us where we came from in Greece, and I said I was from Dimetica. One of the men jumped up, hugged me excitedly and said he too was from there. He took me to his bunk and sat me down. He wanted to know what my father did, and which street we had lived on. I had to come up with answers. I said my father was a butcher, and that we lived above our store, which was on Demosthenes Street. I picked the name of a famous Greek philosopher, hoping that a street had been named after him. My friend couldn't place the street, and I started describing that it was behind a church, confident that every Greek town had at least a few churches. He started saying, oh yes, he remembered a church with some streets behind it, and a butcher's shop nearby. I confirmed that that was my father's. My newfound friend offered to share his food with me, and, in short, took me under his wing. In the course of our conversation, I understood that he was part of a community of affluent Greeks living in Budapest. They were merchants, businessmen, and artisans. The Soviet occupation forces had rounded them up, accused them of dealing in the black market and arrested them. They were now going to be deported to Greece.

The Hungarians didn't provide any food or drink for the prisoners, but the Greeks who had money bribed the guards to bring them food. Although we had no money at all, they generously shared what they had with us. My friend from Dimetica even pushed a wad of Hungarian money on me.

After two days we were told that the following day we would all be taken to the Greek consulate, to arrange for our deportation to Greece. We understood that though we had bluffed our way with the Soviets, the Poles, the Hungarians, and even our cellmates, there was no way we could fool the Greek consulate. We had to find a way out.

The next morning more prisoners, including women, were brought from other places. Altogether there were about a hundred and fifty people. We were organized four abreast and told to march through the streets, guarded by about twenty Hungarian policemen. As we approached a busy intersection crisscrossed with tram tracks, we were told to stop and wait because of the traffic. We were a very peculiar-looking group—mostly well dressed and cheerful, but at the same time under guard. The Greeks were happy to be going to their

The major in charge of the camp was becoming uncomfortable with the friendship developing between the Jewish refugees and the Palestinian brigade. Because of the British policy of keeping the Jewish refugees from entering Palestine, he was afraid that this alliance would result in illegal infiltration into Palestine. He issued an order to close the gates of the camp, and to allow only people with permits to go in or out. When we heard of the new regulation, the Jewish refugees decided on a hunger strike. We were in the courtyard when the food was brought to us, we spilled the soup on the ground. We built a podium from planks of wood lying around, and Markh, who was one of the leaders of the strike, began to speak. At the end of his speech he led us in singing Israeli songs. The British major ordered his soldiers to disperse us from the courtyard. They lined up, their rifles ready, and started coming toward us. But we didn't budge. With arms raised, we began shouting at them that if they wanted to kill us, then go ahead and finish what the Nazis had tried unsuccessfully to do. Knowing what the Jewish refugees had gone through, the soldiers were reluctant to harm us and stopped. They made no effort to push us out of the courtyard. The frustrated major, seeing that he had lost control of the situation, asked for several of our leaders to come to him for negotiations. Markh was among them. In the end, the major agreed to reopen the gates of the camp on condition that the Palestinian brigade would not enter any more. We could go out any time we pleased. Life in the camp returned to normal.

Several weeks later we met with two sergeants who had been sent by Captain Pilsdorf to take us to Italy. They took the four of us, along with three other people, and gave us British uniforms, but without the official insignias. We got into a canvas-enclosed pickup truck and they drove us through Austria toward Italy. At the Italian border a British military policeman stopped the vehicle and checked the papers, which said that we were returning to our unit from furlough. To make sure that we really were Palestinians, they began to ask questions about the geography of Palestine. When one of the girls was asked where Mount Carmel was, and she said Jerusalem, the soldier took her off; Mount Carmel is near Haifa, not Jerusalem. The rest of the group guessed the answers correctly and were let through.

consulate, and broke out in Greek song. A large crowd gathered around us, trying to find out what was happening. We took this opportunity to slip out of the line and merge into the crowd. We jumped onto the first passing tram, and I paid the conductor with the money my friend had given me. The ticket had a map of the city, and a hole was punched in the zone where we had gotten on. That was zone number seven.

We rode in the tram for half an hour, then got off and started asking how to get to Arena Street. It was getting dark when we finally arrived at our destination, 8 Arena, a compound where Jewish refugees assembled and stayed until they moved on. We were greeted with cheers and a lot of excitement. The groups we had left at the train station were already there. Apparently, when Kuperberg, the head of the Aliya there, found out that the guide who was supposed to have met us at the train hadn't come, he'd sent someone else who'd brought all the people over. That's when they discovered that we were missing. Through their connections they traced us to the camp of the undesirables. They tried to have us released, but by then we had already been transferred to the Hungarian police. They were concerned that if our true identities were discovered, the entire organization would be endangered. That was another reason that they were so happy to see us and hear our story.

At the compound Markh discovered Steffi—the widow of one of his closest friends from the Vilna ghetto. Steffi's head was shaven and her huge black eyes dominated her entire face. She was a bag of bones weighing no more than seventy pounds; she had been in a concentration camp which was liberated by the Soviets. Markh immediately took Steffi under his care and included her in our group.

Within the next few days we received a new set of forged papers. We were now Austrian dissidents on our way home from German concentration camps! About fifty of us, broken into small groups, set out again. We took the tram to the train station, passing the seventh zone, where we had been captured just a few days earlier. We created an imaginary scenario, where policemen would arrest us again for some reason, and bring us to the same station. The officer in charge would inspect our papers and say, "Funny, I thought you looked familiar. Last week you were here as Greeks.

Today you are Austrians. What will you be next?" Luckily, we weren't stopped.

We spread out throughout the train so as not to draw attention to ourselves as a group. There were two members of the group who were already familiar with the route. When we got off at a town close to the Austrian border, they led us on foot to a small village and then to the barn of a farmer who was to take us across the border. He was generously paid for his efforts.

At night we set out on foot up the mountains to cross into Austria. We walked all night, carrying whatever we had. I was just behind a young couple, and kept helping the man push the girl up on difficult parts of the trek. At dawn we reached the top of the mountain and began the descent. Our guide told us that we were now in Austria, and showed us how to get down to the small town of Judenberg. He then left us. No one stopped us or questioned us on the way. Judenberg was under British occupation forces; we were finally out of the clutches of the Soviets, and facing freedom for the first time in years.

25

UNDER THE BRITISH

October 1945–March 1946

At Judenberg, as per instructions which we had received in Budapest, we went to an international refugee camp and checked ourselves in as Jews from concentration camps. The camp was run by the British army, headed by a major. He welcomed us and assigned us our quarters in a dorm. We slept in double-decker beds, two to a bed; of course I shared a bed with Musio. Markh and Steffi shared the bed above us. That night we sat up late, talking. Another chapter of our lives had been closed. We were now under British occupation, free of the communist yoke, and didn't have to fear being caught any more. It had been a long, long time since I could sleep peacefully, not having to be alert to any possible danger.

A unit of the Jewish Palestinian brigade, which was part of the British army, was stationed nearby, and as soon as they heard that a group of Jewish refugees had arrived, several of them came to visit us. We all asked about our relatives in Palestine who might be serving in their brigade. It turned out that one of the Jewish soldiers knew a Captain Pilsdorf, the brother of Steffi's late husband. He stationed in Italy. The soldier promised to let Pilsdorf know that Steffi and Markh were alive and in this camp, and a few days later Captain Pilsdorf came to see Steffi and Markh. Their meeting was very emotional. We all spent a day together, he promised to help the four of us get to Italy, where most of the brigade was stationed

By evening we arrived in Milan. We came to 5 Via Unione, which had previously been a Jewish community center but was now a refugee center. There we were overjoyed to meet Rivka Gvint and her mother, whom we had last seen in the woods just before we left with Gvardia. They had survived in the woods until the Soviets came, and then through Aliya contacts found Rivka's brother serving in the Palestinian brigade in Italy. He had arranged for them to come through Europe to Milan.

At the refugee center everyone was always asking around for information about relatives. One soldier suddenly mentioned the name of our cousin Gershon, who was apparenly a soldier in the brigade who had been inquiring about us. Gershon had left us a message saying that he was on his way to Poland to look for his fiancée from before the war, and that on his way back he would come to the center again in the hope of finding us waiting for him.

Italy had capitulated to the Allied Forces about a year before the Germans surrendered. Since then the Italian people had been trying to return to a life of peace and normalcy. Milan had not been ravaged by the war, and we were thrown into what seemed to us the lap of luxury—a beautiful city, well-dressed people, everything available. We were introduced to the Italian ice cream, cassata, and other such luxuries, which we could afford because we were given some money by the Aliya organization. We visited the Duomo, La Scala, and other sites. The people were friendly, helpful, joyous, and exuberant. We heard music everywhere and fell in love with the Italian songs and women.

We spent many evenings discussing our plans. Rivka and Mrs. Gvint also intended to go straight to Palestine with her brother's help, as the immediate families of the soldiers had priority. One evening Rivka recalled the time in the woods when we brought food from our zagatovka, and insisted on leaving it for them. At the time their pride had made her try to refuse it, but when we left she and her mother had cried with joy. That was the first meal they had had in days.

Markh was sent to Rome, to take up some organizational post in the main center of Aliya. Rivka and her mother left too, on their way to Palestine. Musio and I remained, waiting for Gershon.

I was meanwhile sent to Udine, a town near the Austrian border, to meet groups of refugees crossing from Austria, and to escort them to Milan. I was chosen because I still wore my British uniform, and being fair, could more easily pass for a British soldier. I had to travel by train, but didn't have enough money. I was issued a pile of cards saying in English that the holder of the card is a displaced person in a refugee camp. The card was signed, and bore a round red stamp. I was told to try to use these cards instead of tickets. It worked every time. The conductor, seeing me in British uniform, would look at the card, and, not being able to read English but seeing the official stamp, would punch a hole and return the card to me. I began to use these cards instead of tickets for all the groups that I brought in.

Once, on my way to Udine by myself, I accidentally pulled out a card with a hole already punched in it. The conductor refused to take it, since I had already used it. Afraid to show that I had a whole pile of these so-called tickets, I tried to bluff my way. I asked for anybody who spoke English or German to step forward and translate for me. An elderly man who knew a bit of German, whom the conductor called il Dotore, came up to help. I argued that this was a two-way ticket, the conductor wouldn't accept it, and told me that at the next stop he would take me to the station master. Il Dotore was on my side. He appealed to all the Italians in the car to convince the conductor to be reasonable. A heated argument began between those who sided with the conductor and those who sided with il Dotore. It was not my argument anymore. There was such a commotion that when we stopped at the next station, nobody noticed that I got off. From the platform I could still hear loud arguments continuing in the car as the train pulled out. I took the next train, being careful to present a fresh card to the conductor.

Gershon arrived several weeks later, and we recognized each other instantly. He was short and well-built, with a round face and a small mustache. His balding head still had some fair hair; he looked very much like my mother's side of the family. He told us that he had heard from Aunt Ida that we had survived the war and were trying to make our way to Palestine, so he had begun his search for us. He had succeeded in bribing his way into Poland with cigarettes, where he found to his great disappointment that his fiancee had meanwhile married someone she had met in Siberia.

We spent several days together. He took us out and treated us. He was stationed near Naples, and promised to arrange to take me into his unit, explaining that he could only take one person into his camp. Meanwhile, Markh had notified Musio that he had a job for him within the organization in Rome. So the obvious choice was for me to go with Gershon. Since Naples was only about four hours from Rome and we would get to see each other often, this didn't seem like more than a temporary separation. Meanwhile, I would wait in Rome too, until Gershon came for me.

When Gershon left, Musio and I took the train to Rome, using the cards again. We met Markh, and stayed with him in the refugee center in Cinecitta ("Cinema City," the Italian Hollywood). It was about forty-five minutes by tram from the center of Rome.

Markh and Musio began to get paid for their work in the organization, so they rented a room together on Via Gracci, not far from the Vatican.

In October, Gershon came and took me with him to his unit in Madelon, about twenty miles from Naples. It was a Palestinian unit headed by British officers, and was part of a British battalion. The battalion was in charge of all the military maps, which were constantly updated and dispatched to the various units of Field Marshal Alexander's army, at their request. Gershon, who was a civil engineer and an architect by profession, worked on updating the maps. Through his connections, I was hired as a paid civilian employee working in the map dispatch department. Then he arranged, through the Palestinian sergeant major, for me to be incorporated into the Palestinian unit illegally. I was issued a uniform, a bunk, and everything else that all the other soldiers received, even including cigarette rations. The only thing I didn't have was the official papers identifying me as a British soldier. My knowledge of Hebrew was sufficient not to arouse even my colleagues' suspicions, and the only one aside from Gershon who knew that I was illegal was the sergeant major.

On weekends we were free to go to Naples, and a military truck took us there and back. I fully enjoyed all the benefits of being a British soldier in the occupation forces in Naples during peacetime. Being with Gershon gave me confidence: he was quiet, cool, and efficient. He took me around with him, and he taught me how to behave like a British soldier. To avoid attracting undue attention to myself, I was careful to be immaculately dressed and polite. Because of the insignia of the Palestinian unit on my shoulder, it didn't matter that my entire English vocabulary consisted of a few words. I was taught to greet the American soldiers "Hi, Johnny" and British soldiers "Hi, Tommy."

One day, when I was walking along the main street of Naples with two other soldiers from our unit, we were stopped by two British military policemen. I instinctively started trying to think of a way out if they asked us for identification papers. Instead, they scolded my two friends for being sloppily dressed, and, pointing at me, told them that was how a British soldier should look.

It was getting colder, and the only showers in our base in Madelon were outdoors. Gershon suggested going to take a bath in Caserta, where the headquarters of the occupying American and British armies in Italy were located. I hesitated because I didn't have papers, but he said not to worry, he had been there before, and nobody ever asked him for identification. The military policemen at the gate changed every week, and we should just know whether we are greeting "Johnnies" or "Tommies."

We hitchhiked to Caserta, which was about seven miles away, and walked to the headquarters. We greeted the "Tommies" at the gate and walked in. We found a line of soldiers waiting to enter the bath, and took our place. When Gershon's turn came and I was left alone, I looked around and saw another door to a bath, with no line. I went in, filled the tub and luxuriated in the hot water, singing happily. I took my time, as this was my first bath in years. When I was through, and dried and dressed, I went out and saw a line of British officers waiting. That's when I noticed a sign saying this was the officers' bath. Realizing my mistake, and not wanting anyone to approach me, I pulled myself together and walked confidently, as though I belonged there. I saluted, and the British officers saluted in return.

This pattern of not asking questions was typical of the British. Gershon told me I was lucky that time, but to be careful of such mistakes in the future.

Gershon loved music, and every weekend we would go to the magnificent St. Carlo opera in Naples, the second most famous

opera in Italy. For the first time in my life I was exposed to the
beauty of an opera house, and began to look forward to this weekly
luxury. I acquired a taste and love of the arias in *Tosca, Carmen,
Pagliacci,* and others. We also had the time and the peace of mind
to admire the beautiful views, to visit the tourist attractions, and to
enjoy the cultural side of life that I had been deprived of for so long.

I felt pampered by all the amenities available to the soldiers—a
canteen, a dispensary that even gave out free condoms, the Red
Cross cinema with movies in English, which Gershon translated for
me. Everything was free or very cheap for soldiers. Our cigarette rations opened other possibilities for us. We could get anything for
cigarettes—even women offered their services. Yet the British soldiers felt like the poor relations of the American soldiers, whose can-
teens were more luxurious, cigarette rations larger, pay higher, and
uniforms more elegant.

Naples had all the trimmings of a port city: bars, brothels,
drunken soldiers and sailors, and military police from four na-
tions—America, Britian, France and Italy—trying to keep order in
the city. There was a vast difference in both their appearance and
approach in dealing with brawls among the drunken sailors and soldiers. The British, holding their sticks under their arms, and revolvers tucked in their white holsters, would patrol in pairs. They
would try to break up fights by talking, and to separate the fighters without using too much force. The Americans, in white helmets,
with red scarves around their necks, held big automatic pistols on
their hips and swung their large sticks as they patrolled in groups
of three. They were more trigger-happy and aggressive in dealing
with troublemakers, and used their sticks freely. The French patrolled in groups of four. The Italians patrolled in groups of six, and
when they saw trouble a signal was whistled and they would surround the brawlers and attack them from all sides at once. I was a
curious distant observer of these scenes.

In Madalon we were quartered in a school where the class-
rooms were used as dormitories, ten soldiers to a room. Breakfast
was served in the canteen up to 8 o'clock, so most of us got up at
practically the last minute, to be inside the canteen by a minute before eight. One morning, at a quarter to eight, I was getting dressed
and couldn't find my shoes. I asked the other soldiers to stop teas-

ing me and give me back my shoes, or I'd be late for breakfast. Another soldier discovered that he was missing his shirt, another one was missing his underwear, someone else was missing his pants. We realized that at night somebody had come into the room and stolen something from each one. It was nice of the thief not to steal everything from one soldier.

There was a lot of poverty in Naples, and stealing from the military was a way of life. We usually sold our cigarettes in the streets, but one soldier, who drove a pick-up truck, decided he was smarter than all, and would get a better deal in the market. He went there and started bargaining. When he agreed on the price, he handed over his cigarettes with one hand, and in the other got the money, which was counted in front of him. He immediately noticed that the bills in his hand were doubled over, and he had gotten about half of what he had agreed upon. He shoved the money back and demanded his cigarettes, which meanwhile had passed from hand to hand among the surrounding crowd. He tried to chase after the cigarettes, but they disappeared. When he returned to his vehicle, he found that his leather vest and his coat were gone too. He came back to camp without his money, his cigarettes, his vest, and coat.

Orders were issued that all covered trucks had to have an armed soldier sitting in the back, because trucks that went to pick up supplies sometimes came back empty. The population had a system for getting hold of anything in the trucks. The driver would slow down or stop for a child crossing the street, and someone would hop on the back of the truck. As the driver would start moving, the thief would toss out everything he could, and the items would be picked up by others.

Once every few weeks I would go to Rome to visit Musio and Markh. I usually hitchhiked—it would take four to five hours. I liked to be picked up by British officers, because we would travel the whole way without exchanging a word, which suited me perfectly. Once I got a ride with an American officer, who immediately started a conversation, which I could hardly understand. I had to explain in my limited vocabulary that I was a Palestinian, so my English was poor. He was very friendly and on the way invited me to stop for a meal with him. I tried to warn him that it wasn't safe to leave the Jeep unattended, but he waved it off. We went into a small restaurant and had a good lunch. When we came out, there was the Jeep, sitting on wooden planks, minus four wheels. Nobody around knew or witnessed anything! The American officer stayed with the Jeep, and I got another ride from a British soldier.

I supplied Musio and Markh with cigarettes and other necessities from the military canteen. Their lives had fallen into a regular routine. They had a comfortable room and enough to eat. Their job in the Aliya organization consisted of preparing refugees for their illegal immigration to Palestine.

We visited the ancient sites of Rome—the Forum and the Colosseum—and the Vatican. We were awed by the art and architecture, and by the wisdom of the older civilizations. It renewed our faith in the decency of man, which we had lost during the long years of seeing mainly the horrible side of humanity.

In early 1946, the Zionist Organization held a congress of representatives of all the refugees in Europe. It was held in Paris, and Markh was sent to attend; he promised to keep in touch. A few weeks later he sent a message to Musio to join him in Paris. I went to Rome to say goodbye, and we sadly parted at the train station. We didn't yet know where or when we would see each other again—either I would join them in Paris, or they would return to Italy, or we would all meet in Palestine. After so many years and all the experiences we had gone through, I couldn't imagine being without them.

After a month or so, I got a letter from Musio saying that he had found our Aunt Theresa, mother's youngest sister. Before the war she had been a professor of chemistry at the Sorbonne and had also worked for the Marie Curie Institute. She married a French painter and had a daughter. During the German occupation, her colleagues hid her and her daughter in a village near Paris, and arranged papers for her as a Catholic French woman. Ironically, her Catholic husband was meanwhile arrested for having a Jewish wife and sent to a concentration camp. He survived and returned after the war, but his health had been affected. They took Musio in to live with them, and Theresa promised to try to arrange for him to enter the Sorbonne in the fall, without any papers. So he decided to stay in Paris.

Markh found some distant relatives in Paris. He was given the position of editor of a newly formed Jewish weekly, and also decided to stay in Paris for the time being. It seemed that neither one of them had plans to go to Palestine in the foreseeable future. I was going to go to Palestine anyway, so I didn't know when I would see them again. At least they were in the same city and had each other. I felt very lonely without them.

Gershon got his discharge papers and was planning to leave the unit soon. He got in touch with a second cousin of ours, Yehuda Arazi, who was nicknamed "Old Man" because his hair was white, even though he was still quite young. Arazi was one of the leaders of Hagana, the defense organization fighting the British Mandate in Palestine for an independent Jewish state. The British had tried to capture him, and a price was put on his head, but he escaped to Europe and was now organizing the illegal immigration of Jewish refugees into Palestine. He was very daring and creative; he put together entire fictitious British military units which transported refugees through Europe to ships in Italy. He bought or hired the ships, bribed the necessary authorities, and succeeded in sending many ships full of refugees to Palestine.

When Arazi heard from Gershon about me, he promised to take care of me and get me to Palestine. I was sad to part from Gershon, but in his calm way he assured me that we would soon meet again. I remained in the unit, and the only one aware of my illegal status was the sergeant-major. Now I was completely on my own.

In March, 1946, a corporal named Vinogradov came to the base, and sought me out. He told me that he had been sent by the Aliya organization and I was to accompany him on an upcoming voyage to Palestine. On a specific day a week later I was to meet him in Naples, at the Jewish military club. I would not be returning to the base anymore, so I should notify my officer that I was leaving my work as a civilian employee. He said I could mention to my friends in the Palestinian unit that I was going to Egypt to be discharged from the army.

I met Vinogradov at the appointed place and he brought me to an apartment in Naples, where I was introduced to two sergeants. They explained the plans for my departure. During the next two weeks I stayed in the apartment with Vinogradov and the two sergeants. I was taught some English phrases, basic British commands, and patterns of behavior expected from a British soldier. I was given a new uniform with all the badges and trimmings of a British soldier and a stripe on each epaulet saying "Palestinian." I was also given false identification papers and paybook, using the name and military number of a soldier who had been killed. I was asked how many medals I wanted and I said five. So in my papers the sergeants wrote that I was eligible to wear five ribbons on my chest. I memorized the name and background of the soldier whose identity I took.

To become more comfortable with my new identity, Vinogradov and I walked around Naples. I even went into a photo studio and had pictures taken in my uniform.

Early one morning I was picked up by a military pickup truck. One of the sergeants sat in front with the driver; in the back with me were Vinogradov and another soldier. On a side street near the seaport, we waited until a large military convoy came along, we merged unobtrusively and went through the gate into the port. The driver dropped us off on one of the docks, and the sergeant pointed out in the distance a huge military passenger ship, which was supposed to take us from Naples to Port Said, Egypt. Vinogradov, the other soldier and I took our kitbags and rifles, and went off toward the ship.

There were several thousand soldiers waiting to get on. Most of them were Scottish, and stood grouped together according to units. We found the Palestinian unit which we were supposed to join; it was randomly formed of soldiers on their way to Palestine, for discharge or home leave. We stood there for several hours, until all the Scottish units were aboard, then we marched out on the dock leading to the ship. On the pier the Palestinian sergeant-major in charge of us made us form in fours, and one by one we had to board the ship. At the bottom of the gangway stood a British major with his staff. Before going up, each soldier gave his name, and the major checked it off his lists.

This was an unexpected turn of events. Vinogradov became nervous. He whispered to me that usually the officers checked only the number of soldiers, and it would have been easy to cause confusion and sneak me on. But as my name was not on the passenger list, we had a problem. We discussed what to do. I considered leaving the scene, but we were the only group left on the dock, and I was afraid that my walking away would attract too much attention.

Vinogradov conferred softly with a few of the soldiers, then came back to me and said, "Don't worry, don't ask questions, just do what I say. When I say go, you take your kitbag on your back and the rifle in your hand, and go up the gangway without stopping."

With all my senses on alert, I looked around. After a few minutes I saw a soldier running down the gangway, shouting to the major that he had to come down to pick up his second kitbag, and his name was Mizrahi. At that instant another soldier ran up, and to the major's question, said his name was Mizrahi. The first Mizrahi came up again with his kitbag and told the major that he had already been counted. A third soldier came down, and a fourth was going up, all of them claiming their name was Mizrahi. The major said the other man was Mizrahi. "Oh, that's my cousin," was the reply. The major got really confused, searching through his list. At that moment Vinogradov pushed me and said, "Go!"

As per plan, I confidently hurried up the gangway, without glancing at the major. At the top of the gangway, just as I thought that I had made it successfully, a huge sailor blocked my way. He called down to the major, "What about this soldier?"

The major looked up at me and shouted, "What's your name?"

The first word that popped into my head was "Pick." "How do you spell it?" asked the major. Just at that instant two more soldiers calling themselves Mizrahi started running, one up and one down the gangway, and the bewildered major, trying to sort out all the Mizrahis, gave up looking for my name. He asked the Palestinian sergeant major at his side whether he knew me. The sergeant major, whom I had never seen before, looked up at me, and probably out of solidarity to a fellow Palestinian, said yes. "Okay," the major called to the sailor, and turned to sort out the Mizrahis. The sailor gave me a card with a serial number and the location of my bunk. I settled in. Vinogradov also came aboard and had a bunk not far from mine.

About half an hour after all the soldiers were on the ship, we heard an announcement over the loudspeakers calling all the troops to assemble according to units on the deck. When we were all there, the major started counting the soldiers, unit by unit. A Scottish colonel, dressed in his kilt, came up to the major and they began an agitated conversation. I asked Vinogradov what it was all about. He translated that the colonel wanted to know why we were all assembled there, and the major explained that there was some miscalculation among the Palestinian troops. "My men have been standing around since morning, and are tired," the colonel objected. "If there is confusion among the Palestinians, why are you keeping my Scots here?"

The major saluted and dismissed all units except the Palestinians. I removed the Palestinian strip from my epaulets, and walked away with the Scots.

I walked around the outside of the deck and, together with many other Scots, admired Naples at dusk. I wanted to avoid being approached by anyone, so I busied myself at the notice board hanging on the wall. I had no idea what I was reading. Eventually I felt I was spending too much time at the board, and moved away. A friendly Scotsman came up to me and started talking, waving his arm toward Naples. I understood he was admiring the beautiful view, and kept nodding at him, smiling at him, saying yes, yes, yes. Then I walked away, and waited impatiently for the Palestinians to be dismissed so I could join them.

At last they were free to go, and I met Vinogradov by his bunk. He told me that according to the cards that we each held, there was an extra man aboard. They counted again and again, and couldn't find the mistake, and gave up.

We were all assigned daily duties, working in the kitchen and cleaning the ship. The sergeant-major, who knew by now that I was illegal, didn't give me any duties. On the second day of our voyage, one of the soldiers from our unit complained to him that he noticed that I wasn't doing anything, and suspected that I was illegal. Unless I shared in the duties, he would complain to the officer in charge. Vinogradov told me about it, and said that he had taken care of the matter. When I asked how, he said simply that at night two strong guys brought the soldier to the rear of the ship, picked him up and held him over the water. They then said if he opened his mouth, they would drop him overboard and there'd be no extra man on the ship. Nobody would notice that he was gone. He promised to keep his mouth shut, and he did.

On the third day, at night, we were in our bunks when we heard over the loudspeaker that there would be an inspection. Each soldier was to stand by his bunk, with his paybook in his hand. I folded up my book and took my kitbag over to Vinogradov's bunk. Then Vinogradov led me to the ship's hold, and covered me up with a tarpaulin. He said he would come back for me as soon as inspection was over. About two hours later he returned for me, and I unfolded my bunk and went to sleep. None of the soldiers in the entire huge hall where we slept, who each could see what had transpired, ever mentioned it. To my luck, it was typical of the British not to meddle in other people's matters.

On the morning of the fifth day we arrived in Port Said. It was easier to leave the ship because we were merely counted going down, without identifying names, and it wasn't difficult to slip out unnoticed.

We were brought to a military camp and settled in. Vinogradov taught me how to ask in English for a pass to go into the city, the next morning I went to the sergeant-major's office, saluted, and used my newly acquired vocabulary. The sergeant-major checked my attire, and asked for my name. He looked at my false identification papers and issued the requested pass for a twenty-four hour leave. Vinogradov and I left the base together and went to see the town.

This was the first time I saw the Middle East—mosques, donkeys ridden in the middle of the streets and dragging carts, traffic jams with drivers honking constantly, the streets crowded with men in turbans and robes, the long pants with the crotch practically at the knees, and women with covered faces. The outdoor cafés filled with men only, the monotonous rhythm of Arabic music blasting through speakers and the smell and filth were very different from what I had experienced in Europe. We sat down in an outdoor café and ordered hot pita bread with humus and tahina. Vinogradov taught me how to dip into these chickpea and sesame spreads with a piece of pita, using no utensils. I enjoyed the taste, and when it was finished, I asked for another portion. I watched as the Arab waiter took my dirty plate, and without rinsing his hands, dipped his hand in a pot full of humus, and slapped another portion onto my plate. He elegantly shaped the humus with his hand, made a hole in the middle with his thumb, and put an olive in. Compared to the lack of hygiene I had experienced during the war, I wasn't repulsed, and ate it all.

We then went to the Jewish military club and asked to see a man named Motke whom Vinogradov knew. We were directed to another room, where we found Motke in the uniform of a British sergeant. Vinogradov introduced me to him, then parted warmly from me and left me in Motke's care.

Motke told me that it would take several days until I got new false papers showing that I was going to Palestine on home leave. Meanwhile, I was to stay at the club. He gave me some Egyptian money so I could go out, if only briefly, for food and other essentials. He wanted to avoid any chance of my being stopped for any reason by military police.

I stayed at the club in Port Said for three days. By that time my new papers were ready, and again I had to learn a new name and take on another identity. Motke introduced me to three other soldiers who would be traveling with me. Toward evening we went to the station and took the train to Rehovot in Palestine. We had to cross the Sinai Desert and, because of the incredible heat, the train made the crossing at night. Even though I had papers saying I was on home leave, my companions advised me to pretend to be asleep during the check at the border. It was safer not to test the validity of my papers unless it was absolutely necessary. When we reached the border between Egypt and Palestine, the train stopped, and civilian inspectors and military police came aboard. I was "fast asleep" on a bench, my body and head covered with my coat. I heard them talking, and someone lifted my coat. I was softly snoring. "He's so sound asleep," one of them said, "he must be very tired. Leave him alone." He covered me again, and they left.

Selim, in 1946, disguised as a British soldier, en route to Palestine (Israel), where he remained for the next thirty years.

Headquarters of Selim's brigade in the Polish army. Moshe Markh is third from left.

In Rome, 1945. Left to right: Markh, Musio, Cousin Gershon, Selim.

In Budapest, 1945. Left to right: Selim, Steffi, Markh, and Musio.

26

IN PALESTINE

April–June 1946

We arrived at Rehovot in the morning. I had been instructed to reach a kibbutz, Givat Brenner, and ask for the head. My companions directed me to the correct bus and went their own way. I arrived at the kibbutz around noon, and someone led me to the head of the community. I told him briefly about myself, and gave him my kitbag with my British uniform, my fake papers, and my rifle and ammunition. He gave me khaki shorts, a blue short-sleeved shirt and sandals. I also got some money—a five pound note—but no identification papers. A girl from the kibbutz was told to escort me to Tel-Aviv, and to help me find my relatives.

After lunch we boarded the bus to Tel-Aviv. We found the apartment at 9 Shalag Street, where mother's oldest sister Ida lived with her husband and her younger sister Estera. There was nobody at home, the girl spoke to people in the other apartments, and was told that my relatives really did live there, but were out. One of the neighbors said my aunt had a brother Noah living close by, and gave us the address. We arrived, and the door was opened to us by Noah's wife Fella. "You are Selim, aren't you?" she cried out immediately. We embraced, and out came my uncle and their daughter Sarenka whom I hadn't seen since they visited us one summer in Raciaz before the war. We thanked the girl for all her efforts, and she left.

For years I had functioned like a robot, alert and wary, using my instincts to escape danger, but not allowing my emotions to take control of my actions. Suddenly a flood of feelings overwhelmed me. Finally, after all these years of dreaming of being in Palestine, here I was, reaching out to my closest living relatives. I went into their little apartment, and we talked and talked for hours. After a while Uncle Noah went to notify my Aunt Ida of my arrival.

This was in April 1946 on the eve of Pesach, on Seder night. This holiday celebrates the liberation of the Jews from slavery in Egypt thousands of years ago. I, too, was now liberated. After years of being persecuted and hounded, adapting constantly to changing situations, I was now free to start leading a normal life.

That night I went with Noah's family to Ida's house for the Seder. She was in her seventies, white haired and very stately. She was the matron of the entire family, and her home was its acknowledged center. Ida's three sons and their families were already there when we arrived, and they all showered me with warmth and attention, something I had not experienced in such a long time that it overwhelmed me. There was a lump in my throat, and I felt an irrational need to get out of the apartment for a short while, to gain control of my emotions.

My grandmother, my mother's mother, shared a room with her youngest daughter Estera in the same building, and I went down to see them. I felt I could handle one or two people at a time better than a larger group. Although she was very old and frail, my grandmother was alert and interested in everything that was going on. She wanted to know about her daughter, Hannah, my mother. Although I couldn't go into all the horrible details, she was so devastated by the news of her daughter's death that Estera had to give her medicine to calm her down. She also inquired about her other sons and daughters in Europe. There was very little I could tell her. I knew that one of her daughters, Rujia, had survived. And that her other daughter, Teresa, was in Paris, and that Musio was with her.

At the Seder table I told the rest of the family what had happened to my parents, and we mourned their memory together. We all cried and prayed for them. I told them when I had last seen anyone from the family, and described some of Musio's and my experiences. During the Seder services, each person traditionally drinks four glasses of wine, but I finished off a whole bottle of cognac which was on the table. The family must have been shocked and upset, wondering whether they had an alcoholic on their hands. Reading the story of Moses leading the Jews out of Egypt, and remembering the last Seder I had with my parents in Kurzeniec, I needed something to help me numb my feelings. The sadness of my great loss was mixed in with the joy of meeting my relatives, and of fulfilling my dream of being in Palestine. I couldn't cope with the intensity of my emotions. Sometimes when I drank during the war, I found that it helped me blur the reality of the moment. That evening I grabbed at the bottle of cognac, and everything after that at the Seder table became blurry in my memory. I slept that night on the living room couch in Aunt Ida's apartment.

The following morning, I went to meet my Aunt Sarna. She was the sister closest in age to my mother, and my mother's favorite. Sarna and her husband and son had spent numerous summers with us in Raciaz. I remembered her very vividly. Her husband, a veterinarian, had recently been run over and killed by a British military vehicle. Her son Ami was a teenager, going to high school. They lived in Kfar Mallal, a village not far from Tel-Aviv.

We had arranged to meet in a café on the shores of the Mediterranean, a short distance from Ida's house. My grandmother, Ida and her husband, Noah and his wife, and Estera came with me. We were all sitting and looking at the street, waiting for Sarna. But she came from behind and embraced me from the back. She told me later that she didn't know how she would control her feelings on seeing me, so she decided to sneak into the cafe from the back and watch us for a short while until she could face me. I recognized her instantly, she looked so much like my mother.

I sat with my three aunts, my uncle, and my grandmother, surrounded by love and care, having coffee and cake overlooking the Mediterranean Sea. I could hardly believe that it was not a dream.

We discussed my future. Sarna suggested that I move in with her. Because I didn't have any identification papers, it would be safer to be in a village, away from a busy city. The British were constantly on the lookout for illegal immigrants being smuggled into the country. Though they managed to catch some boats, they knew that some succeeded in reaching shore. The smuggled refugees tried to blend into the Jewish population, so the British were always checking identification papers, which were to be carried at all times. They set up check points along the roads, in a different place every time. So how was I to get safely from Tel-Aviv to Kfar Mallal? Ida suggested that her oldest son, who worked at the electric company, would take me in the company car to Sarna, via side roads. There I would remain in seclusion until I had some kind of identification.

Noah remembered that one of my Uncle Avigdor's sons was born in Jaffa, Palestine, but that later they all went back to Poland. We were with them in Warsaw during the war, and crossed over with them into Soviet-held territory. Then we lost touch, and nobody had heard from them since. We all assumed that they had perished. Noah suggested that he go to the hospital in Jaffa and get a copy of the birth certificate, which he would then give to me. I would assume my cousin's identity, and that would enable me to get official identification papers. Everybody agreed that that was top priority; until I had the papers, I would not leave the village of Kfar Mallal.

The next day I moved to Sarna's home as planned, taking side roads to avoid the British. Sarna was wonderful to me. We spent evenings talking; she wanted to know everything that had happened to us, and about her most beloved sister. In turn, I heard stories about my mother's youth. Ami helped me to get adjusted to the lifestyle and mentality of the Jewish youth. By including me in his activities, I made friends with people I met through him. Sometimes Ami and I would go across fields to the village cinema, and on the way back would pick watermelons to take home. The first movie I saw in Palestine starred Bing Crosby, and I have had a soft spot in my heart for him ever since. More relatives came to meet me on Saturdays. It was a bit complicated at first to keep track of all the cousins, second cousins, and others, who added up to about sixty people.

I showed Sarna the bulge in my stomach, which I had kept tightly bound at all times. She was horrified. She brought home a doctor friend to check it, and he insisted that I needed surgery as soon as possible, and instructed me to refrain from any physical activities until then. He said that instinctively I had done the right thing by binding my body tightly, and that was what had kept the stitches from my appendix operation from tearing open. As soon as I had my identity card, he would arrange for me to enter the hospital. He warned me that it was a serious operation, and I would not be able to do anything strenuous for weeks after.

Noah went to Jaffa and got a copy of the birth certificate, then went with me and another cousin to the Jewish registration office. There they swore before a clerk that the birth certificate was mine, that I had lost my original papers, and would need a copy. I was photographed, made to fill out and sign a mountain of papers, and given a temporary card on the spot. My papers were sent to the British authorities, and a few weeks later I received my permanent identity card from them. When I finally became a "legal" citizen of Palestine, I bore my mother's maiden name and my cousin's date of birth.

I began to think of my future. I felt somewhat like a savage thrown into an unfamiliar society, sorely lacking in education and sophistication. The qualities I had developed while maturing into manhood—the ability to adapt to drastic lifestyles, and the wits to cope with survival situations—were not greatly needed or appreciated any more. Decency, honesty, and consideration—the values that had been instilled in me by my parents in what seemed like another lifetime—were there, under layers of different coping skills developed during crises. Survival and revenge, my most basic needs, had become obsolete.

My adolescence had slipped by without my going through the normal stages of growing up. My education was cut short after six grades of elementary school, and I had no experience in the game of dating or even in everyday relations with other people in a civilized society. After spending close to seven years at war, here I was at the age of twenty-one, my dreams fulfilled—I was in Palestine, reunited with relatives. Now I had to acquire totally different skills and habits, to learn a profession and become self-sufficient, to learn tact in dealing with people, finesse. I had to overcome my need to rely on drink so as to be able to feel relaxed. For years I had dealt with transitions of status—from persecuted to fighter to refugee to free member of society. Now it was time to adapt to a new reality once again. First of all, I needed to find a job, and to continue with my education.

Sarna went all out, using her connections and friendships to help me get work. I had meanwhile looked into available evening classes, to catch up on my education. Sarna took me to her friend, who was in charge of a company supplying bottled gas and home ranges. After a brief interview, he offered me a job repairing customers' ranges, to start after I had recuperated from my operation. I would get a bicycle to get to customers' homes around Tel-Aviv, after a certain number of repairs a day, the rest of the day would be mine. It was a good arrangement for me, because if I worked efficiently, I would have more time to study. I enrolled in the fall evening classes at the Montefiore School, to prepare for examinations for a high school equivalency diploma. The length of the course would depend upon my abilities. But first I needed to have my operation.

In June I was successfully operated on. It amazed me that there were no complications or permanent damage after years of neglect. Afterward I was sent to a convalescence home for six weeks, and told to be careful not to do anything strenuous. I was not in physical pain but was not allowed to be active, so for the first time in years I had a lot of time on my hands.

I knew there was something important I had to do. This was when I sat down and compulsively wrote down what had happened to me in the last seven years. I spent hours writing furiously each day in notebooks brought to me by Sarna. I wrote in Polish because at that time it was the language I knew best. I did not have the tools and the skill to write my story as well as I would have liked. But I knew that over the years the details of all that I had been through would be erased or blurred. It was vital to write it all down then, while the memories were still fresh in my mind. When I was through putting it all down on paper, I felt that I had completed my mission and was ready to start a new life in my own homeland.

EPILOGUE

I fulfilled my dream of living in the Jewish homeland—indeed, after changing my name to Shalom Yoran and recovering from my operation, I stayed for more than thirty years. When the State of Israel was established in 1948, I joined the air force and learned aircraft maintenance and engineering. I met my wife Varda, who was also serving in the air force, and began raising our two daughters. After the service I forged a twenty-two-year career with the Israel Aircraft Industries, where I was eventually named senior vice president and managing director of the maintenance and overhaul division.

In 1979, we moved to Long Island, New York, where Varda and I live today. I am currently chairman of a private aircraft trading and servicing company. My brother Musio, now Maurice Sznycer, remained in Paris. He is professor of Antiquities and Epigraphy of West Semitic Languages at the Sorbonne and is world-renowned in his field.

During the years I lived in Israel, I renewed contact with some of my closest friends from the partisan days, several of whom are mentioned in this book, and our friendships have deepened over the years. Wherever they ended up, all of my friends married and raised families.

* * *

Moshe Markh (Kalchaim) stayed in Paris for a number of years, writing and editing a Jewish newspaper. He then relocated to Israel, where he continued working in journalism and became spokesman for the Jewish Agency. Today, Moshe is actively involved with issues and organizations pertaining to the partisans.

Yacub (Shafran) married Hannale after the war. They moved to Israel, where he became an electrical engineer and had his own business selling and servicing electrical appliances. His health failed him and he passed away several years ago. Hannale continues to be involved with Holocaust-related issues and is frequently invited to speak at high schools.

Zalman (Gurevich) is a lawyer by profession. He moved to Israel and later relocated to Germany, where he is a successful businessman. Interested in the cultures of remote countries, Zalman travels extensively.

Shimon (Zimmerman) married his childhood sweetheart Riva. They settled in Israel after the war, where Shimon owns and operates a farm. He recently lost Riva due to heart failure.

Shimon (Glazer) (who had shared the zemlianka with us during the war) joined his brother in Brazil after the war, and has his own men's wear business.

Rivka Gvint (Dodik) lives in Israel. She settled there with her mother and continued to care for her until her mother's death.

Shurka Bogen (Alexander Bogen) resides in Israel, and is a well-known artist. He exhibits extensively, in Israel and abroad.

Old Man Kupper and the older son Grisha were found lifeless in the woods. The younger son Mulek survived and settled in the United States after the war. I met him once many years ago.

In 1995, I visited Minsk and finally received my partisan medal, fifty-one years after I arrived there to get it, but was drafted into the Soviet army instead. It took half a century for the medal to catch up with me.

Left to right: Zalman, Selim, and Musio, telling Biruk's daughter how her father had helped them survive by not revealing their hiding in his barn fifty years ago.

The barn belonging to Ignalia Biruk (still standing fifty years later) where Selim, Musio, Zalman, and others hid during the akzia in 1942.

Selim (in the middle) with his grandson and Musio in front of a preserved zemlianka. In the foreground is a long-extinguished partisan campfire.

Selim revisiting Commander Markov's preserved headquarters zemlianka, 1995.

In Kurzeniec, the town where Selim's parents were among the 1,040 Jews killed during the akzia in 1942, a memorial was erected in 1995 on the site where their ashes remain.

Selim, Hannale, and Musio visiting the War Museum in Minsk, 1995.

GLOSSARY

AK: National Army; Polish partisan command formed by the exiled Polish government in England

akcia: "action" in Polish; a term used by the Nazis for the extermination of a specific village or town

drezina: a hand-driven cart used by repairmen working on railroad tracks

Einsatzgruppen: Nazi mobile killing units

Gebietskommissar: a German officer nominated as county chief over annexed or conquered territory

Gestapo: Nazi secret police in charge of internal security

heder: Jewish religious school

Herrenvolk: master race

hutor: a solitary, primitive farmhouse built of logs, usually situated on the fringe of a forest

isrebitel: "destroyer" in Russian

Judenrat: Jewish council set up as a liaison between the Germans and the Jews of a given village or town. The Judenrat received the Germans' orders and enforced them amongst the Jewish population.

KGB: Soviet secret service, wielding great power and greatly feared by all levels of the Soviet population

Kol Nidre: opening prayer of the Yom Kippur services

kolkhozy: farming cooperative

miest: "revenge" in Russian

Nazi: a member of Hitler's political party

NKVD: Soviet secret service; precursor to the KGB

oblava: seige in which the Germans surrounded a forest and combed through it, killing or capturing those found there

otriad: a single partisan unit

progul: truancy

Proizvodstvennaya Gruppa: a Jewish industrial group in the woods which consisted of skilled craftspeople who worked for the partisans

puszcza: a dense, almost impenetrable forest stretching for miles

Raycom: Soviet district party committee

razviedka: the special reconnaissance and scouting arm of a partisan unit

SD: Sicherheitsdienst; one of the Nazi security forces

SS: the Nazis' military arm, separate from the regular army

shamash: caretaker of the synagogue

specgruppa: a small partisan unit created for a specific missions

starshina: sergeant-major

valenki: Russian army boots made of felt with leather soles

Wannsee Conference: a meeting in Wannsee attended by all branches of the Nazi government, where the plan for the "Final Solution"—total extermination of the Jews—was formed and activated

Wehrmacht: German army

zagatovka: a mission to acquire provisions and supplies for the partisans

zemlianka: an underground shelter in the forest where people in hiding lived

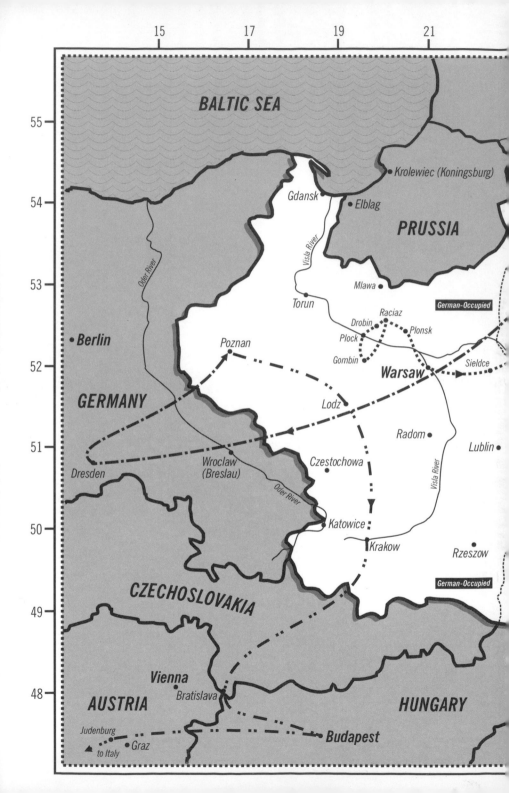

15	17	19	21

BALTIC SEA

55 —

Krolewiec (Koningsburg) •

Gdansk •   • Elblag

54 —

PRUSSIA

Odra River

Visla River

53 —

Mlawa •

Torun •

German-Occupied

• Berlin

Raciaz

Drobin

Plock • • Plonsk

Poznan

Gombin

52 —

Warsaw   Sieldce •

Lodz •

GERMANY

Radom •   Lublin •

51 —

Wroclaw
(Breslau)

Czestochowa •

Dresden

Odra River

Visla River

50 —

Katowice •

Krakow •   Rzeszow •

German-Occupied

CZECHOSLOVAKIA

49 —

Vienna

48 —

Bratislava

AUSTRIA   **HUNGARY**

Judenburg   • Budapest

▲ to Italy   • Graz